W9-BTF-367

The Daily You

The Daily You

How the New Advertising
Industry Is Defining Your
Identity and Your Worth

Joseph Turow

Yale UNIVERSITY PRESS

NEW HAVEN & LONDON

Copyright © 2011 by Joseph Turow.
All rights reserved.
This book may not be reproduced, in whole or in part, including illustrations, in any form (beyond that copying permitted by Sections 107 and 108 of the U.S. Copyright Law and except by reviewers for the public press), without written permission from the publishers.

Yale University Press books may be purchased in quantity for educational, business, or promotional use. For information, please e-mail sales.press@yale.edu (U.S. office) or sales@yaleup.co.uk (U.K. office).

Set in Adobe Garamond and Stone Sans types by IDS Infotech Ltd.
Printed in the United States of America.

Library of Congress Cataloging-in-Publication Data
Turow, Joseph.
The daily you : how the new advertising industry is defining your identity and your worth / Joseph Turow.
    p.   cm.
Includes bibliographical references and index.
ISBN 978-0-300-16501-2 (hardback)
1. Consumer profiling. 2. Marketing—Technological innovations. 3. Customer services—Technological innovations. 4. Advertising. I. Title.
HF5415.32.T945 2011
659.1—dc23
2011028202

A catalogue record for this book is available from the British Library.

This paper meets the requirements of ANSI/NISO Z39.48–1992 (Permanence of Paper).

10 9 8 7 6 5 4 3 2 1

To Judy

Contents

Acknowledgments

This book explores a new advertising industry in the making and its effect on how we see ourselves and our world. I owe a lot to the many business practitioners, journalist-experts, and public-interest advocates who answered my questions about the thicket of technology, business processes, and government policies that are guiding the fascinating transformation. Several of these generous individuals wished to remain anonymous. I am thankful for the opportunity to acknowledge the others together with the firms that employed them when we talked: Matt Apprendi (Collective Media), Don Batsford Jr., (31 Media), Denis Beaujejour (Mariemount Community Church), JC Cannon (Microsoft), Jeffrey Chester (Center for Digital Democracy), Stephanie Clifford *(New York Times)*, Peter Eckersley (Progress and Freedom Foundation), Carol Garofalo (Collective Media), Bob Gellman (privacy consultant), Alec Gerster (Initiative), Matt Greizer (Razorfish), David Hallerman (eMarketer), Saul Hansell *(New York Times)*, Eduardo Hauser (DailyMe), Darren Herman (Varick Media Management), Tom Hespos (Underscore Marketing), Imran Iziz (Microsoft), Brad Johnson (Advertising

Age), Michael Katz (Interclick), Joakim Kent (Omniture), Yaakov Kimelfeld (Mediavest), Scott Lang (WPP), Jeremy Lau (Real Networks), Edmund Lee (Advertising Age), Ying Lee (Microsoft), Kirk McDonald (Time Inc.), Jack Neff (Advertising Age), John Nitti (Zenith Optimedia), Eric Picard (Microsoft), Ariel Poler (TextMarks), Jules Polonetsky (Future of Privacy Forum), Andy Pratkin, (WPP), Paul Rostoski (LucidMedia), Marc Rotenberg (Electronic Privacy Information Center), Jay Sears (ContextWeb), Ted Shargalis (X+1), Dou Shen (Microsoft), Mark Stewart (Kraft), Michael Stich (Bridge Worldwide), Rohit Thawani (Publicis), Rishad Tobaccowala (Publicis), Jonathan Trieber (RevTrax), Nat Turner (Invite Media), Kurt Unkle (Publicis), Tim Westergren (Pandora), Brian Wieser (Magna), Debra Aho Williamson (eMarketer), and Edwin Wong (Yahoo!).

In many cases, I contacted sources because they were mentioned in, or wrote, helpful articles I read in trade magazines or because they appeared on panels at industry meetings I attended. The industry meetings were useful for confirming, extending, or refuting what I learned in the trades. I have been reading *Advertising Age* for decades (I started subscribing as a teenager), and I have been a regular visitor to online newsletters about the ad-driven digital world such as *Online Media Daily, PaidContent.org,* and *AdExchanger* from virtually their inception. In addition, the Nexis and Factiva databases have made it practical to explore particular topics in depth across a wide range of industry periodicals (such as *Adweek, Multichannel News,* and *Progressive Grocer*) and government-agency publications. I have also bene-fited from reports from media and marketing consulting and research firms such as Forrester Research, eMarketer, Bernstein Research, and Magna. The Omniture advertising-optimization company kindly let me study its *Test and Target* training manual. I am also grateful for the many explanatory reports and white papers that firms in the digital-marketing space released during the past several years.

Colleagues from various academic disciplines have been crucial to teaching me, critiquing my ideas, and offering sage advice about various aspects of marketing, the digital environment, and/or privacy. Warm thanks are due to Jack Balkin, Pablo Boczkowski, Danielle Citron, Laurie Cranor, Peter Decherney, Peter Fader, Ellen Goodman, James Grimmelmann, Keith Hampton, Eszter Hargitai, Chris Jay Hoofnagle, Elihu Katz, Jennifer King, Greg Lastowka, Matt McAllister, Aleecia McDonald, Kathy Montgomery, Monroe Price, Sheizaf Rafaeli, Rivka Ribak, Jonathan Smith, Jeffrey Sonstein, Lokman Tsui, Joel Waldfogle, Kevin Werbach, and Christopher

Yoo. My thinking on topics in this book has also benefited from research help by students Aymar Jean Christian, Deb Lieu, Alex Sastre, and Nora Draper at the University of Pennsylvania's Annenberg School for Communication.

Michael Delli Carpini, dean of the Annenberg School, has provided an encouraging environment for research through his personal style and his adjustment of the faculty course load with an eye toward the production of knowledge. A sustained amount of my writing took place at Oxford University via a Lady Astor Lectureship from the university. I'd like to thank Professor William Dutton of the Oxford Internet Institute, who was a supportive host. Thanks also go to Jeffrey Schier, my copyeditor, whose meticulous reading (and rereading) of the manuscript led him to ask penetrating questions and offer valuable suggestions. Alison MacKeen, my editor at Yale University Press, has been kind, critical, demanding, astute, and extremely encouraging—all at the same time. I am very fortunate to be working with her.

The Daily You

Introduction

At the start of the twenty-first century, the advertising industry is guiding one of history's most massive stealth efforts in social profiling. At this point you may hardly notice the results of this trend. You may find you're getting better or worse discounts on products than your friends. You may notice that some ads seem to follow you around the internet. Every once in a while a website may ask you if you like a particular ad you just received. Or perhaps your cell phone has told you that you will be rewarded if you eat in a nearby restaurant where, by the way, two of your friends are hanging out this very minute.

You may actually like some of these intrusions. You may feel that they pale before the digital power you now have. After all, your ability to create blogs, collaborate with others to distribute videos online, and say what you want on Facebook (carefully using its privacy settings) seems only to confirm what marketers and even many academics are telling us: that consumers are captains of their own new-media ships.

But look beneath the surface, and a different picture emerges. We're at the start of a revolution in the ways marketers and media intrude in—and shape—our lives. Every day most if not all Americans who use the internet, along with hundreds of millions of other users from all over the planet, are being quietly peeked at, poked, analyzed, and tagged as they move through the online world. Governments undoubtedly conduct a good deal of snooping, more in some parts of the world than in others. But in North America, Europe, and many other places companies that work for marketers have taken the lead in secretly slicing and dicing the actions and backgrounds of huge populations on a virtually minute-by-minute basis. Their goal is to find out how to activate individuals' buying impulses so they can sell us stuff more efficiently than ever before. But their work has broader social and cultural consequences as well. It is destroying traditional publishing ethics by forcing media outlets to adapt their editorial content to advertisers' public-relations needs and slice-and-dice demands. And it is performing a highly controversial form of social profiling and discrimination by customizing our media content on the basis of marketing reputations we don't even know we have.

Consider a fictional middle class family of two parents with three children who eat out a lot in fast-food restaurants. After a while the parents receive a continual flow of fast-food restaurant coupons. Data suggest the parents, let's call them Larry and Rhonda, will consistently spend far more than the coupons' value. Additional statistical evaluations of parents' activities and discussions online and off may suggest that Larry and Rhonda and their children tend toward being overweight. The data, in turn, result in a small torrent of messages by marketers and publishers seeking to exploit these weight issues to increase attention or sales. Videos about dealing with over-weight children, produced by a new type of company called content farms, begin to show up on parenting websites Rhonda frequents. When Larry goes online, he routinely receives articles about how fitness chains emphasize weight loss around the holidays. Ads for fitness firms and diet pills typically show up on the pages with those articles. One of Larry and Rhonda's sons, who is fifteen years old, is happy to find a text message on his phone that invites him to use a discount at an ice cream chain not too far from his house. One of their daughters, by contrast, is mortified when she receives texts inviting her to a diet program and an ad on her Facebook page inviting her to a clothing store for hip, oversized women. What's more, people keep sending her Twitter messages about weight loss. In the meantime, both Larry and Rhonda are getting ads from check-cashing services and payday-loan companies. And Larry notices sourly on auto sites he visits that the main articles on the home page and the ads throughout feature entry-level and used models.

His bitterness only becomes more acute when he describes to his boss the down-market Web he has been seeing lately. Quite surprised, she tells him she has been to the same auto sites recently and has just the opposite impression: many of the articles are about the latest German cars, and one home-page ad even offered her a gift for test-driving one at a dealer near her home.

This scenario of individual and household profiling and media customization is quite possible today. Websites, advertisers, and a panoply of other companies are continuously assessing the activities, intentions, and backgrounds of virtually everyone online; even our social relationships and comments are being carefully and continuously analyzed. In broader and broader ways, computer-generated conclusions about who we are affect the media content—the streams of commercial messages, discount offers, information, news, and entertainment—each of us confronts. Over the next few decades the business logic that drives these tailored activities will transform the ways we see ourselves, those around us, and the world at large. Governments too may be able to use marketers' technology and data to influence what we see and hear.

From this vantage point, the rhetoric of consumer power begins to lose credibility. In its place is a rhetoric of esoteric technological and statistical knowledge that supports the practice of social discrimination through profiling. We may note its outcomes only once in a while, and we may shrug when we do because it seems trivial—just a few ads, after all. But unless we try to understand how this profiling or reputation-making process works and what it means for the long term, our children and grandchildren will bear the full brunt of its prejudicial force.

The best way to enter this new world is to focus on its central driving force: the advertising industry's media-buying system. Media buying involves planning and purchasing space or time for advertising on outlets as diverse as billboards, radio, websites, mobile phones, and newspapers. For decades, media buying was a backwater, a service wing of advertising agencies that was known for having the lowest-paying jobs on Madison Avenue and for filling those jobs with female liberal arts majors fresh out of college. But that has all changed. The past twenty years have seen the rise of "media agencies" that are no longer part of ad agencies, though they may both be owned by the same parent company. Along with a wide array of satellite companies that feed them technology and data, media agencies have become magnets for well-remunerated software engineers and financial statisticians of both sexes.

In the United States alone, media-buying agencies wield more than $170 billion of their clients' campaign funds; they use these funds to purchase space and time on media they think will advance their clients' marketing aims. But in the process they are doing much more. With the money as leverage, they are guiding the media system toward nothing less than new ways of thinking about and evaluating audience members and defining what counts as a successful attempt to reach them. Traditionally, marketers have used media such as newspapers, magazines, radio, billboards, and television to reach out to segments of the population through commercial messages. These advertisers typically learned about audience segments from survey companies that polled representative portions of the population via a variety of methods, including panel research. A less prestigious direct-marketing business has involved contacting individuals by mail or phone. Firms have rented lists of public data or purchase information that suggests who might be likely customers.

The emerging new world is dramatically different. The distinction between reaching out to audiences via mass media and by direct-response methods is disappearing. Advertisers in the digital space expect all media firms to deliver to them particular types of individuals—and, increasingly, *particular* individuals—by leveraging a detailed knowledge about them and their behaviors that was unheard of even a few years ago. The new advertising strategy involves drawing as specific a picture as possible of a person based in large part on measurable physical acts such as clicks, swipes, mouseovers, and even voice commands. The strategy uses new digital tracking tools like cookies and beacons as well as new organizations with names like BlueKai, Rapleaf, Invidi, and eXelate. These companies track people on websites and across websites in an effort to learn what they do, what they care about, and who their friends are. Firms that exchange the information often do ensure that the targets' names and postal addresses remain anonymous—but not before they add specific demographic data and lifestyle information. For example:

• Rapleaf is a firm that claims on its website to help marketers "customize your customers' experience." To do that, it gleans data from individual users of blogs, internet forums, and social networks. It uses ad exchanges to sell the ability to reach those people. Rapleaf says it has "data on 900+ million records, 400+ million consumers, [and] 52+ billion friend connections." Advertisers are particularly aware of the firm's ability to predict the reliability of individuals (for example, the likelihood they will pay their mortgage) based on Rapleaf's research on the trustworthiness of the people in those individuals' social networks.

- A company called Next Jump runs employee discount and reward programs for about one-third of U.S. corporate employees. It gets personal information about all of them from the human relations departments of the companies and supplements that information with transactional data from the manufacturers it deals with as well as from credit companies. Armed with this combination of information, Next Jump can predict what people want and what they will pay for. It also generates a "UserRank" score for every employee based on how many purchases a person has made and how much he or she has spent. That score plays an important role in determining which employee gets what product e-mail offers and at what price.
- A firm called The Daily Me already sells an ad and news personalization technology to online periodicals. If a *Boston Globe* reader who reads a lot of soccer sports news visits a *Dallas Morning News* site, the Daily Me's technology tells the *Dallas Morning News* to serve him soccer stories. Moreover, when an ad is served along with the story, its text and photos are instantly configured so as to include soccer terms and photos as part of the advertising pitch. A basketball fan receiving an ad for the same product will get language and photos that call out to people with hoop interests.

These specific operations may not be in business a few years from now. In the new media-buying environment companies come and go amid furious competition. The logic propelling them and more established firms forward, though, is consistent: the future belongs to marketers and media firms— *publishers,* in current terminology—that learn how to find and keep the most valuable customers by surrounding them with the most persuasive media materials. Special online advertising exchanges, owned by Google, Yahoo!, Microsoft, Interpublic, and other major players, allow publishers to auction and media agencies to "buy" individuals with particular characteristics, often in real time. That is, it is now possible to buy the right to deliver an ad to a person with specific characteristics at the precise moment that that person loads a Web page. In fact, through an activity called cookie matching, which I discuss in detail later, an advertiser can actually bid for the right to reach an individual whom the advertiser knows from previous contacts and is now tracking around the Web. Moreover, the technology keeps changing. Because consumers delete Web cookies and marketers find cookies difficult to use with mobile devices, technology companies have developed methods to "fingerprint" devices permanently and allow for persistent personalization across many media platforms.

The significance of tailored commercial messages and offers goes far beyond whether or not the targeted persons buy the products. Advertisements and discounts are status signals: they alert people as to their social position. If you consistently get ads for low-priced cars, regional vacations, fast-food restaurants, and other products that reflect a lower-class status, your sense of the world's opportunities may be narrower than that of someone who is feted with ads for national or international trips and luxury products. Moreover, if like Larry and Rhonda you happen to know that your colleague is receiving more ads for the luxury products than you are, and more and better discounts to boot, you may worry that you are falling behind in society's estimation of your worth.

In fact, the ads may signal your opportunities actually *are* narrowed if marketers and publishers decide that the data points—profiles—about you across the internet position you in a segment of the population that is relatively less desirable to marketers because of income, age, past-purchase behavior, geographical location, or other reasons. Turning individual profiles into individual evaluations is what happens when a profile becomes a reputation. Today individual marketers still make most of the decisions about which particular persons matter to them, and about how much they matter. But that is beginning to change as certain publishers and data providers— Rapleaf and Next Jump, for example—allow their calculations of value to help advertisers make targeting decisions. In the future, these calculations of our marketing value, both broadly and for particular products, may become routine parts of the information exchanged about people throughout the media system.

The tailoring of news and entertainment is less advanced, but it is clearly under way. Technologies developed for personalized advertising and coupons point to possibilities for targeting individuals with personalized news and entertainment. Not only is this already happening, the logic of doing that is becoming more urgent to advertisers and publishers. Advertisers operate on the assumption that, on the internet as in traditional media, commercial messages that parade as soft (or "human interest") news and entertainment are more persuasive than straightforward ads. Publishers know this too, and in the heat of a terrible economic downturn even the most traditional ones have begun to compromise long-standing professional norms about the separation of advertising and editorial matter. And in fact many of the new online publishers—companies, such as Demand Media, that turn out thousands of text and video pieces a day—never really bought into the old-world ideas about editorial integrity anyway. What this means is that we are entering a world of intensively customized content, a world in which publishers and even marketers will package personalized advertisements with soft news or entertainment that is tailored to fit both the selling needs of the ads and the reputation of the particular individual.

The rise of digital profiling and personalization has spawned a new industrial jargon that reflects potentially grave social divisions and privacy issues. Marketers divide people into *targets* and *waste.* They also use words like *anonymous* and *personal* in unrecognizable ways that distort and drain them of their traditional meanings. If a company can follow your behavior in the digital environment—an environment that potentially includes your mobile phone and television set—its claim that you are "anonymous" is meaningless. That is particularly true when firms intermittently add off-line information such as shopping patterns and the value of your house to their online data and then simply strip the name and address to make it "anonymous." It matters little if your name is John Smith, Yesh Mispar, or 3211466. The persistence of information about you will lead firms to act based on what they know, share, and care about you, whether you know it is happening or not.

All these developments may sound more than a little unsettling; *creeped out* is a phrase people often use when they learn about them. National surveys I have conducted over the past decade consistently suggest that although people know companies are using their data and do worry about it, their understanding of exactly how the data are being used is severely lacking. That of course shouldn't be surprising. People today lead busy, even harried, lives. Keeping up with the complex and changing particulars of data mining is simply not something most of us have the time or ability to do. There are many great things about the new media environment. But when companies track people without their knowledge, sell their data without letting them know what they are doing or securing their permission, and then use those data to decide which of those people are targets or waste, we have a serious social problem. The precise implications of this problem are not yet clear. If it's allowed to persist, and people begin to realize how the advertising industry segregates them from and pits them against others in the ads they get, the discounts they receive, the TV-viewing suggestions and news stories they confront, and even the offers they receive in the supermarket, they may begin to suffer the effects of discrimination. They will likely learn to distrust the companies that have put them in this situation, and they may well be incensed at the government that has not helped to prevent it. A comparison to the financial industry is apt. Here was an industry engaged in a whole spectrum of arcane practices that were not at all transparent to consumers or regulators but that had serious negative impact on our lives. It would be deeply unfortunate if the advertising system followed the same trajectory.

Despite valiant efforts on the part of advocacy groups and some federal and state officials, neither government rulings nor industry self-regulation has set policies that will address these issues before they become major sources of widespread social distress. Part of the reason for the lack of action may be that neither citizens nor politicians recognize how deeply embedded in American life these privacy-breaching and social-profiling activities are. Few individuals outside advertising know about the power of the new media-buying system: its capacity to determine not only what media firms do but how we see ourselves and others. They don't know that that system is working to attach marketing labels to us based on the clicks we make, the conversations we have, and the friendships we enjoy on websites, mobile devices, iPads, supermarket carts, and even television sets. They don't know that the new system is forcing many media firms to sell their souls for ad money while they serve us commercial messages, discounts, and, increasingly, news and entertainment based on our marketing labels. They don't realize that the wide sharing of data suggests that in the future marketers and media firms may find it useful to place us into personalized "reputation silos" that surround us with worldviews and rewards based on labels marketers have created reflecting our value to them. Without this knowledge, it is hard to even begin to have broad-based serious discussions about what society and industry should do about this sobering new world: into the twenty-first century the media-buying system's strategy of social discrimination will increasingly define how we as individuals relate to society—not only how much we pay but what we see and when and how we see it.

Until now, the advertising industry's new media-buying processes have been virtually hidden to all but a relatively few practitioners in the field. No books have been written about the business, and while some excellent trade publications follow its developing story continuously, the particulars they present are more or less opaque to those outside the industry. A few experts in the media-buying field, in fact, told me that they don't try to explain the details of what they do to their clients, the advertisers, or their bosses in the upper reaches of their advertising agencies. They simply wouldn't grasp it. All the clients and the bosses care about, these media buying experts added, is whether they reach their targets with an appropriate return on investment. But from a consumer perspective, from the standpoint of a society aiming for transparency and fairness, this black-box approach is not acceptable. We need to understand the industrial forces that are defining our identities, our worth, and the media environments we inhabit so that we can decide what, if anything, to do about them. Academics, advocates, and government leaders must know enough about this business and its workings to be able to ask hard questions and formulate realistic policy suggestions when they are needed.

The aim of this book, then, is to describe the brave new world that is the media-buying system, especially as it relates to the internet and emerging digital technologies. The chapters that follow detail the media-buying system's tangled history, reveal its logic and operations, identify the problems it poses for individuals and society, and suggest solutions. Chapter 1 starts by challenging the common assertion, made not only by marketers but by many academics, that the consumer is king in the new media environment. This idea is most closely associated with Nicholas Negroponte's pioneering and still influential account of *The Daily Me*. In his 1995 best seller, *Being Digital,* Negroponte predicted that the power of digital media would give citizens an unprecedented degree of control over their media environments. He illustrated this new control with the hypothetical example of *The Daily Me,* an online newspaper whose content would be customized to suit the interests and beliefs of individual readers. Many years later, as I show here, the content customization that Negroponte predicted is taking off. The crucial difference, however, is that much of the content is not being customized and personalized by consumers themselves. Advertisements, discounts, information, and entertainment are increasingly customized by a largely invisible industry on the basis of a vast amount of information that we likely don't realize it is collecting as a result of social profiles and reputations it assigns us and never discloses, and about which we are likely ignorant.

This book attempts to address this knowledge and power imbalance. By looking under the hood of the internet and other digital media, we see that media buyers play key roles in whether, when, and how people's worth is constructed in that world. To recognize such immense power is not to deny the spaces and opportunities for freedom, participation, and creativity that several scholars identify in the new environment. But it does make clear that the ruthlessly commercial logic and obscure social profiling practices of the new media-buying system are what dominate the emerging digital world.

Why and how did the system develop? The first chapter finds answers in the rise of huge agency conglomerates in the United Kingdom, United States, and France during the 1980s and 1990s. They separated media planning and buying from their historical roles within the ad agency and made them stand-alone businesses. That led to new "media agencies" that competed with one another for clients by stressing their ability to evaluate and predict consumer responses with sophisticated statistics. When the internet came along, they saw its interactive environment as terrific terrain for expanding their numerical understanding of audiences—and for using the measures and labels directly to sell products.

Chapter 2 describes how two technological innovations, "the click" and "the cookie," became the key mechanisms around which media buyers, marketers, technology firms, and online publishers (that is, firms that create or distribute news, information, or entertainment) planned their digital future. They tried to develop mutual understandings of how to measure the number of people at particular online sites and evaluate the worth of the people and the sites to marketers. The click provided marketers with a way to directly track individuals' actions with ads and other content. The cookie allowed publishers and marketers to recognize a computer—and sometimes a person—with which they had previous interactions. It also allowed them to store information about targets' movements across thousands of websites. With the click and the cookie as a start, media buyers and their allies placed a key proposition at the heart of the new system: help marketers identify measureable ways to know, target, and consider the impact of commercial messages on audiences as never before, even in the face of vocal public worries about privacy invasion.

Chapter 3 shows how the compulsion to learn increasing amounts of information about online individuals escalated as the near-manic desire by online publishers to prove their utility to media buyers continued into the 2000s. This trend coincided particularly with the rise of Google's search engine. Unlike the approach of most publishers, which charged a fee for the display of an ad, Google charged advertisers only if an individual clicked on an ad adjacent to the search results. Media buyers agreed with Google's claim that consumers' keywords were insights into their direct interests. Moreover, Google's pitch that clicking on an ad was a significant indicator of individual consumers' interest fit exactly with advertisers' increasing insistence on direct measurability. The search engine quickly garnered more than half of the money advertisers spent online. As thousands of publishers worked furiously to attract advertisers in order to win some of the other 50 percent of the media buyers' spending with new forms of display advertising, they turned for help to new types of organizations—online ad networks, data providers, and data exchanges. These companies promised to help them boost revenues by presenting advertisers with yet more information about the individuals in their audiences. In the interest of raising publishers' rates with advertisers, publishers asked visitors to register, tracked them, bought information about them, shared much of it (often anonymously) with advertisers, and affiliated with networks of sites that claimed to help advertisers reach their targeted individuals wherever they went.

Chapters 4, 5, and 6 describe how the contemporary business of profiles and valuations of individuals is escalating in unprecedented ways. Chapter 4 shows how marketers increasingly use databases to predict which of the two classifications (target or waste) they should use to categorize particular Americans. Those considered waste are ignored or shunted to other products the marketers deem more relevant to their tastes or income. Chapter 5 explores how media buyers' pressures are leading publishers to accept the idea of customizing news and information based on the characteristics of people that advertisers would want to see. The chapter suggests how consistently shared notions of profiled individuals will lead publishers and advertisers to place anonymous persons they reach into "reputation silos." The content that they will stream to these individuals will have different values based on marketers' evaluation of their lifestyles, offline and online activities, social relationships, and demographics.

These activities aren't tied to the Web. As Chapter 6 shows, they are spreading quickly to other digital media. Although social-media and gaming sites such as Facebook and Pogo have their roots in the traditional Web, their use outdoors is exploding with the rapid spread of multimedia mobile devices. Not surprisingly, these devices are a particularly fertile arena for tracking in the interest of sales and services. The competition for digital dominance in a social-media world is even affecting the biggest medium of all, the home television set. This chapter discusses a mini-industry of companies that exist to analyze social relationships on the Web and elsewhere and to predict which individuals are worth pursuing for what products and with what incentives. The aim is to help marketers follow the targeted individuals across as many geographical locations and devices as possible. The ultimate goal is to pinpoint a consumer with a particular reputation, decide what offers to surround her or him with, and track the results. Call that tracking the *long click*. It means, for example, being able to follow a person's response from the initial presentations of a product in Web ads through a gauntlet of purposeful marketing encounters: an article sent to her that integrates the product into the piece; a commercial extolling the product sent to that person on her home TV when she is watching; and discount offers for the product based on the individual's location as determined via her mobile phone. The target's ultimate purchase of the product with a swipe of a frequent-shopper card, credit card, or debit card identifies a marketing success—and gets the individual to offer up still more data for various parties to add to the person's profiles and reputations.

Chapter 7 crystallizes the social and policy issues these and related activities raise. Social discrimination via reputation silos may well mean having sectors of your life labeled by companies you don't know, for reasons you don't understand, and with data that you did not give any permission to use. Do your eating habits suggest you will soon spend a lot on health care? What do your age, income, and lifestyle indicators suggest about the value of cultivating you as a cruise line customer—and what do they imply about the minimum discount that you would need to purchase a cruise? What does your household profile suggest about the kinds of commercials your children should receive? What does your Facebook page suggest about your reliability as an employee, or as a borrower? The questions will be as varied as advertisers' interests, and as detailed as the data they can garner about us.

National surveys I have conducted suggest that Americans firmly reject this direction of marketing and media when they are made aware of it. What, then, should be done? Is industry self-regulation sufficient to achieve the kind of information respect individuals suggest they want, or are national regulations necessary to ensure it? I address these questions in Chapter 7. My argument is that a mixture of responsible industry initiatives and government laws is necessary if we are to develop a twenty-first century communication environment that reflects the openness of the democracy we would like our society to be.

Before getting to policy matters, though, the particulars that drive this important debate need to be laid out. How have we gotten to the point of worrying about how marketers shape our digital reputation? What exactly are the processes that ought to concern us, and how do they operate? The answers are part of a compelling story that begins with the academic, business, and public fascination with the internet's potential.

Chapter 1 The Power
Under the Hood

During the early days of the Web the pattern was set for advertisers to turn profiles of Web visitors into decisions about their marketing value—in other words, their reputation. Nicholas Negroponte might have charted that potential in *Being Digital*, his best-selling 1995 guide to the new order, but he didn't. Neither did the public intellectuals who followed him. The result was that marketers' growing power remained hidden from public view—and it remains so to this day. At a time when concerns about privacy and the creepiness of Web tracking are making headlines, the under-the-hood forces that generate these effects remain largely unknown. It's crucial to recognize how a new advertising system arose to transform the media and our sense of self—and in the process how it has created our rising sense of unease about digital intrusiveness.

Being Digital came out only a few months after the release of Netscape Navigator, the Web browser that began to open gates to the internet for non-techies. Negroponte headed the Massachusetts Institute of Technology's Media Lab, a hothouse for computer-based inventions supported by major corporations. His prognostications garnered wide respect in the mainstream media, and the fact that he over-looked advertisers' power hardly raised critical comments. He enthused instead about how communication technologies of the early twenty-first century would give us power to define ourselves; they would allow us to become the captains of our own attention, to focus our interests on what we value. "Your telephone won't ring indiscriminately," he wrote. "It will receive, sort, and perhaps respond to your incoming calls like a well-trained English butler."[1]

Negroponte took for granted that creators of the new media technology would tilt it toward individuals' interests rather than toward those of the commercial or governmental spheres. It also made sense to him that users of the new media technology would revel in that individualism. His model for the individual's control of meaning was a virtual newspaper he foresaw called *The Daily Me*. A prototype in the Media Lab was a project (called "Fishwrap") that was available to MIT's population only. Fishwrap was actually not as individualistic as the phrase *daily me* implies. People did receive the kinds of stories that they said they wanted and that the Media Lab's computer inferred based on previous choices. In addition, they received news that others in the MIT community believed important. Still, Negroponte, his supporters, and his critics underscored the power of the users to decide the limits of their social attention, for good or bad. "The services are egocentric," noted the *American Journalism Review* in April 1997 about commercial versions of *The Daily Me* in the wake of Fishwrap. "A user chooses what he or she wants to read and can filter out other information." The developments seemed to displace the traditional attention-setting function of editors, a point that concerned traditional journalists, who worried people might ignore socially significant agendas. *AJR* put the concern this way: "Customized online news services allow readers to receive content tailored to their interests. But do readers risk missing important developments that don't fit their profiles?"[2]

Pro or con, the idea that individuals would hold power over media desti-nies in the twenty-first century got a lot of traction. An important book to trumpet the idea positively from economic and legal standpoints was Yochai Benkler's *The Wealth of Networks*. A book jacket blurb by University of Virginia communication professor Siva Vaidhyanathan accurately described it as "a lucid, powerful, and optimistic account of a revolution in the making." Underscore the word *optimistic*. As Benkler saw it, the technological openness and flexibility of the internet would allow individuals unprecedented oppor-tunities to collaborate outside of traditional business frameworks toward the creation of an astonishing new world:

A series of changes in the technologies, economic organization, and social practices of production in this environment has created new opportunities for how we make and exchange information, knowledge, and culture. . . . [N]ewly emerging practices have seen remarkable success in areas as diverse as software development and investigative reporting, avant-garde video and multiplayer online games. Together, they hint at the emergence of a new information environment, one in which individuals are free to take a more active role than was possible in the industrial information economy of the twentieth century. This new freedom holds great practical promise: as a dimension of individual freedom; as a platform for better democratic participation; as a medium to foster a more critical and self-reflective culture; and, in an increasingly information-dependent global economy, as a mechanism to achieve improvements in human development everywhere.[3]

Paralleling Benkler's bold claims for the collaborative efficiencies afforded by new information platforms were assertions that the new technologies provided people with previously unheard of levels of power to follow their individual interests. Some pointed to the bad side of that power, others to its positive implications. Cass Sunstein took a negative slant in his book *Republic.com* and in related writings. "The most striking power provided by emerging technologies is the growing power of consumers to 'filter' what they see," he stated, in an often-cited line.[4] To Sunstein, the ability to customize news sites by topic, to skip unpalatable topics, and to find comfort in like-minded ideological blogs meant that people can live in idea cocoons of their own making, or of their making in collaboration with people who agree with them—what Sunstein called "cyber-polarization."

Henry Jenkins saw these same individual powers quite differently. In *Convergence Culture* and other works, his focus was on very active contemporary audiences who often push media companies to include them in their activities across multiple platforms, from television to magazines to fan conventions. It was a celebratory view that reveled in people's growing influence on their symbol-making environment.[5] What concerned Jenkins was not ideological polarization but teenagers' awareness of what is appropriate when wielding the liberating technologies of the digital revolution. "The world has suddenly developed a printing press for every person on the planet," he told Singapore's *Straits Times* in response to consternation in that nation about a young woman who posted nude photos of herself on her website, "but it has not prepared its culture to be responsible or imagine the consequences of suddenly becoming media makers."[6]

Jenkins overreached in his assertion: there surely are places where not everyone has even the most widespread digital medium, the cell phone— places, in fact, where those who have phones cannot afford to charge their batteries frequently. His basic point, though, is quite reasonable. Digital technologies *are* providing more people than ever with the tools to be media makers and so to reach out to more people than ever. Similarly clear in the new media landscape is the proposition that individuals are captains of their own interpretations and increasingly use them as starting points to create culturally exciting or politically dangerous worlds of understanding for themselves and others.

Yet his contentions, and those of others about digital-powers-to-the-people, beg important questions that the proponents of such views almost never raise: How broad and deep is this power by individuals and volunteer networks of collaborators compared to the large institutional brokers of cultural and political power in society? Is the new individual or group autonomy the central force that will shape the way Americans and others learn about the world and realize opportunities to benefit from it, or will other emerging factors be more important, more decisive?

The basic concerns are certainly not new with the digital age. Since at least the late 1920s, academics have disagreed about the primacy of human agency versus the power of media industries in shaping people's views of the world. Until quite recently, despite an ocean of writing about media over the past century, virtually separate worlds of media scholarship existed with different assumptions about individual autonomy. These scholars argued different worldviews but rarely clashed directly over particular cases that would try the claims of individual autonomy versus institutional power. So, for example, a raft of major quantitative studies beginning in the late 1920s at Ohio State University, Columbia University, and the U.S. military showed that personal background characteristics and social relationships led people to interpret what they heard, saw, or read from the media in their own ways, as well as to choose the content that would provide the gratifica-tions they wanted. Media, they concluded, have far more limited power to change people than many in society thought. Around the same time, a stream of critical sociologists and political economists inflected by Marxist perspectives argued that individual autonomy actually paled in the face of powerful business institutions. Sometimes generating detailed content anal-yses of media output as evidence, they insisted that the capitalist system, working with government, deeply influenced the broad social and cultural agendas from which audience members had the opportunity to choose their materials.

Similar sets of opposing academic insights converged on qualitative cultural studies. From the 1940s through the 1980s, left-leaning interests in historical and textual aspects of popular culture underscored the importance of understanding the industrial production of culture to lay bare the dynamics of institutional power. Yet by the 1980s disappointment that powerful culture-producing systems wouldn't respond to demands for substantial change coincided with quite a different view: that the actual meaning of a media article, song, sign, or video came not from its institutional creation but in its interpretation by the individual receiver, who could be often seen to create interpretations that resisted authority.

The work by Negroponte, Benkler, and even Sunstein fit neatly into this corpus as it relates to the new digital environment. While their views hold much prominence, several critiques that have emerged present an institutional perspective. One line, drawing from critical political economy, points to the huge corporations that control the content people are supposedly using autonomously. A second stream of writings on the digital world dives more directly into the human-agency fray. They see the liberating experiences that Jenkins and others have mentioned as actually part of strategies for exploitation. It is, for example, quite logical to explore Facebook and other sites that rely on content generated by the sites' users as examples of free labor in the interest of corporate profits.[7]

A few scholarly attempts accommodate both the models of individual power that Negroponte, Benkler, and Sunstein profess and the corporate-power approaches that others have advanced. Dutch theorist José van Dijck argues for seeing audience members as both independent and exploited, "as facilitator of civic engagement and participation, . . . as a producer, consumer, and data provider, as well as [in a] volatile position in the labour market."[8] Van Dijck's formulation certainly points to an important mixture of elements of individual autonomy amid corporate control. It falls short, though, of suggesting ways to map the relative importance of each. That's where understanding the contemporary media-buying business becomes critical.

The following pages show that the centrality of corporate power is a direct reality at the very heart of the digital age. In previous writings I have followed the rise of audience targeting and database marketing and suggested that marketers and ad agencies have pivotal roles in shaping a new media world. This book goes further to show how a specific system of organizations within marketing is most responsible for the transformation that is taking place. The following chapters look under the hood of what advertising executives often call the media-buying ecosystem to reveal the forces driving the evaluations of audiences. These processes are in turn leading marketers and media firms to reconfigure the entire media structure and its relationship to the ways audiences are profiled, valued, and surrounded by various forms of content. It is through this analysis that we can best understand the pressures on and strategies of search sites such as Google; portals like Yahoo!; social-media sites such as Facebook; myriad digital "publishers," from Huffington Post to CBS.com; smart phones such as the Android, iPhone, and BlackBerry; traditional radio stations; magazines; and supermarket coupons—as well as the convergence of these, and far more.

Ironically, while Henry Jenkins believes that the new system is rooted in an empowering of the audience and a respect for it, this project unpacks a fundamental lack of audience respect on the part of the media-buying system even as its practitioners use rhetorics of consumer power to hide it. None of this denies the spaces for independence of individual and group action that Negroponte, Benkler, Jenkins, Sunstein, and others identify in the new environment. It becomes clear, though, that these spaces are constrained and channeled by industry logics shaped by new media-buying mindsets that speak directly to whether, when, and how items are presented to particular audiences for attention. Increasingly, it is the media-buying system that is the prime mover in the emerging digital world.

Media buying is probably not the first thing you think of when someone mentions the advertising business. The commercial messages that surround us—the industry's most obvious products—make up its public face. They can also generate considerable controversy. Particular ads have, for example, been charged with propelling children to eat too much, encouraging women to be too thin, or urging people to demand their doctors to prescribe expensive drugs. Ads are also sometimes viewed as entertainment in and of themselves—a phenomenon that is especially striking in the yearly fixation on commercials that show up during the Super Bowl. The unending love-hate relationship with commercial appeals also shows up in a broad array of academic writings by communication researchers, anthropologists, cultural-studies analysts, and social historians on ways to understand how advertising messages "work" in society.[9]

Advertising-industry leaders try to use popular and catchy commercial images and expressions to embody their business as a whole and generate goodwill. The Advertising Walk of Fame, on New York's traditional ad capital, Madison Avenue, has become a high-profile way to define the industry for the public. In 2009, the AOL running man and the Budweiser Clydesdales entered the Walk in the category of brand characters. They beat twenty-four other nominees, including Smokey Bear and the Vlasic stork. In the slogan category, the winners were "Like a good neighbor, State Farm is there," for State Farm insurance, and "Virginia is for lovers," for Virginia tourism. They topped two dozen other nominees, including "Just do it," for Nike.[10]

These collective memories may well be useful for the industry, and scholarly analyses of advertisements may well be illuminating for what they say to and about their intended audiences. Yet lavishing attention on what trade parlance calls the "creative" side of the business leaves out essential aspects of advertising's social role. At base, advertising involves payment for attempts to persuade people to purchase or otherwise support a product or service. The definition suggests two sets of activities in addition to the creation of a persuasive message. One, traditionally called media planning and buying, revolves around the provision of funds to pay for placement of the notice. The other, part of marketing research, entails evaluating whether and how the message worked. Both areas of ad work have evolved substantially over the past century or so; so has the creative side. The advertising playbook says that practitioners from "creative," research, and planning/buying should work together for maximum impact of a campaign, and often they do. Nevertheless, the center of gravity in the industry has moved so that the media-buying and planning function has taken outsized importance. The forthcoming chapters describe such fundamental shifts around media buying and the research to define its success (what are often called *metrics*) that they are causing advertising-industry and media-industry executives to fundamentally rethink the very nature of their businesses, their relationships with advertisers, their dealings with media firms, and their approaches to audiences.

The changes are particularly momentous with the large consumer-oriented marketers, companies such as Procter and Gamble, Kraft, General Motors, and Nestlé, that have developed cozy relationships with television, magazines, radio, billboard companies, and newspapers over the past century. The trade magazine *Advertising Age* estimates that in 2009 the top one hundred consumer advertisers in the United States spent around $90.7 billion on advertising.[11] Those advertising expenditures are the fuel not only for commercial messages about their products but also for great portions of entertainment, news, and information in the United States and around the world. It follows that decisions by them and their ad agencies to shift even a small portion of their buys to the digital media—around 15 percent and growing quickly in 2010—validated the new data-gathering models for media buying and pushed them ahead. At the same time, the reallocation of money to the Web, video games, and mobile handsets reinforced the process of devaluing traditional ad vehicles, particularly print newspapers and magazines.

Although these changes are today associated with digital media, they are rooted in the pre-Web era. During the 1980s and early 1990s, many companies decided to restructure media planning and buying into stand-alone businesses within the advertising industry. Looking back at the slow ramp-up to media buying's current prominence, we can see a growing desire to measure and label consumer responses as part of the new media agencies' need to justify expectations of their parent companies. The latter were encouraging major advertisers to consolidate unprecedented amounts of money into their new buying subsidiaries. As part of their desire to distinguish themselves from other firms, media-agency executives boasted about a continually growing quantitative audience knowledge and about their agencies' abilities to measure their advertising clients' audience responses as well as the specific benefits—returns on investments—that the agencies' clients were getting for their expensive campaigns. To attract clients, executives exhorted the new divisions to develop proprietary technologies and models that predicted audience behavior in traditional media—television, magazines, radio, newspapers—that had never been subject to such evaluative gymnastics. The claims were thin in the beginning, but the underlying logic took on a life of its own. When the internet came along, media buyers saw its interactive environment as terrific terrain for expanding their numerical understanding of audiences—and for using the measures and labels directly to sell products.

The new approaches to measurement, along with the creation of specialized media agencies, clearly were responses by advertising-agency executives to the new realities of their industry's relationship with clients and media in both Europe and the United States. Although many were flummoxed by media buying's newfound prominence, historical precedent did exist for such a trend. In the nineteenth and early twentieth centuries agency executives considered media buying complex and so media buyers were respected, often powerful, figures. During network radio's heyday, from the late 1920s through the 1940s, advertisers typically owned the programs they sponsored, and media departments often produced them for their clients. That "full-sponsorship" model withered in the 1950s, however, during television's first decade, as the networks and local stations owned the shows and agencies bought slots in and around them based on the numbers of viewers tuning in. The criteria to evaluate the purchase of radio ad time, as well as the purchase of ad space in magazines and newspapers, became similarly straightforward.

By the 1960s the media-buying process had become so predictable for national advertisers that many considered the task of buying print space and broadcast time for clients a paint-by-numbers activity. Advertising agencies built their reputation instead on their creative work. While an agency's research department was appreciated as a vehicle for helping copywriters and art personnel develop their ideas, most industry practitioners took planning and buying units for granted. They understood that a large part of overall agency revenues typically derived from the then-standard 15 percent commission that was determined by the amount its buying division spent for the media time or space occupied by the advertisements the copy and art department created. But they also knew that most of the buying work was conducted by low-paid recent college graduates, most of them female, who pored over boring television ratings and periodical circulation data in conjunction with advertising charges to determine the key measure of an ad vehicle's efficiency: CPM (or cost per mil), the price for reaching a thousand members of the target audience via that outlet. The challenging part of this job, which was done by the head media buyers, was hardly creative by Madison Avenue's definition of the word; it involved tough bargaining to lower the CPM, interspersed with the kinds of backslapping and dining with competitors that might be unseemly if it didn't produce results for clients. "Let's be honest—media buyers have always suffered from a sort of Rodney Dangerfield status in the ad world," an *Adweek* reporter wrote in 1998. "Sure they handled the lion's share of the client's money, but when it came to getting respect, they ended up with zilch."[12]

Nevertheless, because media buying was a financial engine, agency leaders before the 1980s considered the activity a critical and inextricable part of the agency structure. Yet in the 1960s and 1970s, media-buying independents (those disconnected from advertising agencies) emerged in Europe and

North America. In France, Gilbert Gross launched what became a buying powerhouse, Carat. In Canada, Peter Simpson launched Media Buying Services and set up a London office. In the United States Dennis Holt began Western International Media. And in the United Kingdom, which became the epicenter of this mini-movement, Allan Rich and Don Becket launched The Media Business, and David Reich started The Media Department. The clients that these and firms like them found were not the blue-chip advertisers that full-service agencies on both sides of the pond coveted. Independents tended to attract direct-marketing companies that created their print ads or TV commercials themselves and needed an intermediary to buy space or time for them. Ron Popeil, whose Ronco company invented the Veg-O-Matic food slicer and who called himself the "Greatest Salesman of the Century," was the archetypal client. Western International managed to work at the higher end, representing movie producers such as Clint Eastwood, who needed Western to place commercials for their films.

The ad-industry establishment did not worry much about the clients these independents were winning. Their concern was that independent media buyers would undermine the lucrative commission system because they were charging a lot less than the 15 percent that the full-service agencies were demanding. The concern was especially high in Britain, where the independent-media movement was particularly strong during the 1960s and 1970s. "They were called cowboys, crooks, conmen and several other words beginning with C.," a reporter recalled.[13]

The first moves toward mainstream acceptance of stand-alone buying firms occurred in 1975 in the United Kingdom. Richardson-Vicks had placed its Oil of Olay brand with a small London agency that, R-V felt, was doing good creative work but which had lost its capacity to perform media buying adequately. The marketer had other brands at the U.K. subsidiary of the full-service U.S. agency Benton and Bowles, and the client asked B&B's media director, Ray Morgan, if he would help out by taking on the Oil of Olay account as a piece of media-only business. Morgan agreed; there had been precedents for that sort of activity in London. But then he took a novel step. He asked the agency management if he could reconstitute the media department as a stand-alone division within the group so that he might get other media-only clients. His request was approved, and, because Mercury House was the location of B&B's offices, he called the division Mercury Media.

The establishment of Mercury Media made it acceptable for blue-chip advertisers to link up with media-only agencies. Another buying firm with connections to the advertising establishment, John Ayling & Associates, began in 1978. Ayling focused on the needs of creative boutiques that were emerging in London in the early 1980s, shops such as Bartle Bogle Hegarty and Leagas Delaney. They didn't want the cost and responsibility of media departments and found that their respectable clients had no problem with Ayling picking up those duties. "Suddenly," Ayling recalled, "we were working with different sorts of clients—the likes of Audi and Levi's. Along with what Morgan was doing, it gave the sector even more credibility. There was a feeling that the earliest independents just booked airtime. We were doing media."[14]

Ray Morgan's activities over the next few years moved the stand-alone firm into a new era of bigness and consolidation. He went fully independent in 1985 when he and his team left Benton and Bowles to start Ray Morgan & Partners with a roster of major clients such as General Foods, Johnson Wax, and Richardson-Vicks. Then, in 1988, Maurice and Charles Saatchi bought Morgan's business. The Saatchi brothers were proponents of the advertising agency holding company, the notion that dominance in all parts of the industry could be achieved by buying a number of full-service agencies with worldwide networks, great creative boutiques, and allied businesses such as public relations outfits. The first agency holding company, Interpublic, was actually founded in 1960. Its creator, Marion Harper, Jr., aimed to get around a major obstacle of an ad agency's growth: client conflicts. Advertisers had long established the principle that if an agency represented one type of firm—a car manufacturer, for example—it should not represent another of the same type out of both respect and a concern for leaking sensitive information. Harper was sure he had hit on a solution: Own two or more advertising agencies that operate separately but feed the revenues to the central firm. He would do the same thing with marketing services firms— research companies and brand-consulting outfits, for example. Interpublic under Harper grew quickly to include two hundred offices in a hundred cities and forty-eight countries. Things turned disastrous, though, as his inability to cope with the umbrella firm's skyrocketing overhead brought the company to the brink of bankruptcy in 1967.[15] Harper was forced out in disgrace, and while Interpublic eventually righted itself the entire episode convinced ad executives that a holding company was not a sustainable goal in their business.

Yet the idea reemerged during the 1980s. At that time, consolidations were the norm in many industries. The Saatchis, who had been in the agency business since 1970, saw the logic of extending consolidation to marketing communication. They argued that multinational companies would seek all possible economies of scale by using a single provider of not only advertising but also public relations, marketing, research, and consulting. Often using their company's stock as payment, the brothers bought solid agencies in Britain and, beginning in 1982, began a shopping spree to get hold of a raft of U.S. firms in the advertising, public-relations, and research fields, a number of which had important worldwide networks. To those who scoffed that Saatchi & Saatchi would be better off growing internally than acquiring firms, Charles Saatchi noted in 1985 that well over half of the agency's growth recently had come internally, but he also defended the acquisitions. "If you're going to offer global advertising, you need to establish a credible network," he said. "You can't just open little offices all over the world. There have been takeovers in communications—the Interpublic Group was assembled that way—but we've attracted more attention because we're an English firm doing lots of things American."[16] In 1986 the Saatchis' purchase of New York–based Ted Bates Worldwide made them owners of the world's largest advertising holding company. It also brought them close to a promise they had made in 1984: that within two years the firm would be among the top-ten agencies in the top-ten international markets.[17]

It was this outsized confidence in their understanding of their business that led the Saatchi brothers to merge Ray Morgan & Partners with the media-buying activities of their three U.K. ad agencies into one subsidiary, which they called Zenith Media. Its new structure kept much media planning for the clients in the agency (a vehicle to let the agency keep the commission) but subcontracted media-buying decisions to Zenith, which was staffed by 150 people. At the time it was easily the United Kingdom's biggest media buyer, handling $1.2 billion worth of advertising—18 percent of the British market.[18] The Saatchis argued that Zenith's clout was a necessary balance to the concentration of power among European media owners such as Rupert Murdoch's News Corporation, which in the late 1980s controlled 35 percent of Britain's print media.[19]

The merger caused consternation among London's small independent media houses and full-service agencies. They argued it would lead to intractable conflicts of interest in which competing clients from the three agencies now would have access to buying work for rival advertisers. What's more, they continued, separating planning from buying would lead to a decline in the skills of media-buying companies. The Saatchis responded that far from dumbing down the quality of media planning and buying, Zenith would work to cultivate both skills by bringing about £100 million of independent buying and planning billings directly into the agency.[20] Moreover, they asserted, the firm's size and salaries would attract smart buyers. That would be necessary for "handling an increasingly complex media"[21]—the expansion of commercial broadcast channels and the spread of cable television, satellite TV, and VCRs that were in the 1980s multiplying viewing options in homes throughout Western Europe. As for the conflict-of-interest concern, the Saatchis argued that Zenith had set up impervious walls that would not allow competing clients to know what media their competitors were buying.

In Britain observers saw the creation of Zenith as an indication of a profound change in the buying game. The U.K. trade magazine *Campaign* said that "the media buying industry is being shaken to its foundation." It suggested "forthcoming major structural changes whereby the size of market share controlled by agencies will become increasingly important in future years."[22] But while heavyweight media-buying firms (or joint ventures between advertising firms) began to spread rather quickly through Western Europe and parts of Asia, freestanding buying operations failed to get traction in the United States until the mid–1990s. One longtime *Campaign* writer suggested that it was because "over in the US . . . the business culture is more conservative."[23]

Part of the issue in the United States was a fear of client conflicts. Several major advertisers refused to come near a media-buying unit that also bought space or time for a competitor. Another reason for the hesitation was a long-time belief that the full-service agency was the best model to take care of client needs, integrating creative, research, planning, and buying. In contrast to Zenith and other U.K. media agencies, the heads of most U.S. versions that began to develop insisted that they had to be involved in planning as well as buying. They argued that as the stewards of an advertiser's media investment, they rightfully should be responsible for both.[24] That sort of worry often led full-service agencies to balk at handing over strategic planning even to a media shop under the same corporate umbrella. They feared "simply turning into creative boutiques."[25]

The early 1990s certainly saw attempts to find models of the consolidated media-buying operation that would be palatable in the United States. Zenith and Carat tried, with quite mixed results; they attributed some of their rough spots to being unprepared for the U.S. media market's much greater variety and complexity than that of Europe. A combined media operation of two homegrown U.S. ad agencies, Ogilvy & Mather and J Walter Thompson, was also not greeted with open arms by all clients. The O&M/JWT combination was engineered by their owner, a London-based marketing-services holding company named WPP. It was run by Martin Sorrell, who had helped the Saatchis build their empire with a similar buying philosophy though also with a bit more financial caution. Larry Cole, Ogilvy & Mather's media director, put a positive spin on "the alliance" to *Advertising Age:* "We can move inventory between various clients, and cover periods when one advertiser has fewer ads running than another," he said. Yet others pointed out that many kinds of conflicts could lower the effectiveness of bargaining with media firms when several clients with different interests were involved. "Let's see what happens when it's 3 in the morning during the upfront [TV marketplace] and Sprint [a JWT client] and IBM [an O&M client] want a deal with some network to close, but Ford [a JWT client] and American Express [an O&M client] don't," said one network TV executive. "That's where the rubber hits the road." There was also the more traditional client-conflict issue. For example, O&M had recently won the GTE phone company account while JWT was steward of its competitor, Sprint. *Advertising Age* reported that "one executive close to the situation" said GTE would not join the media-buying alliance partly because of Sprint's presence.[26]

Through the 1990s, though, resistance to stand-alone media-buying units that consolidated huge budgets began to fade in the United States as it had in Europe. (The U.S. media units included the planners.) Both the agency side and the client side realized that the plusses outweighed the minuses. The agencies involved were a handful of towering holding companies that were increasingly collecting advertising-agency networks, regional ad agencies, creative boutiques, public-relations agencies, promotion shops, branding companies, and far more in organizational structures than only those who knew and loved them well could understand. The decade saw enormous struggles for position and control, with four dominant worldwide holding companies emerging: Omnicom and Interpublic, based in New York; WPP, based in London; and Publicis (which had absorbed the Saatchis' holdings), sited in Paris. In addition to these were two firms with French pedigrees, great renown, and strong reputations as buying authorities: Aegis, based by then in London, and Havas, based in Suresnes, France.

Part of the philosophy of these companies was to offer the services of any one of their subsidiaries to an interested marketer on an à la carte basis. Media planning and buying could operate that way and become profit centers rather than service activities. Bringing in huge amounts of money had become an economic imperative in the face of clients' determination to lower commissions substantially. The 15 percent commission on media purchases had pretty well disappeared. In a still-small but growing number of cases tightfisted clients were forcing agencies to forgo commissions altogether and instead get paid for the cost of the work plus an agreed-upon margin. In 1999 the head of DDB Worldwide complained that advertisers were typically paying between 5 percent and 15 percent and wanted to push down payments to 6 percent of media expenditures for creative and 3 percent for media buying.[27] Some at the time said that because of the rabid competition among agencies for business, media-buying commissions were already typically 2 percent to 3 percent at full-service agencies. Holding companies realized that if they could bring together lots of clients with huge budgets into freestanding media-buying firms, they could charge fees even lower than those and still be quite profitable. In the late 1990s, *Adweek* reported that the U.S.-based independent media agency CIA routinely racked up margins of 12 percent to 15 percent. The publication noted that Aegis-owned stand-alone Carat typically posted margins as high as 22 percent.[28]

Clients, too, were beginning to see the benefits of consolidating their buying under one roof rather than spreading it out across the several agencies doing their creative work. It was a time of huge growth in the number of TV channels available to the home viewer, increasing popularity of the internet, increasing product-placement possibilities in television and other media, and new attention to targeting segments of the audience. With an awareness that two-thirds of their ad budget was going to media spending, major marketers such as P&G, Coca-Cola, and Nestlé were scrutinizing their advertising dollars in search of efficiencies and innovative ways to reach their customers. "Clients are focusing on a line in their budget that they didn't pay much attention to for years," said Mike Moore, executive vice president and director of media development at the MacManus Group.[29] That became easier when clients decided to be somewhat more lenient in their definitions of client conflicts. P&G, with among the toughest approaches to conflicts, in 1999 allowed its roster shops to join holding companies with agencies that worked for key competitors—with the one exception of its archrival Unilever.[30] Procter and Gamble's decision marked acceptance of the agency world's movement toward a handful of powerful corporations with multiple marketing-communications capabilities.

What's more, advertisers realized that the megamergers might bring efficiencies to large clients by offering many services under one roof. And "increasingly," noted *Adweek* in 1998, "major marketers have decided they can receive greater impact from their ad dollars by realizing the economies of scale that come from unbundling and consolidating their media budgets within a single shop."[31] For the holding companies, attracting all the billings of a major marketer into a media firm would be the kind of coup that would justify foreswearing competitors. That logic made headlines in 1997 when P&G consolidated its $1.2 billion TV billings into a single media shop, MediaVest.[32] A way around the conflict problem would be for a holding company to create two or more media-buying outfits, a process that took on steam through the 2000s. Holding companies also showed a willingness to create media planning and buying units dedicated to particular clients—GM Works at Omnicom, for example, and Ford MotorWorks at WPP. "I think you'll see more of that," said Bob Brennan, chief operating officer of Chicago-based Leo Burnett media-buying division, Starcom USA. "The fact is that you've got to be able to plan media so discretely and react on a real-time basis to what's going on in the marketplace that having it all in one place is going to be the way of the future."[33]

To Brennan and his counterparts in big media shops, the past decade had already transformed their business. Brennan recalled in 1999 that when he entered advertising twenty years earlier, "successful marketing was all about [a] great creative [side], because you dealt with a very static media environment, and the only way to really break through and build a brand was to have a great message. Today, the media environment has so changed that you can't have a great brand unless you have great creative and great media. When we started in the business, 95% of your success was great creative, and 5% was great media. I don't know that it's 50–50 now, but it's much closer to 50–50 today than it was when we started."[34]

By the late 1990s the consolidation of media buying had reached a point at which the number of huge media agencies was declining. "We have been shocked by the speed at which the industry is consolidating," said the head of Carat's U.S. business, David Verklin, in 1998. "If you're not one of the [top] four or five [companies], you're probably looking over your shoulder and getting nervous."[35] Having gotten to that point of power and status, the leaders of the biggest media shops looked for ways to maintain and extend their growing centrality to the advertising world. They knew they were in an age in which the clients with the biggest accounts—global corporations—were obsessed with quantifying their return on their marketing investments and demanding accountability from agencies while allowing them rather small profit margins. Media-buying executives therefore began to position their firms as places where the massive scale that came from consolidating media holdings would mean not just buying clout. It would signal worldwide planning capability, quantitative research expertise, and advanced technological know-how. In short, these executives claimed, only the very largest media agencies would have the depth of resources to serve and maintain marketers' jumbo accounts adequately. "You need to be wherever your clients do business, with capabilities that handle everyone's expectations," argued Alec Gerster, chairman of WPP's MediaCom. "You need scale and size and intelligence."[36] With this requirement giving just a few firms a step up in the bidding, their executives argued that their outfits had more than bargaining clout (which their competitors also had). They had special knowledge to drive their clients' returns on media investments. "When you get to that size and scale, the model needs to be less Western International Media and more Andersen Consulting," asserted David Verklin in 1997 when he was managing director of the Hal Riney & Partners ad agency.[37] A year later he was heading Carat's U.S. business and continuing to argue the importance of sophisticated thinking about complex issues. "You have to take things to the next level. It needs to be more than 'We buy a ton of media,'" he added. "You need to think about your job as managing messages [and] you need to learn a lot more about a client's business."[38]

The trend away from commissions in favor of flat fees for all kinds of advertising work, including media, increased the need for greater accountability. "If you can demonstrate value, you can attach a price for the product," the MacManus Group's Moore said. One tack in that direction, said Stephen King, general manager of Zenith Media's U.S. division, was the U.S. unit's "breadth and depth" with specialized divisions such as merchandising, sports marketing, national broadcast, and interactive medium.[39] Increasingly, though, the new media shops were explicitly touting that they had proprietary research about the right consumers to target as well as special technology to decide how to reach them. The combination, they claimed, would generate high return on the investment of media dollars. The cost of research on media audiences had skyrocketed exponentially as the media universe exploded from three to six national TV networks, plus hundreds of new independent stations and cable outlets, not to mention new arrivals such as internet advertising. Executives in media firms owned by global agency conglomerates argued that their massive size and global reach meant they could afford unmatched proprietary research that would boost sales results. Jon Mandel, chief negotiating officer at MediaCom, Grey Advertising's media agency, proudly told *Advertising Age* that his firm spent more on research than it did on any other factor except personnel.[40] And when Interpublic bought Western International Media and merged it with its Initiative media-buying operation, executives let the trade press know that "an immediate post-merger research bonus was realized when the media management firm was able to tap into Initiative Media's proprietary research on how consumers relate to advertising."[41]

Leadership in computer-driven solutions was another tack through which the biggest media shops looked for ways to maintain and extend their growing centrality to the advertising world. Each big media-buying firm wanted to show that it could lead the ad industry in finding exclusive, quantitative ways to plan media and measure success. The basic aim was not new. One of the great ambitions of media buying during the second half of the twentieth century was the creation of a model that would optimize advertising expenditures to reach intended audiences across a variety of media. Quantitative attempts at that "media optimization" had taken flight with the arrival of mainframe computers in the offices of the largest advertising agencies in the early 1960s.[42] The idea was that available broadcast ratings, periodical-circulation data, media-cost information, research findings, and executives' intuitions about audience reactions could be integrated into formulas. They would yield the optimal mix of print and broadcast outlets through which to advertise—and the dollars to be spent on each.

Optimization had doubters, who said it simply pretended to be scientific. They noted that at the core of some optimization formulas were simple beliefs by executives about how much weight to give different media for their ability to persuade different audiences. Other formulas tried to use experimental tests to come up with "objective" weights for the impact of different media. Some executives argued that even if the experiments were applicable to the larger population (a big if), these weights too were problematic because they didn't take into account that "impact relationships among media would be influenced by the product category, the creative execution, the audience of the medium, the medium's environment (e.g. the mood created, the credibility of the publication, etc.), and the payoff measure [for example, recall of the ad or purchase of the advertised product] which the impact weight reflected."[43] A slim amount of research, and a lot of industry lore, suggested that certain content environments somehow encouraged commercial recall better than did others—for example, audiences could better recall commercials for pain relievers when they were placed in TV dramas than when the ads were placed in TV comedies. These considerations too had to enter the optimization models.[44]

Erwin Ephron, a respected advertising consultant, wrote in 2000 that the data underlying optimization and other sorts of advertising research was dubious. "Science is giving way to convenience in the way we gather all of our numbers. Who but an opportunist would try to measure 200 magazines in a single survey [as MRI research was doing]? Who but a cynic would still use a household diary [as Nielsen was doing for TV and Arbitron for radio]? And the pressure to count and quantify increases each day. The scientist in us wants a rational approach to decision-making based on substantial data. But the guy who does the work in us understands that much of the data we need will never be available, and much of the data we have are not substantial. The discomfort is not in making do with deficient data. It's with our growing need to make the numbers up."[45]

In the eyes of Ephron and other critics, building optimization weights into formulas based on these ideas simply lent bad research and executives' guesses a spurious aura of quantitative legitimacy. Ephron well understood the organizational vectors pushing media firms to use those technologies. "In advertising, made-up metrics is the backside of accountability," he noted. "Management pressure to reduce 'judgment calls' to get more rational spending decisions creates systems that require numbers that just aren't there."[46] Despite these cautions, advertisers, agencies, and independent media firms (especially Carat in France) kept trying to improve on the models with better guesses and more research. Exploiting client concerns about the increased complexity of the media-buying environment, including the internet, the media agencies of the holding companies touted proprietary computer analyses of data that allowed them to be accountable to their clients with the best return on investment. Grey's MediaCom, for example, billed its global media-planning system, known as Maxis, as the "first and only optimization system to utilize fourth-generation technology." Young & Rubicam's Media Edge buying unit promoted its Brand Asset Valuator system to clients in its media presentations. "Whatever you call them," noted *Adweek,* "none of these optimizers comes cheap; Carat executives boast that their firm spends nearly $33 million each year on developing new research technologies."[47]

David Verklin, Carat's U.S. boss, risked antagonizing copywriters and art directors by proclaiming that world-class planning and buying were where advertising's true creativity were now to be found. Creative agencies were predisposed to building campaigns around certain well-known television and print vehicles. They did this both in response to tradition and because they continued to believe in the strong impact of these vehicles over other media along with cost-per-thousand (CPM) numbers that looked favorable because they reached so many people. Verklin and others argued that these a priori choices by creative department personnel based on broad generalizations about impact and audience size might not be best as media choices proliferated, from internet to cable TV. The buyers contended that people's involvement with so many media outlets called for strategies that would follow audiences across different platforms and that would utilize a wide spectrum of marketing-communication activities, not just advertising. The real key to efficient return on the client's spending was to be media-agnostic at the start and let research and optimization technology point to the right mix. "Before we figure out advertising strategy we need to figure out communications strategy," Verklin told *Advertising Age*. "For example, maybe given a limited budget, we should do only trade advertising for a client. Or maybe it is better not to use advertising at all and just use public relations. We are trying to help a client figure out the appropriate communications strategy and then turn it over to the advertising agencies."[48]

Carat scored a coup in 2001 when Philips Electronics decided to place its $600-million media-buying and planning account with that company and at the same time dictated that Philips's creative agencies had to take their instructions from Carat about what commercial messages to create for what media. "We want to turn the process on its head," said Mark Kerray, head of Philips's Global Brand Management in Amsterdam, adding that Philips was looking to Carat to help it find more nontraditional advertising and media vehicles. Philips, like many other companies with big budgets, had relied heavily on TV and print, and was now looking for new avenues.[49]

That was exactly what advocates of the huge new media-buying houses wanted to see happen. "These new media entities can handle the complexity needed to really understand who an advertiser's target is and move us away from CPMs to something that looks a lot more like return on investment," said Stephen Heyer, CEO of cable-delivered Turner Broadcasting System in

2001. At that point Heyer clearly hoped to benefit from media buyers' evident willingness to take money from broadcast network television budgets.[50] Still, the environment for the large media-buying units was not at all settled. Traditional attitudes and organizational structures within many advertising clients often short-circuited buyers' media-agnostic perspective, sided with agency creative personnel about the power of standard television and print, and lessened the need to bring huge media budgets into one organization. At the same time, the still-consolidating agency-holding companies were piling more and more media-buying units from ad agencies they acquired into two or three giant media-buying operations per holding company. With the bringing together of many clients came huge expectations for husbanding large proportions of their media budgets so that small profit margins could translate into huge revenues. The trick for the big buying operations going into the twenty-first century would be to keep big money coming in by highlighting their quantitative knowledge of the audience, accepting accountability for return-on-investments—and demonstrating results.

It was a daunting goal. But just around that time, a medium they had only recently begun to consider, the Web, gave them the golden opportunity to do all these things and more by simply focusing on the audience's click of a button. Along with their advertiser-clients, media agencies' early involvement with publishers in the new medium was rocky, marked by both enthusiasm and disappointment on all sides. It was in these early interactions that the essential weakness of Web publishers in the relationship—along with their willingness to track audiences and even mold content to secure sponsorships—was born.

Chapter 2 Clicks
and Cookies

The May 17, 1993, issue of *Adweek* featured an essay urging the advertising industry to colonize the internet. Its author, business writer and researcher Michael Schrage, was sure major advertisers would turn the internet into their next great vehicle. Writing at a time when media buyers saw the internet as both primitive and anti-commercial, Schrage adopted a tone that was both admonitory and celebratory. He began by invoking the hot media properties of the day to flag the superiority of the internet: "A uniquely American network that's growing faster than John Malone's TCI ever did; that's even more global than Ted Turner's CNN; and is light years more interactive than Barry Diller's QVC. It's called Internet." He continued:

> Advertisers and agencies take note: It has the potential to become the next great mass/personal medium. No one really "owns" it; no one really "manages" it. Nonetheless, over the past five years the Internet has exploded into a multimedia phenomenon that deserves the serious attention of anyone who wants to understand what the future has to look like.

. . . Virtually every major university, corporation and government agency in the world is on it. Now that it's being privatized, the Internet is rapidly opening up to the tens of millions of personal computers. Forget Prodigy, CompuServe and America Online. What the world's telecommunications networks are to telephones, Internet is becoming for personal computers.

Pick a media metaphor, any metaphor—direct mail, telemarketing, broadcasting, narrowcasting, interactive multimedia—and the Internet is flexible enough to handle it. Want to put the L. L. Bean catalogue online? And let people place custom orders with their American Express cards? Why not advertising-sponsored electronic mail? Technically, the Internet could do it today. Want to do a direct electronic mailing? Electronic classifieds? Interactive animated brochures? It's already happening.[1]

Schrage noted that talk radio already existed on the internet. ("The neat aspect is that you can capture only the snippets of the show that you want and file them into your PC for retrieval at your leisure. No plans yet to get Rush Limbaugh.") He foresaw that video would follow radio and "the Internet may well be a driving force in making tomorrow's PCs even more TV-like." He argued that in view of the heavy downloading of pornographic pictures, the future was bright: "Where 'adult' services begin, mainstream programming is sure to follow." Schrage ended his essay with a prediction about media buying: "That's why the Internet is like the early days of radio. The technology is there and accessible; more people are logging on; big ideas are just waiting to be born. It's exciting. My bet? By the end of 1996, at least two major advertising agencies will be designing ads and recommending Internet buys for at least a dozen of their Fortune 1000 clients."[2]

Nearly two decades later, it's clear that Schrage's predictions about advertisers' ability to reach people through the internet, and even his internet-buying recommendations, were remarkably accurate. But what he failed to foresee, or at least to note, in 1996 was that Madison Avenue's movement into this new world would be quite rocky and uncertain. A key reason for this was the struggle to create media-buying criteria to legitimate the new medium. What audience characteristics should advertisers demand that website owners deliver? What kinds of measurements ("metrics") should advertisers require of websites to prove that they reached the right audiences in a profitable manner? In 1993, systematic measurements of internet audiences simply didn't exist. Media buyers initially had little clue how to evaluate their advertising spending in the new online world.

Not that it was a top-of-mind issue for the major media-buying agencies and their clients. During the 1990s, these clients saw online work as low-budget and experimental, a probe into a future in which the effects of advertising could be far more measurable than with traditional media. As for media buyers, many were in the throes of developing the freestanding planning-and-buying profit centers described in Chapter 1. In so doing, one of their primary goals was to improve the metrics available to them regarding audiences for television, magazines, radio, newspapers, and other traditional media. To these media-buying agencies the internet was a marginal consideration. They competed in that space with small start-up firms that were often devoted to both online creative work and buying.

Nevertheless, when media buyers did place persuasive messages into the digital space, they employed the hardball, quantitative approaches to efficiency and measurement that they were working to establish throughout the media system. From the beginning of their involvement, they saw an audience member's click—a concept Michael Schrage didn't invoke—as the central proof of value. To them the click was the attribute that distinguished the internet. With traditional media, agency practitioners had to use general circulation figures and program ratings to make decisions about where to place their advertisements. They had no way to know, for example, exactly how many people would really see a magazine ad or watch a television commercial. The click was compelling for media buyers because they saw it helping them implement the increasing measurability—read quantification—of advertising that was part of the additional value they claimed when talking to clients about their new stand-alone business models. Further, though more subtle, the click was a tangible audience action that media buyers and advertisers could use as a vehicle to ease their historical anxiety over whether people notice their persuasive messages or, even more, care about them. At the very least, they hoped, it would finally eliminate the legendary client complaint: "I know that half of my advertising works, but I don't know which half."

Despite the availability of the click, media buyers and their clients oscillated between enthusiasm and pessimism. The story of the Web's first few years is one of ambivalence regarding its role for advertisers. On one side was optimism that an ability to track responses through clicks would make the "on line" space the great new place to reach out to audiences. On the other side was a continual worry that ways to think about clicks, and techniques to measure them, were flawed and raised more questions about accountability than answers.

The concerns led to indecisiveness about measuring audiences on websites and continual changing of the definitions for success. The indecision was reinforced by practices within the advertising industry that separated key media-buying decision makers from those involved with the Web. It was exacerbated by a desire by interactive media buyers and their clients to push down online ad prices rather than give the new medium slack. And it was furthered by continual comparison of the Web to television, to the former's detriment. Major advertisers saw television as the consummate branding medium—a major way to create likable personalities for their products. They suspected that the Web, at the time visible only on a computer with a small screen, would never rise to the status of a serious branding vehicle. Because of the clicks it might be useful for rather basic forms of direct marketing. For a time the nation's largest advertiser, Procter and Gamble, and its internet-buying firm, media.com, advocated this position.

Yet the creators and distributors of content on the internet—they would be called internet "publishers"—believed the rhetoric claiming that the internet would become the new big medium. They doggedly kept trying to find favor in the eyes of leading advertisers. They had little choice. Having rather quickly decided that their audiences wouldn't pay for their online content, they looked to media planners and their clients for long-term survival. The publishers became sellers of a "banner" form of advertising—essentially a rectangular box positioned either vertically or horizontally across the Web page—on which a site visitor could click. Websites used all sorts of click-related metrics to make Web audiences stand out to advertisers and argue valuable returns on investment. They tried new ways of counting clicks. They tried new ad formats and technologies to spike clicks on ads. They tried to find ways to understand why visitors went to their site so that marketers could target among them efficiently. They joined up with firms that charged advertisers for people's clicks on ads around the Web, traced what visitors were doing across many sites, and drew conclusions about them so marketers could select among them efficiently. And when media buyers and major marketers still grumbled that the results were not what they wanted, the Web publishers and their partners in click metrics went back to learn even more detailed information about their audiences.

A major irony of this one-step forward, half-step backward period for Web marketing was that advertisers turned the very phenomenon that was supposed to make the internet their best vehicle—its interactivity—into a liability. Web publishers simply could not persuade buyers that the Web met their new bar for acceptable quantitative measurement. Many buyers scoffed that internet metrics lent less insight into target audiences than did the measurement schemes of traditional media. Some advertising executives, in fact, dismissed Web audiences as unattractive precisely because of their interactive habits. One result of that irony was a determination by Web publishers to show Madison Avenue it was wrong. They and their technology allies placed a key proposition permanently at the heart of the new system: help media buyers identify measureable ways to know, target, and consider the impact of commercial messages on audiences as never before, even in the face of vocal public worries about privacy invasion.

In 1994, the start of the Web's first commercial decade, most companies considered the internet out-of-bounds for advertising campaigns. In those years it was primarily a text-based medium; pictures and sounds could be downloaded and opened only through special software. The internet was therefore not amenable to the large display ads and audiovisual commercials that were used in traditional media to build brand images. More important, to marketers internet users seemed fiercely protective of what an *Advertising Age* writer in 1993 called a "culture . . . which is loath to advertising."[3] The "usenet" discussion groups that populated this world had created strong norms against sending obvious and persistent sales messages. People who went against the norms were "flamed"—subjected to barrages of angry replies. Nevertheless, in this environment advertisers still found ways to reach internet users. The key, said those doing it, lay in subtlety. They often used the euphemism *information provider* and emphasized the helpfulness of the activity.[4] But most firms wanting to reach people "on line" tended to do so via Prodigy, a dial-up information and entertainment service founded in 1984 by CBS, computer manufacturer IBM, and retailer Sears, Roebuck and Company. Its revenues came from subscriptions and advertising. In the early 1990s, Toyota, for example, had a Prodigy area where Toyota owners could communicate with one another and the company. Sara Lee Corp.'s L'Eggs hosiery offered catalog shopping on Prodigy. Straightforward ad banners touted companies of various sizes and types; advertising, often with low-resolution graphics, was said to take up as much as one-third of Prodigy's available viewing area.

To people in the advertising industry of the early 1990s, Prodigy represented one facet of what they called "interactive." Used in this way—as a noun rather than an adjective—interactive referred to a raft of new technologies that had arrived in the 1970s and 1980s and had the ability to go beyond the one-way flow of traditional media to encourage potential customers to learn more about their company. These included CD-ROM, computer-driven store kiosks, interactive television, and online services such as Prodigy and interactive TV versions called videotex. A smattering of major marketers found it appealing to reach out to people they figured were well-heeled, highly educated consumers who adopted these tools. The firms were joined by a number of big ad agencies, often those that had them as clients and that considered the area small but possibly promising, and, in any event, both the agencies and the clients could be portrayed as cutting-edge. Ogilvy & Mather's interactive division, Ogilvy Direct, had the deepest roots. The agency started this division in 1981 to create marketing material for Time Inc.'s new teletext enterprise (teletext was a technology for broadcasting printed information, such as news reports and sports scores, to television sets equipped with a special decoder). Although Time discontinued the venture in 1983, Ogilvy Direct survived. Led by Martin Nisenholtz, it developed into an operation with forty employees that in 1994 had ongoing projects on one or another interactive medium with Equitable, Forbes, House of Seagram, Kraft, General Foods, Campbell Soup, Hewlett-Packard, and American Express. Ogilvy's size and breadth was unusual, though. In 1994 *Advertising Age* rated major ad agencies in terms of their digital expertise and found none that came close to Ogilvy and many that seemed primarily to pay lip service to the area.

Nisenholtz acknowledged the skepticism of even his own account executives toward suggesting to their clients that they spend media-buying money on vehicles they might not understand. "Account-management people only want to work with you if they trust you," he told a reporter in 1994. "They're not going to open their kimonos and allow you access to their clients unless they know you're going to deliver."[5] Promoters of interactive businesses offered another reason for the agency establishment's skepticism and reluctance to buy space on the new technologies. A DDB Needham account executive put it bluntly in a letter to *Adweek* that same year: "Agencies have resisted all forms of new media," wrote Jonathan Anastas, because they feared "erosion of commissions, expensive capital investments during a recession, loss of creative control and fewer awards. Repeatedly, clients have asked for 'new thinking' only to get media plans loaded with expensive TV campaigns and four-color spreads." He added, "Shame on any agency executive, creative or media professional who hasn't explored Internet at least once."[6]

Interest in the medium that most in the ad world had considered off-limits had already begun to bubble up, however. Michael Schrage's 1993

Adweek piece was an example; while organized as a set of predictions, the essay was also an exhortation. About a year later an *Advertising Age* editorial echoed it, arguing that "with anywhere from 10 million to 30 million relatively well-educated, affluent and cutting-edge online users, the Internet would seem to be a heavenly place for advertising."[7] *Advertising Age* didn't say where it got its numbers; the Forrester Research internet consultant firm in 1995 estimated that only 250,000 to 500,000 consumers were dialing into the Web from home.[8] The inconsistent audience claims underscored the invisibility of people in the Web space. Optimism abounded, though. Forrester predicted the number would reach twenty million by 2000.[9] For its part, *Advertising Age* enjoined marketers to abandon their notion that Web users eschewed commercialism while it urged them to retain the assumption of the Web audience as elite: The magazine acknowledged that marketers exposed to tales of flaming by "a cyberspace community peopled by academics and intellectuals" might view the Web as "advertising hell." But it noted that "the truth is the Internet is already flooded with commercial traffic and transactions. It is becoming more and more a mass medium whose real-world users are accustomed to having their information subsidized by advertisers." The editorial advised its readers on the importance of respectfully opening "a clear dialogue between the 'net community and the ad community."[10]

The thrust of the editorial was seconded and extended a month later in a widely heralded speech by Procter and Gamble's CEO, Edwin Artzt, to the American Association of Advertising Agencies. P&G was the largest U.S. advertiser and historically a powerful force in the media system; the company had pioneered the soap opera on radio and television, for example. Artzt said he still believed in the importance of broadcast TV to reach huge numbers of people at the same time to sell products such as "four hundred million boxes of Tide." Yet he felt it important to consider a variety of methods beyond the major TV networks to get the "broad reach" the firm needed. Procter and Gamble had already begun to use customer segmentation and target-marketing techniques. What worried P&G's chairman primarily was not that new technologies would encourage more targeted advertising. Rather, it was the "chilling thought" that emerging technologies were giving people the opportunity to escape from advertising's grasp altogether.[11] He noted that, instead, the personal computer could be "a formidable future vehicle for advertising and even programming." He reminded his audience that the advertising industry had worked in the past to shape the media to its needs. "We may not get another opportunity like this in our lifetime," he said. "Let's grab all this new technology in our teeth once again and turn it into a bonanza for advertising."[12]

Artzt didn't mention the internet specifically; he gave equal weight to CDs, online services, and other devices, some presumably not yet imagined. Rather quickly, though, mainstream marketers and their agencies came to see the Web as the embodiment of where Artzt was telling them to go and take control.[13] Executives at P&G, in particular, took his words as a cue to encourage experimentation with the new medium.[14] A crucial technical development that helped the process along was the creation of programs facilitating the interface between the user and the internet called the "browser"—especially Mosaic in 1993 (a month before Schrage's piece appeared in *Adweek*) and Netscape Navigator (a more user-friendly browser) in fall 1994, a few months after the *Advertising Age* editorial and Artzt speech. These programs made it easy to see graphics as well as text; previously people who wanted to download pictures had to combine files in viewers such as LView. The browsers introduced the idea of a "Web site" to the general public, where photos, drawings, and ads could be seen immediately. Clicking on them as well as on highlighted sentences would activate hyperlinks that transport the user to other parts of the site or the Web. Such links represented a new way of accessing knowledge, including information from marketers.

Web publishers themselves were certainly interested in getting marketers' business. A large part of the reason was that the overwhelming majority of websites didn't charge visitors to enter. Broadly speaking, the reason was clear. In the mid- and late-1990s, publishers were in a race to show advertisers who had the most users, and if they wanted that kind of scale they couldn't charge a fee.[15] Yet even in 1995, an analyst for Forrester contended that eventually the free-access model of websites would have to give way to fee-based services. "This can't go on indefinitely the way it is," she said. "You will probably see different models developing, and we think there will certainly be a 'bundle' level, where customers pay for a set bundle of content."[16]

The bundling didn't happen, but over the next few years several high-profile Web publishers did try to charge access fees using various approaches, and they failed painfully. One tactic was to require payment for what people were used to buying off-line; for example, some daily newspapers took this route, believing the pundits who claimed that news was "the perfect commodity for making money on the Internet."[17] Quickly, though, they concluded that people would not subscribe to online editions. Also attempted was a mixed subscription model—free and "premium." ESPNNet, the online version of the sports TV network, tried this and found that it couldn't coax many visitors to pay $4.95 per month for the extras. Some publishers adopted yet another strategy: give the product away free until people seem to be hooked on it, and then start charging them. Observers concluded that this didn't work, either. The *Wall Street Journal* became known as the most successful of this sort, though industry experts didn't consider it much of a success. The paper allowed free access to the site until the site reached 650,000 registered users in September 1996. It then asked subscribers to pay $29 a year for the online version, while it charged nonsubscribers $49. Online readership immediately plummeted to 30,000 and then rose again to 50,000—still less than 10 percent of the initial number—by the end of the year. It wasn't a great model for publishers, most of which did not possess the *Journal's* reputation and role as a professional tool. The poster child for an even more dismal result was *Slate,* Microsoft's sophisticated Web-only culture magazine. It threw in the subscription towel in February 1997 after switching only a month earlier from free access to a $19.95 annual subscription rate. The magazine's editor, Michael Kinsley, wrote a letter to his readers titled "Slate Chickens Out." Kinsley admitted what many people had already predicted: If he started charging anything for *Slate,* no one would read it.[18]

This was a dispiriting development for publishers and editors who hoped that the internet would signal a new venue for both subscriptions and advertising. In 1997, a columnist for Canada's *Globe and Mail* newspaper asked why people wouldn't pay Web publishers. Some analysts, he said, "suggest that once users had become accustomed to free content they became unwilling to give it up." Other observers, he added, point to demographic factors. "The Web audience—largely white and middle-class—is too demanding and too critical to pay for content," he wrote, without elaborating on precisely what he meant.[19] Both explanations fit with a historical view: Free or virtually free content was a feature of so much North American content throughout the twentieth century. Magazines and newspapers charged readers between 20 percent and 50 percent of the cost of producing each issue, with the rest (including a profit margin) paid by advertisers. And U.S. television and radio stations were free to their listeners; marketers picked up the entire tab. The underlying message to generations of

Americans was that content should be presented cheaply or at no charge. So with a new medium in which content was still often rather simply presented and many sites were indeed free, internet users saw no reason to pay anything. Websites, eager for visitors and hoping to sell space to advertisers, capitulated rather quickly. Early on, they did ask people to register to use the sites, requesting information that would entice advertisers. But many sites found that internet users shied away from doing that, and that others lied when registering. Many sites stopped even that imposition on visitors.

Some publishing sites turned to selling things to make money. A few began to sell their promotion of other sites via "hot links"—hypertext connections in their site that sent users to another site.[20] For most, though, traditional forms of advertising seemed the logical place to turn. Sometimes an advertiser would pay for a message stating that it was sponsoring a site or a page on a site. Then, on October 26, 1994, the popular technology magazine *Wired* began to sell pictorial banners in large quantities on its new website, HotWired.[21] A 1996 *Advertising Age* article claimed that this was the first application of banner advertising on the Web. Clicking on the ad would activate a link to the advertiser's own website. HotWired tempted visitors to interact with the ads by asking the question "Have you ever clicked here?" *Advertising Age* said that the gimmick "was very effective in attracting the user's attention."[22]

Despite superficial similarities to ads in other media, the clickable ads represented an unprecedented format. Like print ads, Web commercial messages appeared in various sizes; as opposed to column inches, the dimensions of Web ads were measured in terms of the computer screen's pixels. At the same time, Web ads, like TV ads, were wedded to time; yet while the duration of television commercials was set by the networks and agencies buying them, the practical duration of an internet ad depended on the person staring at the computer. A click on the address box, the back button, or a different ad, and a company's ad might well disappear.

Other Web publishers followed with clickable banners. Generally, they sold the ads by the cost-per-thousand (CPM, or cost per mil) model that was standard for newspapers, magazines, and other traditional media. According to that standard, when a media agency agreed to pay a certain amount to place an ad, the agency evaluated the cost in terms of the price to reach one thousand people. So, for example, if a magazine ad costs $50,000 to reach ten thousand people, the CPM is $5. Assuming all other conditions are equal, that is a more efficient buy than a magazine ad that costs $50,000 and reaches five thousand people, because in this case the cost per thousand is $10.

Because it was impossible in the traditional model to determine whether an audience member saw the content or the ad, CPM was based simply on general circulation—the number of copies of newspapers sold, for example, or the Nielsen rating of a television program. A website, by contrast, would charge a price based on the *advertising impressions* served to an actual person. Websites defined an impression as an advertisement that was sent to an individual who had clicked on a site's page.[23] Because at the time it wasn't possible to determine whether clicks were by the same or different individuals, sites judged every click separately. Costs per thousand impressions varied greatly depending on the presumed nature of a site's visitors. Sites that continued to require registration could often charge higher prices than nonregistering sites because they offered greater visibility of the audience. An *Advertising Age* reporter found that that "web CPMs at major sites generally range from $10 to $80."[24] If accurate, the numbers were generally higher than typical broadcast network rates, which at the time hovered between $5 and $15. Of course, websites charging even $70 CPMs would earn far less money than the TV networks because online audiences were so much smaller.

In adopting the cost-per-thousand model, Web publishers recognized the importance of being able to tell potential advertisers as much as possible about site visitors who might click on a banner ad. Since sites accepted that people didn't want to register (or lied when they did), they decided to obtain this information surreptitiously, and a new business came into being. In September 1995, *Adweek* noted that "a scant year-and-a-half after the World Wide Web was born, companies are scrambling to offer data-crunching systems that can tell Web site proprietors and the advertisers that have begun to enrich them how many people are logging onto their sites, who they are, where they're coming from, what they're doing once they get there, and how long they stick around."[25] In other words, publishers were hiring companies with systems that could analyze the click traffic coming into their websites.

The leader in this area was the Internet Profiles Corporation (I/Pro), which had Nielsen as a partner and counted Hearst, Netscape, and Playboy among its fifty customers in 1995.[26] Its I/COUNT service let website proprietors monitor their own sites' usage, delivering such data as number of visits, pages viewed within each site, and basic data about users' geographic location and system configuration. Its I/AUDIT service collected these data, analyzed them independently, and then delivered a monthly or quarterly report that guaranteed to advertisers the accuracy of the traffic data.[27] To Ariel Poler, I/Pro's founder, it was this process that distinguished the new medium. "There's no question that the Web is the most measurable of all media by far," he enthused in 1995.[28]

To substantiate this claim, Rick Boyce, Hotwired's vice president for advertising, enthusiastically told a trade-press reporter what he and his advertisers could learn from an I/Pro report about a Hotwired page with an AT&T banner across the top. "In a particular week, this page was served 11,955 times," he noted. "Of the 11,955 views, 576 clicked on that banner and went through. So you start to get at an ad effectiveness-type measure, which is really critical—what we're able to see is ad wearout. It's not at all uncommon to see what I call the 'click rate' decline over time." Boyce was clearly emphasizing the dual value of his site—as a point to display the ad and as a place where the visitor could click on the ad to learn more. The latter action, he suggested, was the responsibility of the advertiser—in this case, AT&T— which needed to bring the attitude of a direct marketer to this new form of display advertising. AT&T needed to realize that as the click rate starts to dip, it should adjust its message in an attempt to reinvigorate the click numbers. "AT&T has been on our site for 40 weeks and has not changed once," he said disapprovingly. "If they'd gone into this with a mind-set that was in touch with what's happening in the content area, they could really have maximized their investment. Agencies need to begin retraining themselves to a different model. The old model is, the ad's done, let's go on to the next project. In this medium, the ad's never done. It can never be done."[29]

Boyce's enthusiasm notwithstanding, many advertisers were not convinced that they could learn enough about visitors to publishing websites to justify spending lots of money on display ads. Two problems stood out in particular. One was simply the possibility of fraudulent data. As *Adweek* noted, "Web-auditing today is roughly equivalent to ABC, Fox and the USA Network each sending their own ratings points to Nielsen directly, and asking the ad industry to trust them to report their audience honestly." Concern about this difficulty led to discussions of independent entities such as the Audit Bureau of Circulation taking over the audit side of I/Pro's business, but nothing had yet happened. (Eventually ABC did offer audits.) The second problem was that neither websites nor I/Pro in September 1995 had the ability to track individuals. I/Pro could infer individual "sessions" by their streams of click patterns but couldn't be sure if the clicks represented particular visitors. Moreover, Poler admitted, in the absence of visitors' registering, "we can estimate how many visitors came to the site, but we can't tell if it's a repeat visitor versus a new visitor. The technology doesn't let you get 100 percent accurate numbers. There's no standard yet for keeping track of a visitor throughout his or her session."[30]

These sorts of concerns soured some media planners on the idea that display ads were the way to use the Web. Erica Guen, the head of strategic media resources at the Saatchi & Saatchi agency, stated flatly in 1995 that on publisher websites "you're going to know a great deal less than you can know about users in other media." Her preference was to see the Web as totally different from the traditional media space. The goal should not be to advertise on websites with independent content but to create websites for advertisers that would gauge their success not through audits but through the building of relationships with customers and potential customers. She offered the example of a loyalty program instituted by Toyota Interactive on Prodigy. The site offered bulletin boards, chat sessions, and product information to members who accessed the service by typing in their vehicle I.D. number. A year later, she said, the company had tracked sales of five hundred new Toyotas to customers who'd participated in the program. "More and more," she asserted, "I'm only going to use my Internet presence to strengthen relationships with consumers—and that's not something that's measured in numbers of users, but in terms of quality of measurements."[31]

How much emphasis to place on advertisers' websites versus display ads was a topic of much discussion among media planners and their clients. Their hesitancy about Web advertising was reflected in data the Jupiter Communications internet-consulting firm released in mid-1996. Jupiter found that the Web business had gone from virtually zero to in 1994 to $71.6 million in the first half of 1996. It expected Web spending to zoom past $300 million by the end of that year.[32] From fall 1994 through July 1996, forty-six of the top one hundred advertisers purchased ad space on the Web. Yet Jupiter found that only eleven of the top media advertisers in traditional media ranked among the top fifty Web spenders during July 1996. Telecommunication and computer companies trying to sell internet-related services or wares showed up on the list, but a lot of the spenders were simply Web companies trying to draw visitors from other websites to their own sites so that they could sell ads at high prices. These Web companies were using money they received from venture capitalists, who hoped the sites could ratchet up sales and then go public, providing them with huge windfalls. Nontech marketers appeared in abundance, but they were spending rather little cash.[33] Advertising practitioners realized that with such a profile of corporate patrons, the Web didn't have a chance to get the really big money to compete with television, radio, magazines, and newspapers. "Web publishers know," an *Advertising Age* reporter wrote, "that for Web advertising to succeed the number of big marketers participating must increase and the amount spent by Web-centric companies must go down."[34]

In late 1995, I/Pro's Ariel Poler thought he had a solution for increasing major marketers' interest in display advertising: a universal registration system that would track a person across all websites he or she visited and report it to marketers who paid I/Pro. Called I/CODE, it would, according to Poler, be a "name-tag system." As he described his plan to *Adweek,* every user logging on to an I/CODE-compatible website would have to enter a user name and password. I/PRO software would then be able to track every page he or she logged on to. And, he suggested, if the user could be convinced, just once, to fill out a questionnaire providing basic personal data—i.e., sex, age, income level—then I/PRO would be able to provide advertisers with detailed demographic information about his or her Web buys. "I sure hope that the standard will be something like I/CODE," he told *Adweek.* "But if I/CODE doesn't fly, we'll have to find other mechanisms that do."[35]

As it turned out, I-CODE went nowhere. Critics doubted that people would sign up, but Poler later recalled that tests with *Playboy* magazine's website attracted a million registrants. He said that the sites were reluctant to sign up with I-CODE because they feared that Poler rather than they would own the data.[36] As he suggested, though, the marketing logic of the day was demanding this kind of information. The coming years would move in I/CODE's direction incrementally and without going to the trouble of getting visitors' permission.

The "cookie" marked the beginning of this shift. Ultimately it would do more to shape advertising—and social attention—on the Web than any other invention apart from the browser itself. Its profound significance seems not to have been apparent at the time to Lou Montulli, who created the cookie while working for Netscape Communications in 1994 to solve a marketing problem. Montulli was charged with devising a better "shopping cart," which enables a website to keep track of the different items that a customer sets aside for purchase. Without a way to identify the customer, every click to put an item in the cart would appear to the online store as if it were originating from a different individual. Consequently, a person would not be able to buy more than one item at a time. Previous attempts to solve this problem involved storing information about the ongoing transaction in the Web address, or uniform resource locator (URL), of an individual's browser, which could be read by the store to differentiate between what each individual customer was buying. These methods didn't work very well, so technicians in the server division asked Montulli to come up with something better.[37] His concept, which he refined with the help of John Giannadrea, another Netscape employee, was a small text file—a "cookie"—that a website could place on a visitor's computer. The file would have an identification code for the visitor and other codes detailing the person's clicks during the visit. The next time the person used the same computer to access the website, tags on the browser would recognize the cookie. By decoding the information the site would learn where the user of that computer had clicked previously, what had been purchased, and even what had been placed in the shopping cart even if the shopper had decided not to click through to give payment information and complete the purchase.

Montulli named his invention a cookie because the concept seemed similar to what computer programmers called "magic cookies": packets of data a program receives and sends out again unchanged. By itself the cookie could not distinguish between different people using the same computer; Montulli and Giannadrea made a conscious decision to have the cookie work without asking the computer user to accept or contribute information to it. Consequently, this seamless approach had an ominous downside: by not requiring the computer user's permission to accept the cookie, the two programmers were legitimating the trend toward lack of openness and inserting it into the center of the consumer's digital transactions with marketers.

Netscape installed cookie-placement capability into its Navigator browser in late 1994. Microsoft incorporated it into its first Internet Explorer browser, released in 1995. The head of Microsoft's browser efforts, Michael Wallent, suggested that to compete with Netscape Navigator his company needed Web publishers and advertisers to conform to Internet Explorer's specifications; otherwise large numbers of internet users would not adopt this browser. If online companies were to support Explorer, he recalled in 2001, Explorer needed to support cookies: "I don't think anyone ever thought that cookies were anything that could be excluded in the browser and have that browser become a success in the marketplace."[38]

Most directly, the cookie allowed websites to quietly determine the number of separate individuals entering various parts of their domains and clicking on their ads. Yet the major advertisers that were experimenting with the internet in 1996 made it clear that knowing this was not enough. "We're not buying banners right now because there's no adequate measurement factor out there," said Mike Perugi, communications specialist for Dodge Division in October 1996.[39] Underscore the word *adequate;* entrepreneurs certainly kept trying to find measurements that they hoped would satisfy traditional marketers. Server-side measurement firms such as I/Pro could make visible certain types of information about a visit, but not much about the specific characteristics of the audience. To fill that void, audience-side companies emerged to bid for media buyers' research money. The audience-side group aimed to create a ratings system that was similar to Nielsen's television and Arbitron's radio ratings. So, for example, PC Meter (later called Media Metrix), a subsidiary of the research firm NDP, systematically audited the computers of a panel of ten thousand U.S. households to determine what sites they visited. It charged ad agencies and websites an annual subscription to its findings starting at $50,000. Another such company, @plan, polled forty thousand Web users with partner Gallup Organization and charged $65,000 annually for access to its data. For the more frugal buyers, advertisers, and Web publishers, the research company Relevant Knowledge said it could do the job for $10,000 annually with a five-thousand-person panel. As had become typical with the arrival of new Web metrics, those involved in Web ratings depicted the activity as a major advance that would finally bring major marketers to treat the Web as an established rather than a still-experimental advertising vehicle. "There is an absolute crying need for third-party neutral information that will help advance this new medium," said Matt Wright, CEO of @plan, when describing his new firm's anticipated contributions toward that end. Jeff Levy, CEO of Relevant Knowledge, was even more direct. "The large package-goods companies are not going on the Web right now because there is no reliable standard [for measuring Web usage]. If we can give those people the tools to understand the Web, they will spend a lot more than $300 million or even $5 billion to chase 44.7 million individuals," he said, referring to Relevant Knowledge's projected number of individual Web users online in the United States in 1997.[40]

And yet big marketers still weren't overly enthused. 3M Co.'s Buf Puf skin-care product brand, which launched a website for teens in April 1996, received that sort of audience quantification through its ad agency, Martin/

Williams Advertising of Minneapolis. "We've been able to track not only the 'hits' but what the audience is seeking beyond the home page," said Buf Puf's brand supervisor. "We're interested in the overall number of user sessions, which we calculate has been in the range of 1,000 daily." Buf Puf, like many website owners, invited visitors to supply information about themselves, including e-mail addresses, and their reaction to the material posted on the website. The brand manager said that this information was more valuable to Buf Puf than was the actual number of visitors. "Having numbers is great, but it's not telling us much," she told *Advertising Age* later that year.[41]

Part of the problem was that media buyers and their clients didn't know what to make of the value of clicks, or even user sessions (clicks that cookies showed as being from one individual's visit). "What does it mean when 1,000 people visit your site?" asked Farris Khan, interactive consumer marketing coordinator at General Motors Corp.'s Saturn division. "Is it better or worse than 100,000 people seeing your TV commercial?"[42] It was not an idle philosophical issue. Apart from comparisons to traditional media, it led to questions about whom to target with websites (for example, should the target be potential customers or brand loyalists), the relative value of a website with many pages versus a website that allowed visitors to obtain the desired information quickly and leave, and the utility of a website versus a banner ad. Those ads, too, were raising major questions. Media buyers and chagrined website publishers were finding that after an initial flurry of high activity the number of clicks on banner ads dropped dramatically. In 1996 I/Pro reported only a 2.1 percent average click-through rate. Moreover, a five-hundred-person survey by Market Facts for *Advertising Age* found that 42 percent of online users said they never look at ad banners.[43]

It was, in fact, the low percentage of clicks along with the dearth of information about people who saw Web ads without clicking that led Procter and Gamble to a decision in April 1996 that shook Web publishers. Together with its interactive agency media.com (a subsidiary of Grey Advertising's MediaCom), P&G used audience-side ratings rankings to solicit proposals from major websites to place banner ads for sites built around its products.[44] The catch was that P&G would accept only those proposals that jettisoned the standard cost-per-thousand model and agreed to base advertising fees on the number of times an ad was clicked and that visitor sent to a P&G site. Media.com executives had urged their client to take this conservative buying route; they figured they could, given P&G's clout.[45] They knew that lots of people would see the ads and not click, so they would get a residual display audience without cost. But in justifying the move the buyers complained that site costs per thousand were outrageous in view of the lack of sufficiently detailed data about visitors and the lack of interactivity with them that was supposed to be the attraction to marketers of the online environment. "If you can't articulate a message with sufficient depth and create awareness, we will maintain that it's not what the medium's about," said Alec Gerster, the head of media buying at Grey. "Then I shouldn't be spending money there, I can go and buy outdoor." He added: "You know if someone's entering the [sponsor's] site, you're probably getting pretty good value. It's someone who's interested, who wants to find out more."[46]

P&G announced it had made deals with Yahoo! and a few other big Web names. Yet executives representing many site publishers initially registered shock and put up lots of resistance. AOL refused the deal. Because it was the largest internet service provider, its leaders had the advantage of believing (correctly) that its ability to supply P&G with millions of customers gave it clout. As an internet service provider (ISP) with "walled gardens"—websites exclusively for its users—AOL also knew more about its audience than other sites knew about theirs. Still, one of its executives repudiated the P&G approach, which other marketers tried to copy, on principle. "What we are telling advertisers is that with a click-through standard, if TV advertising had developed on an inquiry-only basis, [the medium] would have elevated into nothing but infomercials," and in the process would have alienated much of the audience.[47] An *Advertising Age* editorial agreed, noting "the dirty secret of Web publishing: Banners just don't get clicked. On many Web pages, they're mere billboards. And if they're not clicked, they're not interactive." P&G, the editorial said, was right to see the internet as "all about interactivity. Viewing it as a place to put a pretty picture is the wrong attitude entirely." But the editorial suggested that P&G and other marketers find new ways to succeed rather than make demands that would ensure their failure. Calling the internet "the biggest and brightest ad medium to come along in years," the editorial reminded its readers that "this is a fledgling economy. . . . Birds with clipped wings will never really be able to fly."[48] It was a wise exhortation that marketers and their agencies never quite followed.

P&G backed off from its click-through demand. Instead, in a quiet compromise implemented by other firms as well, the packaged-goods giant sometimes pursued deals that combined clicks with CPMs. One version, called a *hybrid purchase,* paid mostly on a CPM basis but added certain click-through expectations to the deal. Another, dubbed *performance CPMs,* involved negotiating a lower CPM price sweetened by revenues based on actions (sales, website visits) generated through clicks. P&G and other major marketers also began to emphasize new ways to encourage consumers to click on the ads. They were prodded by publishers, who claimed that they could not be blamed if Web users weren't clicking on what most observers agreed were uncreative banners.

Advertising agencies that focused on creative campaigns for the Web reveled in the term "beyond the banner" as an indicator of the new focus. It referred to new forms of ad units that transcended the static company logo and message in a banner ad. Some were interstitials, ads that covered the entire screen after a click while a new Web page was loading. A short-lived company called PointCast began to push news, information, and advertising through a downloadable screen saver. Its ads were animated and invited users to click to the sponsor's website. A reporter commented that "even if they don't jump to the marketer site, they still have an interactive experience with the brand."[49] A more long-lasting tactic was to create intermediate websites so that a person who clicked would not be afraid that this act would spirit him or her from the site on which the ad sat. Those banner ads carried Flash animations or Java applets—small interactive modules—that users could play without leaving the original website. AT&T's ad agency bought spots for these sorts of ads across the Web in order to invite users to its 1996 Olympics site. Similarly, in ads for GM's Oldsmobile division on Packet. com, when a user passed the cursor over the site's navigation bar, applets popped up with information about the car.[50] Sun Microsystems tried to be even more alluring with its banner. It featured both a marketing message and a picture of the director of the company's science office. If you clicked on the marketing message, you would go to Sun's site; if you clicked on the picture you would hear an interview between the science-office director and the popular ("web-hot") writer Howard Rheingold.[51]

Pizza Hut's 1996 Web promotion, created by BBDO and overseen by its director of media services, stood out in the category of using an ad to collect e-mail addresses and begin the kind of relationship with customers that Erica Gruen had described as the real utility of the Web. Targeting college-age men, the company eschewed driving them to its own website in favor of a deal with ESPN SportsZone's online home. Along with regular banner advertising on the site, Pizza Hut created three games—Baseball Challenge, Pigskin Pick'em, and NCAA Tournament Challenge—each requiring participants to register, which included providing an e-mail address. A couple of months after launching the games, Pizza Hut sent e-mails to 327,000 players, thanking them for participating in the games and offering them online discount coupons for pizza. Pizza Hut's agency measured the results in clicks but made clear that they were far more efficient and meaningful than standard banner click-throughs. Said BBDO vice president Frances Laufer:

> [W]ithin three days after the e-mails were sent out, 14.4 percent of the recipients, or 47,115 users, had visited the coupon page. Of those, nearly 40 percent completed a form stating that they wanted more information or offers from Pizza Hut. It's too early to tell how many actually tried the "totally new pizza."
>
> Within 10 days of the blanket e-mail, 79,000 SportsZone regulars, or 24 percent of the original group, had visited the coupon page. This can be compared to the pull from 1.5 million guaranteed impressions the Pizza Hut banners receive per month, which have about a 2 percent click-through rate. In effect, the coupon initiative drew nearly three times the responses to a banner ad. The cost to achieve this? Roughly $500,000 a year for the entire package, which includes development fees for the games, banners and maintenance.[52]

"We went after the user by giving them an experience that was relevant to them," explained Laufer. "There's a game they can play every week. That was the strategy—to brand ourself [*sic*] and leverage the Internet. It's not just a Pizza Hut ad there. Otherwise we're not making use of the medium for what it could be."[53]

Results such as Pizza Hut's helped focus attention on new ways to think of relevant interactive measures to get visitors to click on ads and identify themselves. It didn't solve the problem accountability-oriented media buyers had with even websites such as ESPN SportsZone. The Web was supposed to be "the most measureable of media," and yet most websites knew little about who was coming to them, while at the same time many insisted on CPM charges that were at best on par with traditional media and at worst substantially higher. Those prices were floated even though the sites knew almost nothing about whether people were attending to the ads unless they clicked on them. Ironically, despite the hoopla about the new medium, marketers believed that they obtained more information about audiences from traditional media than from internet sites. "What advertisers ultimately seek," wrote a reporter in 1996, "are the kinds of in-depth demographic and psychographic information about Web page users that television, magazines, radio and newspapers provide about their viewers and subscribers."[54]

The pressure to present data to help advertisers account for costs increased as major advertising agencies became involved. In 1996 advertisers spent $300 million to advertise online, according to Jupiter Communications.[55] The amount was apparently enough, and the direction sufficiently upward, that in 1997 a number of major advertising companies began digital buying units after years of hesitation. Previously, the buying department that handled traditional media had also handled Web work. Web enthusiasts saw the creation of separate departments as real progress toward management's understanding that the new world needed special handling. "As clients require more capabilities, we're listening to what they want," said Rishad Tobaccowala, president of Giant Step, advertising agency Leo Burnett's new interactive subsidiary. "It makes a lot of sense for the interactive media experts to be here rather than at Burnett."[56] Similarly, Grey Interactive spun off its media.com division as a separate entity available to solicit clients for strategy, planning, and buying in the interactive space. David Dowling, director of the new unit, said that clients were demanding more online media expertise. "Media continues to increase in importance in (the online) area," he said. Marketers that built websites are looking for creative ways to promote them, he said, adding, "We can benefit from being a separate entity. There's a lot of opportunity in this area."[57]

One practical need buyers and publishers noted was standardized ad sizes and shapes so that agencies would not have to spend substantial time sizing ads repeatedly to fit sites' varied specifications. Web publishers worried that the difficulty of doing this may have deterred media buyers from certain sites. Two new industry groups that represented publisher interests—the Coalition for Advertising Supported Information & Entertainment (CASIE) and the Internet Advertising Bureau (IAB)—were working separately on guidelines; eventually they would co-release a set of eight standardized banners. But the real pressure on the Web-specific media buyers was to show their clients—and presumably traditional media buyers in their agencies—that they were pushing for the data they needed to serve their clients. Joe Philport, an executive at Competitive Media Reporting, which assessed national advertisers' media buys, suggested that the Web world was trying his clients' patience. "We know that advertisers aren't going to wait forever . . . to know how their Web site ranks [with audiences] compared to the competition."[58]

Entrepreneurs looked to the cookie as the natural vehicle to learn more and more what people were doing without having them knowingly raise their hands. Cookie inventor Montulli confessed to mixed emotions about this development. He and co-inventor Giannadrea originally had taken steps to limit the information sent back to the website. Montulli recalled that he considered and rejected an idea for creating a single identification number that a person's browser would use in all Web explorations. That would have made the cookie a universal tracking mechanism, a phenomenon he wanted to avoid.[59] To make sure companies that had not inserted the cookie in the browser could not update or alter it, Netscape Navigator 2.0 also baked a "same origin policy" into the cookie structure. This meant that while any party could note the existence of a cookie in a visitor's browser, only a site that created the cookie could read or change it.[60]

Montulli and Giannadrea did decide to design the cookie so its creator could detect it across all the sites the creator controlled. Savvy marketing entrepreneurs quickly realized that if they received permission to place cookies across sites, they could note what individuals did after they went to one site. If a cookie were detected at one of the related sites, the marketers could serve an ad to that individual's screen in sync not only with the topic of the current website but with those visited previously. Data about what the cookie owner learned about the individual could be added to the cookie (or stored on a server and linked to the cookie), and revenues could be shared with the participating sites. The challenge was to incorporate many sites to create an ad network. Technologists called cookies in these networks third-party cookies because they could be controlled by an entity separate from the website on which they appear or from their advertiser. The advantage of a wide-ranging network to an advertiser was the high likelihood of noticing a computer with a related cookie.[61]

By the fall of 1996 and early 1997 advertising networks had emerged "in a big way," according to a trade writer of the time. Part of the reason was that the Forrester Research consulting firm endorsed the entity as an easy and efficient way for Web publishers to sell advertising.[62] Networks would share their revenues with the sites on which they served the ads. In fact, the idea of aggregating sites to sell ads was so popular that even content providers such as Starwave, CNET, and Yahoo! gave advertisers the ability to buy ad space across their domains and, through cookies, infer whether the ads were going to new or repeat visitors. Nobody in these articles mentioned whether the people followed would want that to happen. Some observers saw the practice of linking sites to sell commercial messages as merely an extension of ad representation in traditional media. *Adweek* called it one of the early signs of new media "convergence," noting that the television advertising representation firms Petry and Katz were involved in packaging groups of sites for clients just as they packaged stations for television commercials. Petry noted that it could serve ads to a bit more than sixty sites in May 1997; Katz had fourteen affiliates, including Netfind, which was America Online's search service, and AOL.com itself.[63]

It quickly became apparent that a major problem for these aggregators was scale. In traditional media, buyers for major advertisers were accustomed to buying huge numbers of people by contacting just a few media firms. With the internet, audiences were scattered throughout the Web so that a few websites delivered a relatively small number of people. Media buyers, though, wanted both the simplicity of reaching huge numbers with a few buys as well as the ability to take advantage of the targeting of interests that the Web presumably allowed. As a result, while Petry, Katz, and other networks concentrated on small numbers of sites that major advertisers knew and found credible, a growing number of other networks prided themselves on delivering to advertising agencies and their clients huge numbers of people across thousands of sites. Executives at internet groups in major agencies as well as in fledging internet advertising agencies such as Modem Media acknowledged that the chief benefit of such operations was saving the time of staff members who would otherwise have to contact many websites individually. But *Adweek* suggested in May 1997 that issues of measurement and credibility plagued them, and that networks buyers who used these operations were fooling themselves. "The ad networks are like young adolescents," the article stated. "They have grown to considerable size physically, representing dozens or even thousands of sites, but they haven't evolved intellectually to the same extent. They have yet to assure buyers that their targeting works, for one thing, and no model has presented itself as the ultimate advertising option—one with extensive reach and desirable demographics and quality sites."[64]

The article presented the Commonwealth Network, Cliqnow, and DoubleClick as examples. Cliqnow aggregated its affiliate websites into the five "networks"—on travel, golf, college, financial, and children's topics—and sold ads to advertisers based on the affinity of the topics to the audience they were pursuing. Media buyers, though, said that the differentiation among categories wasn't granular enough for their needs. Commonwealth touted the information it collected through registration of users of its 3,400 small-to-medium website affiliates. Media buyers worried that they didn't know exactly which sites were in the network and that sites they never heard of could post content that wouldn't go well with their clients' ads. DoubleClick was the most elite of the three, a network with popular sites like the AltaVista search engine and the travel booking site Travelocity, and that reported more than five hundred million deliverable impressions per month and claimed high-end internet demographics judging by the sites' registration data. "But DoubleClick has its own hurdles," noted *Adweek*. "Its boast of whiz-bang technology that zips advertisers' messages across the screens of their most desirable eyeballs isn't a claim every buyer believes." Buyers were concerned that DoubleClick still could not guarantee specific types of users and was making assertions about users that couldn't be verified. For its part, DoubleClick insisted it was promising only that ads would be technically well served to a great group of sites. Kevin O'Conner, the firm's CEO, saw the answer to accountability in the impending sophisticated use of cookies. He said that based on DoubleClick's so-far limited use of cookies, it could follow individuals' sequence of clicks (their "clickstreams") and the number of pages opened, and through that infer a few categories of users that advertisers might want to consider. For example, "Someone who signs on to their ISP at 10 am on Fridays is likely to be a home-office type." O'Conner said that more solid attributions about users would await full deployment of its cookie technology.[65]

Many internet advertising network and buying executives shared this expectation that cookies would soon solve the problem of audience identification and verification. Consequently, they were aghast when a working group from the Internet Society's Internet Engineering Task Force identified third-party cookies as a considerable privacy threat. Founded in 1992 by internet pioneers Vint Cerf, Bob Kahn, and Lyman Chapin, the nonprofit organization aimed to provide direction in internet-related standards, education, and policy. The Task Force advised that cookies "should be shut off unless someone decides they're willing to accept them."[66] Opponents of this opt-in proposal were quite happy with the approach of the then-current Netscape browser (with a dominant 70 percent of the market) and Microsoft Explorer (with most of the rest). Both allowed users to change their "cookie preferences" manually to show an alert when a site was trying to deliver a cookie, but they could not stop cookies. The online marketing executives noted that building the engineers' restrictions into the browser would affect not only ad networks, which dealt with thousands of sites. It would also prevent Web publishers with multiple sites, such as CNET, News.com, and

Download.com, from using cookies across their firm's own domains to follow and serve ads to visitors without their permission. To the cookie supporters that restriction seemed so obviously wrong as to invalidate the whole opt-in proposal.

The fight over third-party cookies was the first time that accountability to marketers on the Web publicly came into direct conflict with the Web's users. Jonathan Rosenberg, CNET's executive vice president of technology, argued it was actually a false choice. He contended that the Internet Society's engineers were conceiving trouble where none existed. "It seems to me it's an extreme reaction from a bunch of people who are saying . . . 'We're going to convince you there is a privacy problem on the Web,'" he told *Advertising Age* in 1997.[67] Sue Doyle, director of marketing at AdSmart, an ad network, went right to the heart of the matter: the future of Web advertising. "What concerns us is the tone of the proposal, which is that advertising is not good for us, so we want to avoid it," she exclaimed. "That begs the question, how is the Web going to be funded?"[68]

When she said this in March 1997, internet ad network executives already were drafting counterproposals and lobbying Netscape and Microsoft directly against accepting the engineers' cookie proposal. By early May, Netscape decided to bow to its commercial constituencies while nodding to the engineers' concerns. The company announced that the next version of the Netscape Navigator browser would still accept all types of cookies. That would enable ad networks and publishers to continue using them to deliver targeted ads and content to internet users. "We are not planning on making any changes at all to the basic function of Navigator with regard to cookies," Lou Montulli told *Advertising Age*.[69] Montulli, who had been a member of the IETF working group and who was feeling strong pressure from its members, did signal a compromise: the next version of Navigator, 4.0, would offer the ability to reject all cookies outright as well as reject only certain types of cookies.[70] "We simply will be adding the ability for the users to make changes to cookie acceptance policies, if they wish," he noted.[71] *Advertising Age*'s reporter suggested that members of the online ad industry, whom he said had been in a "panic" about the proposed changes, should feel relieved. He played down the coming ability to stop cookies, noting that "because the vast majority of Web users never bother to change their cookie preferences, the effect on companies that use cookies as targeting tools will be minimal." The magazine's headline was "Advertisers Win One in Debate over 'Cookies.'"[72]

As it turned out, the intra-industry squabble marked only the beginning of a public debate over the right of site visitors to know what companies were learning about them. Publisher, ad network, and advertising executives stressed that cookies "aren't able to grab an email address" or to probe an individual's computer. Concern escalated nonetheless, fueled by a 1996 article in *MacWeek* about the ways cookies in combination with an advanced writing tool for Web browsers, called JavaScript, could be used on the Netscape browser for the Apple Macintosh computer to "retrieve a user's email address, real name and activity from the Netscape cache file, which documents a user's movement on the Web."[73] Netscape acknowledged the problem and said it was taking steps to remedy it and make the cookie more secure. Web publishers and marketers alike kept repeating that cookies were anonymous, so personal privacy was not at issue. But such incidents and the mere presence of cookies worried privacy advocates that the new medium might threaten its users with the theft of personal information. That same year saw a report from the advocacy group Center for Media Education titled "Web of Deceit," about how marketers were using their websites to pull personal information from youngsters about themselves and family members.[74] The storm it created among legislators led in 1998 to the Children's Online Privacy Protection Act (COPPA), which prohibited websites from receiving personally identifiable information from children younger than thirteen years of age without their parents' permission. Industry assurances of self-regulation halted government attempts to require any information about the marketing activities that were going on behind the screen.

A lot was certainly going on. The arguments in Washington didn't stop a great rush by Web publishers and third-party ad networks in the late 1990s to profile individual Web users in order to attract money to reach them. Whereas in the past ad buyers had relied on the subject matter of a site to infer user interests—much as they did with traditional television programs or magazines—now they increasingly had the opportunity to get more detailed information by analyzing their clicking habits across different sites, or on different pages of the same sites. Cross-site clicking was typically the province of the ad networks, and competition spurred them toward creative attempts to describe people in ways advertisers would like. DoubleClick, for example, came up with a way to use cookies to observe a visitor's behavior and then serve an ad based on that pattern and retarget the same person with an ad for the same product on another venue in its 3,800-site network. Another approach that got press attention was the AdSmart network's collaboration with Engage Technologies. AdSmart classified every page of the more than ninety sites in its network into about 450 content categories. Tracking more than ten million of the AdSmart network visitors via cross-site cookie files, Engage inferred their demographic and personality characteristics and stored those data, linked to the cookies, on its computers. Moreover, using AdSmart's page categorization, Engage could compile detailed profiles of the visitors' interests based on the pages they viewed, which could also be stored on the database. The collected data could then be used to serve relevant ads to individuals when (and if) the cookie in their computer indicated that they were visiting an AdSmart-network site. "We can target users on what we call 'first-time relevance,'" said Paul Schaut, CEO of Engage. "With our system, from the first moment a visitor shows up at a sports site, we already know he's a baseball fan and can start serving relevant ads immediately."[75]

While tracking people across websites made use of cookies, ad networks' desire to track what people did on particular pages of a specific site required them to create a different technology. The challenge was that their ads were not stored on the same computer servers as the pages of the websites onto which the ads were served. When all the elements of a website are stored together on the same computer server, the controller of the website can easily follow a visitor across pages. The server knows and can store the internet address of the user's computer (referred to as the internet protocol, or IP, address) requesting the page via the click. The website's employees can then retrieve the information from the server's activity records—its "log files."

The situation becomes more complex, though, when an ad network that serves an ad wants to know the specific website page on which a visitor sees an ad because the network doesn't have access to the site's server logs. Instead, it uses a technology called a Web bug. As described by Richard Smith of the Electronic Frontier Foundation, a digital consumer rights advocacy group, a Web bug in the late 1990s was a small, invisible graphic, typically only one pixel by one pixel in size.[76] When the user clicked on the page, an advertising image was downloaded. This download required the browser to request the image from the ad network's server that was storing it. That request would include the page on which the ad would appear. In that way, the ad network would know which pages the visitor had browsed, and that information could be connected to that person's cookie ID and stored either on the cookie or on the network's computers.

In fact, an ad didn't have to accompany a Web bug. A marketing firm might simply have purchased permission from the website to place an invisible graphic on its pages that would not download a commercial message but would instead trigger the gathering of information about the visitor yet invisible to him. The purpose was not to advertise but to learn what pages particular audience members were visiting on sites. A similar Web bug in e-mails that used graphics allowed advertisers to note whether and when the messages were opened. Together with cookie developments, server files and Web bugs gave publishers and ad networks an increasing number of ways to note the amount of people coming to their domains and to profile them in ways that might attract advertisers. And, following the precedent the cookie had set, those activities were hidden from the people whose movements were being recorded. Certainly, Web bugs did not have to be invisible. Smith asked, "Why are web bugs invisible on a page?" He answered: "To hide the fact that monitoring is taking place."[77]

And yet, despite the growth of cookies, third-party advertising firms, Web bugs, and server side-audits, *Advertising Age* found in August 1998 that "some [major] advertisers are still hesitant" about buying into the Web. The trade magazine added that "lack of accurate measurement and difficulty tracking return on investment are cited as the biggest barriers to buying online media in a survey conducted by the Association of National Advertisers earlier this year."[78] Jed Breger, media director for Webnet Marketing, whose clients include Cablevision and Network Solutions, stated that "unsophisticated and sometimes even inaccurate measurement systems have been a real hindrance to many marketers and [have] kept them at very stable advertising levels."[79] David Dowling, president of Grey Interactive's media.com, which handled planning and buying for P&G, agreed. "Advertisers will be excited to spend more money online when the medium proves it is accountable," he said.[80] To some commentators, the problem was that many advertisers were unfamiliar with the new techniques to audit the display of ads and the audiences who viewed them. A larger problem, marketers and their agency counterparts agreed, involved a lack of consistency in the measurements that companies were offering. When marketers compared the visitor numbers presented by the ratings firms, the figures often didn't mesh. They also had difficulty making sense of how those data meshed with the data that companies tracking the sites themselves were reporting. "A big part of the confusion out there now is that it's hard for people to make sense of both site-centric and audience-centric data," noted Mary Ann Packo, president of Media Metrix. "We are trying to marry traditional audience data like unduplicated reach and demographics with more site-centric measures like how many pages are viewed or clickstreams."[81]

CASIE and the IAB were trying to push Web publishers toward indus-trywide measurement standards.[82] Publishers and technology firms were also trying to encourage media buyers into following realistic best practices regarding internet ads. *Advertising Age, Business Marketing,* chip maker Intel, and the search engine website AltaVista were among the groups funding a "Camp Interactive" convocation in Beaver Creek, Colorado, where more than three hundred media-buying executives learned ways to think about evaluating websites, generating realistic research-based campaign ideas, and pitching these ideas to clients.[83] Procter and Gamble had the even more ambitious goal of remaking the Web into a packaged-goods marketer's dream. Since the acclaimed speech by Ed Artzt in 1994 executives had puzzled over the best ways to think about the Web's role in their marketing. P&G's insistence on click-through measurement had turned into a public-relations mess. Moreover, the pay-per-click (PPC) model seemed to be focused on a vision of the Web that didn't fit with the company's emerging strategy of differentially targeting particular consumer segments with messages that would enhance brands and persuade at the same time.

P&G's advertising expenditures reflected the firm's lack of confidence in the medium so far. Four years into the presence of the Web as a commercial medium, the company still pitched a relative pittance its way. In the fourth quarter of its 1998 fiscal year, P&G spent $3 million on U.S. internet adver-tising out of an annual $3 billion worldwide advertising budget. P&G watchers pointed out that its approach to television had taken quite a different trajectory. Its commitment to the medium jumped from 2 percent of its ad spending in 1950 to 61 percent five years later.[84]

To Denis Beausejour, the company's vice president of advertising, the issue was very much how to configure the Web so it could conceivably replace conventional television, P&G's advertising mainstay. Beausejour was intensely interested in applying the Web to product awareness. Placing prod-ucts in front of consumers was a crucial activity for P&G divisions. Their customers were continually aware of the competition among companies for their attention regarding cleaning products, health care items, cosmetics, diapers, and other typical purchases. The promise of the Web was that a TV-like ad on a site could stir emotions that would reinforce branding while encouraging clicks that would lead people to learn more and leave their e-mail addresses for coupons and other ways P&G could address them. The reality in the late 1990s was different. Not only were ads not TV-like, the then-key measure of interactivity, click-through rates, were, in the words of an expert, "miserable"—less than one half of one percent. Fixing both problems through creative-enhancing technologies was Beausejour's purpose for a two-day summit at P&G's Cincinnati headquarters in 1998 that brought together senior executives from leading technology companies, advertising agencies, and marketers, including AT&T Corp., Coca-Coca Co., Euro RSCG Worldwide, Levi Strauss & Co., McDonald's Corp., and even P&G archrival Unilever. Sessions of the summit discussed the problems of Americans' dial-up connection to the Web and ways to change that system; the future of computer-chip manufacturing and the Web's ability to process audiovisual materials; and the need for an industry association to foster collaboration among its various sectors in order to speed up the Web's development as an advertising medium.[85]

It became clear there, though, that the central connection most Americans had to the Web, America Online, had no intention of abandoning its lucrative dial-up service to encourage a much less profitable broadband service. The firm had no broadband infrastructure of its own, and tying into broadband providers to boost customer speeds would cost it far more money than it spent on linking to standard phone lines.[86] If it and other dial-up service providers encouraged their members to switch to broadband, their profit margins would plummet. That awareness seems to have dampened marketers' enthusiasm about the Web beating television with branding commercials anytime soon. Rather than utopian expectations, efficiency and pragmatism reigned. In a move that startled the trade, P&G's buying agency, media.com, told website executives that it would purchase ad space on the basis of a flat $5 cost per thousand ad impressions served onto Web pages. The company implied that the amount was similar to what the packaged-goods giant paid television broadcasters for a thousand viewers of a program (the cost per mil, or CPM) around which an ad appeared. The research firm eMarketer found in 1999 that the asking CPM for a thirty-second prime-time commercial was $12. This was at a time when sites were earning an average $36 CPM for Web buys, according to the measurement firm AdKnowledge.[87]

Many in an advertising industry mired in a business recession at the turn of the millennium seemed to agree that Web publishing did not deserve a lot of attention from brand advertisers. In 2001 an article in the *Industry Standard,* a richly produced short-lived print magazine subtitled "The Newsmagazine of the Internet Economy," noted that "about 12 percent of media consumption is on the Internet, yet it accounts for 3 percent or less of overall U.S. ad dollars." One reason, the article stated, was that the segregation of internet marketing from other areas of media spending was making it less likely that traditional media planners would integrate Web advertising into a client's campaign. Traditional planners, "creatives" (copywriters and art directors), and clients didn't mind the omission, according to the article, because "traditional advertisers, it turns out, never really bought into this new medium. They were sold the Web on the basis of fear, convinced that if they didn't jump on the bandwagon, they would go the way of all dinosaurs. . . . These extravagant promises are not easily forgotten—or forgiven." And, noted the article, "As the world waits for broadband and various forms of 'rich media' that promise to make Internet ads akin to TV commercials, many of the marketers holding the purse strings on big campaigns remain unconvinced."[88] The co-CEO and chief creative officer of the large Omnicom-owned BBDO advertising agency expressed the Web's utility in a way that might make online publishers wince: "Today the Net is fine for a discount offer. But nobody has figured out how to build brands."[89]

The spread of broadband allowed for vivid commercial possibilities by the late 2000s. Nevertheless, publishers found that the media buyers for P&G and other large marketers still expected Web CPMs to be cheap. They encouraged competition among internet vehicles to keep it that way, no matter the technology or the website publishers' expenses. Helping them was a search engine called Google. Even though major advertisers didn't consider it a builder of brand images, they joined with thousands of small marketers that saw it as a practical, efficient, and more measureable way than display advertising to lead consumers to clients' products. In response, Web publishers joined a phalanx of firms in the belief that the path to lucrative display advertising would come through giving sponsors more and more information about individual anonymous site visitors. The future of advertising, publishing, and audience targeting on the Web would be shaped by these developments.

Chapter 3 A New
Advertising Food Chain

Starting from zero in 2002, in two years Google made $2.08 billion from the advertising that appeared next to its search engine results.[1] Its rocketing "paid search" business marked the beginning of a new chapter in advertising history and had ripple effects throughout the online and off-line media economy. To understand why marketers would get so excited about search-engine advertising, consider that for decades they had been fixated on what they call the "purchase funnel," or "consumer decision journey"[2]—the multistage trip that people take when they make a purchase, from awareness of product choices to action on those choices. Google's innovations meant that, for the first time, advertisers could reach out to huge numbers of *individuals* as they took consumer decision journeys online.

Marketers hoped to connect those individuals conducting Google searches with products that mirror the interests expressed by the search terms, using two approaches: search-engine optimization (SEO) and paid search. The first aims to exploit so-called organic (nonpaid-for) search results—in other words, the list of websites that appear when you type keywords into the search box. In response to those search terms, Google's formulas determine which sites will appear on the list and, depending on a site's relevance, how near the top. Although many of the relevance criteria are secret, two core values that guide a site's appearance and position on Google's search results are well known: the extent of the site's connection to the search terms and its reputation with respect to those topics. Google's signal contribution to search engines was to define a site with a high reputation as one that has many other sites linking to it. A site that reflects the search terms and has many other high-reputation sites linking to it will appear higher on the organic search results compared with sites with fewer such links. Under SEO, marketers attempt to optimize their position on the organic search results by crafting sites sensitive to Google's rules. For example, to give its site the best chance to appear prominently in the search results when an individual is looking for information about high-definition televisions, Toshiba would want to make sure that its website contains the sort of information about its high-definition TV products that would lead many other sites to link to it. Achieving this goal is difficult, as Toshiba is one of many major high-definition television manufacturers, and none of these companies can control its ranking in Google's organic search results. All these manufacturers are constantly jockeying for better placement, and Google adds to the challenge by continually changing its search formulas.

Google's paid-search advertising system is another way to reach prospective customers, and under this process companies are better able—though still not guaranteed—to ensure that their ads appear. This process involves an auction, as companies bid on search words—perhaps thousands of them—to win the right to have its ads appear prominently alongside the organic search results. For Toshiba the terms they might bid on could be as generic as *HD-TV* and as specific as *Toshiba LED*. To increase its chances, Toshiba's bid might also even include competitors' names, such as *Samsung, Vizio,* and *Panasonic.* Toshiba's digital-advertising agency would present its bids electronically to Google, and the search engine would evaluate it along with those it receives from other companies based on a complex and changing combination of factors, such as the relevance of the product to the firm's bidding words, the bid amount, and the degree of success (measured via clicks) that other such Toshiba ads have already had on Google. Google's paid-search ads have appeared in different places on the search page over the years. Currently Google ranks its auction winners and arrays them immediately above the organic search findings (usually three ads) as well as to the right (up to eight ads). Google's basic business model, though, has remained the same: every time someone clicks on one of these ads, the advertiser pays Google the agreed-upon amount.

This pay-per-click principle was not new when Google's founders, Larry Page and Sergei Brin, launched their paid-search business sometime around 2002. This approach was the same that had intrigued but then frustrated websites and advertisers, including Procter and Gamble, for its low yield. But the Google crew was confident in the advertising model, which built off the approach Web entrepreneur Bill Gross had used for his search engine GoTo. Later called Overture and ultimately bought by Yahoo!, it used a pay-per-click system with click charges set by auction. Google's savvy innovation was instituting an algorithm for choosing auction winners that considered not just the bid price but also the relevance of the ads according to the number of clicks that they or ads like them had registered in previous campaigns. Page and Brin reasoned that awarding auctions for ads that were also based on click records would both benefit Google's revenues and encourage marketers to create ads relevant to users, according to this new definition of relevance. The pair also diverged from the competition by having the search engine carry text ads only. With many users entering Google via slow dial-up connections, Page and Brin worried that ads with pictures would unduly slow the loading of the search results. They also wanted to emphasize their goal of creating the most relevant search experience. They therefore insisted that the ads be no longer than a couple of lines, be informative, and carry no more than ninety-five characters. Initially a vertical line separated the noncommercial (organic) search results on the left side of the page from paid search findings on the right side.[3]

It worked. JP Morgan estimated that by 2008 Google had a 73 percent share of search revenues in a $22-billion global search economy.[4] Many small advertisers aiming to sell products directly off of the click liked the ability to put small amounts of money into keywords that reflected their products, and they accepted the proposition that a click on their ad meant someone at least was paying attention. Although common keywords were cheap in the beginning, Google's increasing traffic as a search engine and expert ability to match search words with ads led to soaring revenues. Research in 2003 by the comScore internet research company for the Internet Advertising Bureau (IAB) found that sponsored-search listings in April and May of that year generated click-through rates of over 16 percent, more than four times greater than those for organic search listings, based on the financial-services and travel-industry ads studied. Over the next few years, the click-through rate plummeted (by 2010 it was less than 1 percent), but the actual number of clicks (and so the payout) remained huge because of the enormous number of searches that internet visitors made at Google.[5]

Although the pay-per-click metric telegraphed Google as a direct-response vehicle, major marketers got in on the act despite the limiting nature of the ads. For example, they saw the additional utility of integrating search campaigns with brand advertising on traditional media. In 2005, General Motors' Cadillac division tied its search campaign to its television ads during the Super Bowl, concluding that the two thirty-second TV spots accounted for a 170 percent increase in clicks on the car's search site ads over the previous week. Cadillac planned to increase its search site ad spending 1,000 percent in 2006.[6]

Reports of the Cadillac and similar experiences in the trade publications and at industry meetings came as unwelcome news for website executives. Search site advertising was yet another development that challenged online publishers' usefulness as an advertising vehicle. Media buyers agreed with Google's claim that consumers' keywords were insights into their direct interests. Google's pitch that clicking on an ad was a significant indicator of individual consumers' interest fit exactly with advertisers' increasing insistence on direct measurability. Moreover, media buyers reasoned that the sometimes-high prices they occasionally had to bid for individual words ("car," for example) were actually cheaper than the pay-per-click model might appear, because even the text ad had display value, and they didn't pay for that.[7]

By 2010 search site advertising was earning about half of all Web revenue. Not all of this amount would flow to non-search-engine websites if Google and the other search engines didn't exist, but the increasing popularity of search by brand-oriented advertisers such as General Motors did suggest that there was direct competition between publishing and search-engine sites. True, organic listings might lead searchers to websites, and sometimes this "side-door" traffic could substantially boost visitors and thus ad revenue. But for most websites it was an uneven and unpredictable way to make a living. The dilemma for Web publishers—companies outside of search-engine sites that serve up and distribute content—didn't stop there. As they worked furiously to attract advertisers in order to win some of the other 50 percent of the media buyers' spending with new forms of display advertising, they turned for help to new types of organizations—online ad networks, data providers, and data exchanges. These companies promised to help them boost revenues by presenting advertisers with yet more information about the individuals in their audiences. What emerged quickly, though, was a new advertising food chain in which publishers—particularly traditional publishers that spent a lot of money on original content—fell dangerously toward the bottom.

As usual, the media-buying developments contained seeds of irony. Publishers were key supporters of the new system. They hoped media buyers would see the utility of their Web pages for drawing target audiences. Despite providing more and more data about their visitors in the hope of gaining revenue clout, and despite the spread of broadband, which could accommodate the videos the P&Gs of the world had said they wanted, marketers and their affiliates kept pushing Web publishers further down the ladder. Neither the advertising trade press nor industry meetings paid attention to the possibility that weakening certain kinds of publishers might harm the role they play as sources of culture and democratic argumentation. Nor did executives engage in debates about whether particular actions might positively or negatively affect diversity and quality of entertainment, news, and information. That the positions of these publishers were not considered stands to reason: in the roiling, competitive digital advertising system, companies struggled to prove efficient return on investment. How we get our politics, where we seek our identity, how we frame ourselves and our relationship to the world—these simply were not part of the business agenda.

In fact, by the decade's end many media buyers didn't even consider websites their focus. The internet industry's laserlike attention to audience data had led to technology that allowed agencies to "buy" (that is, purchase the right to reach) individuals, automatically and in real time, on whatever page they landed. The intrinsic value of any particular website threatened to erode. This decoupling of audiences from context marked a historic shift in deciding what content to support.

At the end of 2009, 92 percent of online households (which represented 72 percent of total U.S. households) possessed some kind of high-speed connection—and the percentage was growing.[8] A result was the increasing number of rich-media and video ads. Created with the help of companies such as Eyeblaster and EyeWonder, the commercial messages could dive directly in front of site visitors with screen-size presentations as the requested page loaded, elastic boxes that spread out when a person moused over them, and TV-style commercials embedded in page banners and joined to the beginning, middle, or end of site videos. The display ads and videos allowed for high-profile image advertising that aims to cultivate awareness of a product and its personality as well as clicks to the product website to learn more. It's the kind of presentation that Denis Beausejour of P&G wanted back in 1998. It's also the kind with the potential for eye-popping involvement that many believe search ads lack. Publishers see this as a competitive advantage against search, which even with video tends to be limited by ads on the sides of results.

Despite this growing capability, and despite the awakening of interest among major corporations in display advertising, many Web publishers still feel trapped toward the bottom of the advertising system's internet food chain. To understand what this means and how it pushed audience labeling and targeting to new heights, we need to examine the forces that shape those who hold power. First, consider that two audience-rating companies, Nielsen and comScore, are central in an odd way to the development of the Web's power structure. You might wonder why the Web needs ratings firms if the sites themselves can audit the number of people visiting them. One reason is that early in the Web's history media buyers decided that they would not trust websites' accounting of their individual ("unique") visitors. Instead they accepted the television industry's model for learning about Web audiences: the survey panel. As the dominant players in that space, Nielsen and comScore place tracking software on computers in homes and the workplace. They use their findings along with what they know about those people (including general media use and shopping patterns) to make generalizations about visitors to particular websites. ComScore reports that its panel includes about two million people "under continuous measurement" globally—one million in the United States and one million distributed across more than 170 countries.[9] Nielsen's panel size is smaller—several hundred thousand—and in fewer countries, but it emphasizes that it creates its sample by using the gold standard: choosing people based on a table of random telephone numbers.[10]

Neither Nielsen nor comScore will explain what kinds of workplaces let their computers be monitored by a ratings firm. (It's hard to imagine big firms and government agencies allowing it.) One doesn't have to dig into the firms' survey methods, though, to realize that they fall short in auditing the traffic to websites. Comparisons between Nielsen and comScore data regarding the websites they rank as most popular typically do show much agreement on the relative rankings of sites in terms of visitors; it would be hard to miss that Google, Facebook, and Yahoo! should be up there. At the same time, the ratings firms often differ by tens of thousands—even more—on the specific audience figures they report for each site. It's not unusual to see, for example, even a site such as MySpace get very different Nielsen and comScore numbers. Nevertheless, media buyers use the ratings to give them a sense of the top-tier sites and their relative sizes.

But just as important as the large number of sites that show up on the Nielsen and comScore lists are the ones that are missing or are way down. While the number of sites that the panels visit is large, the fragmentation of the Web is such that even a survey of over a million people could not capture what writer Chris Anderson has called the "long tail" of the Web: those sites with relatively few visitors that accept ads and may actually be appropriate buys for certain types of advertisers.[11] Advertisers are looking for what they call "scale"—the ability to purchase huge numbers of individuals who fit their targeting needs without the expensive chore of having to cherry-pick them across thousands of Web publishers. The online advertising world is therefore split between premium sites that advertisers recognize and a sea of others with audiences advertisers may want but with much less ability to access media buyers directly. In each category are sites that spend lots of money creating content (so-called legacy publishers) and sites that draw most of their material from visitors (so-called user-generated content) or from other sites. Many of the first type of site are traditional firms that make most of their money in print. Many of the second type of site are rooted to the Web itself. Each type of publisher can present scale to advertisers. The *New York Times* is a legacy publisher with around thirty million unique visitors per month to its nytimes.com website. Huffington Post, by contrast, started on the Web and reaches around the same number of unique individuals per month.

The fortunate publishers that score high on Web ratings charts do have an opportunity to parlay their numbers into advertising by selling ad space on their sites directly to advertisers. For ratings help, sites that might not be well represented in Nielsen or comScore rankings often turn to Quantcast, a measurement company that affiliates with over ten million sites partly as a result of its offer to audit and quantify their audiences. In return, Quantcast loads the computers of the publishers' visitors with cookies that track what they do online. It uses the cookies to find "lookalikes," which are people who seem to reflect the background, interests, and activities of an advertiser's primary targets. They are, Quantcast tells marketers, "audiences who look like your converting customers"—that is, the ones who buy or otherwise respond to the advertisers' requests.[12] It sells the ability to reach the looka-likes to advertisers and shares the revenues with the publishers who let it drop the cookies.

Web publishers that sell directly to advertisers use mixed business models. Some sites offer ads to advertisers on a cost-per-click (CPC) or cost-per-action (CPA) basis. That is, the sponsor pays only if a visitor clicks on the ad or (in cost per action) performs a subsequent deed, such as phoning the company or buying the product. Most publishers, though, sell advertising space on a cost-per-thousand-impressions basis. An industry group defines an impression as "a delivered basic advertising unit."[13] Every time an advertisement loads onto a user's screen, it will be counted as one impression. When publishers adopt the cost-per-thousand-impressions system they get paid whether or not the individuals click on the ads. They use this approach because even though the raw CPC and CPA prices are far higher than CPM costs, the percentage of visitors who actually click on ads is miniscule—far less than 1 percent. The percentage that carries out particular actions is far lower than that. The Google, Bing, and Yahoo! search engines, which charge on a CPC basis, do in fact yield a very low ad-click rate. They can make money charging advertisers on a per click basis because they send out billions of ads each day. Few publishers come close to matching that.

Publishers often try to increase the pages on their sites. They do it partly to increase their chances of showing up in search engine results and partly to give visitors additional reasons to stay. Keeping people on the site longer—the industry term for this is *engaged*—means the publisher will have more opportunity to learn about them and serve them ads. Publishers often take a host of steps to find out about their visitors, including incentives that induce these individuals to reveal their identity; even a thin amount of personal information such as a name, e-mail address, and ZIP code can enable the site to begin a personal file on an individual. For example, nytimes.com has sign-up data from the more than one million individuals who subscribe in one way or another to its service. It encourages nonsubscriber registration by making it a prerequisite to be able to comment on articles, receive news alerts, and sign up for free e-mail newsletters. The website requires registrants to enter an e-mail address and certain demographic information (ZIP code, age, sex, job industry, and job title). It also asks for household income. Meanwhile, nytimes.com tells advertisers that it "has an extensive database of reader-supplied information. Through reader surveys and registration data analysis, we can offer you access to your ideal audience."[14]

Many popular sites, including nytimes.com, add to these data through voluntary surveys that they conduct of visitors on the websites, on the phone, or even through the mail. Nytimes.com has an arrangement with the LinkedIn social-media site to match nytimes.com registrants to their LinkedIn profiles and transfer that information to nytimes.com for its use in advertising.[15] Some publishers, though evidently not nytimes.com, purchase data about their registrants from information vendors such as Experian and Acxiom and append them to their files. The data may directly involve the individual (profession, credit status, number of airline flights) as well as the individual's household (number of kids, age ranges, home value). Information purchased from other companies may help the site make life-style inferences about an individual. So, for example, Nielsen's PRIZM segmentation system might suggest that a person between forty-five and sixty-four years old living in the 19004 ZIP code area has a high chance of being a member of what PRIZM calls the "Upper Crust: wealthy, without kids." People in that cluster "shop at Saks Fifth Avenue, belong to a country club, read *Condé Nast Traveler,* watch the Gold Channel, drive Mercedes SL Class."[16]

Then there is the all-important behavioral data that websites create by placing cookies in visitors' computers—even those who don't register—and making inferences about their interests and even their personalities based on the links they click and the topics they view. A person who tends to read articles about health might be tagged as having specific health interests; a sports reader might be placed in that bailiwick. Sites often hire analytics firms to perform exhaustive analysis of these sorts of data with an eye toward showing why advertisers should find their visitors particularly interesting and consequently pay a lot to reach them.

Nytimes.com reports that it hires Audience Science to track and analyze its site's browsing patterns. While the sentence is tucked away in its privacy policy (where the Times implies that Audience Science uses Web beacons and tags to carry out its work), a glance at what the company does explains why it is critical to nytimes.com's attempts to make its online audience attractive to advertisers. In Audience Science's own words, it analyzes "multiple indicators" to make inferences about visitors: "which pages and sections they have visited, what static and dynamic content they have read, what they say about themselves in registration data, which search terms they use, and what IP [internet protocol] data indicates about them, including geography."[17]

All this can offer advertisers impressive detail when choosing to target people on the site. Moreover, audiences are involved in a continual process of data capture and message presentation. Advertisers and publishers gain usable information about site visitors at the same time they are selling to them. But even major sites such as nytimes.com, with a million individual visitors per month, have found that they can't sell their advertising positions by themselves. Nytimes.com may sell out its front page and other highly trafficked areas of the site. It may also sell "site sessions," which allow an advertiser to "own all display banner positions," except for the home page, that are seen by the targeted individuals.[18] Nevertheless, many positions on the nytimes.com site, including reader comment areas, interest few advertisers and so cannot be sold at premium prices. An executive for the *New York Times* who spoke on the condition of anonymity estimated that these unsold positions constituted approximately 50 percent. He predicted optimistically that the percentage would actually decrease because advertisers would want to reach the select group of people who had chosen to pay for new digital versions of the newspaper. He and others agree that at many sites, even those of big-name off-line publishers, the percentage of advertising space they cannot sell directly is far higher, often close to 80 percent. Some in the industry call this unsold space "remnant ads," though others take exception to the carpet-peddler image the term evokes and instead dub the ads "nonpremium."

Because of this oversupply, virtually all sites link up with at least a few of the hundreds of advertising networks that have emerged to profit from the need for such intermediaries. As Chapter 2 noted, advertising networks came into being pretty close to the Web's big bang. They had developed in the 1990s as a revenue source for websites that didn't have huge visitor numbers and that were running out of venture-capital money. The networks' strategy was to learn a lot about the behaviors and backgrounds of the individuals that their affiliate sites reached, to tag those people via cookies, and then to give marketers the ability to target particular types of people with clients' specific ads when they returned to one of the hundreds, or thousands, of sites on the network. The networks would share their revenues with participating sites. So, for example, the Engage ad network in 1999 reported that it held over thirty-five million profiles. Some of the data came from users' internet protocol (IP) addresses (part of which indicates geographical location). Other data were inferred about the people through their activities (what a person did on sites, as monitored by cookies and Web bugs). The activity-based approach to evaluating visitors and then sending ads to them became known as *behavioral targeting*. Advertisers could buy the right to reach them according to up to eight hundred characteristics. Executives from Engage argued that not only was the firm's segmentation approach useful for ad targeting, it even helped with the click-through rate. Its research found that advertising targeted through user profiling received substantially higher click-through rates than ads served only around content.

Engage eventually disappeared, but the number of networks grew. In 2008 Jupiter Research estimated that approximately 28 percent of online revenue was flowing through them.[19] By then, the four advertising powerhouses of the internet age—Google, Yahoo!, Microsoft, and AOL—had networks that included their own properties and millions of other sites. Google in the early 2000s established AdSense, a network of websites that agreed to allow Google to serve "contextual" text ads on them based on Google's analysis of the content of the sites' Web pages that the visitor was reading. By the late 2000s, it had morphed into the Google Display Network, which serves ads with rich media and video formats to millions of sites.

Apart from the Big Four, approximately three hundred other networks ply their services to websites. Web publishers in search of advertising revenues often affiliate with more than one. ValueClick and Adbrite are among the biggest. Many publishers allow more than one network to place ads on their sites in order to generate revenue from multiple sources. The Huffington Post, for example, allows Advertising.com (owned by parent company AOL), ValueClick, Feedburner, and Google as "advertising partners." These and virtually all other networks use cookies to track the behavior of visitors within and across thousands of websites. In this way they can develop behavioral profiles of individuals and place them into segments that allow targeting of large numbers of people for ads—for example, one segment could consist of women between the age of twenty-one and thirty-four who live on the West Coast and who are in the market for a small car. Using cookies also enables ad networks to "retarget" individuals who had seen an ad on one site with an ad for that product on another site.

The Advertising.com network boasts that it is all about combining niche targeting abilities with the kind of scale unavailable on even the largest website. "Finding your ideal consumer is one thing. Finding millions of them is another. With our targeting solutions, you can extend your message across thousands of sites and reach your customers at scale." In its pitch to advertisers, Advertising.com emphasizes the contextual and behavioral expertise it can offer from its huge number of visitors to AOL-affiliated sites. Advertisers can choose niche networks, such as its community, casual games, or retail channels. They can identify Web users based on behavior segments such as "style mavens" and "family chefs." And they can "pinpoint your customers with other powerful targeting solutions." For example, the company claims it can: "Develop a custom audience segment modeled after visitors to your site (Look-Alike Modeling); find households that have the greatest propensity to purchase specific products or brands (MRI Lifestyle Clusters); if you're sponsoring an AOL page, retarget consumers who have visited it (Sponsorship LeadBack); find your ideal female audiences on the sites they are most likely to visit (Subnet Targeting); find women who are searching for information about fashion or home & gardening; explicitly target households with females present (Age/Gender Targeting)."[20]

The Audience Science Network (which is separate from the work Audience Science conducts for individual websites such as nytimes.com) is equally enthusiastic about its ability to help advertisers. The company says it "accesses 200 billion data insights into 386 million people worldwide." These insights about intent, it states, can fuel marketing that encourages "conversions"— that is, sales, intention to purchase, or other responses marketers want. In addition to behavioral segments, the firm offers targeting and retargeting based on demographics, location, time of day, internet speed, "and more."[21]

Despite these promised benefits, marketers tend to have a love-hate relationship with advertising networks. One reason is that the many networks don't make the names of many sites known to their clients; publishers that sell their own advertising space often don't want advertisers to know that they also sell their ads more cheaply via networks. Moreover, with just a few exceptions ad networks do not guarantee the placement of ads on any particular sites.[22] Consequently advertisers often don't exactly know where their ads appear unless visitors click on them. Sometimes ads appear in e-mails, on minor blog sites, or in other places on the fringes of the Web. Major advertisers tend to be particularly concerned that their ads not be placed among salacious content or content that might reflect poorly on their products. Under such a system, the challenge of delivering the number of promised impressions to the promised targets can be met simply by loading them up repeatedly on a small number of people. To prevent this, the best networks use a process known as frequency capping, which limits the number of times a computer gets served the same ad. But on other networks ads will sometimes be served over and over to the same individuals, much to their annoyance.

Still, marketers and their media-buying agencies like networks because they are extremely inexpensive on a cost-per-thousand-impressions basis—typically between fifty cents and a dollar.[23] Many advertisers use this avenue as a way to simply spray the Web with ads in the hope of direct-response revenues. But major marketers with brand-oriented initiatives have also been using cheap network buys as inexpensive ways to reach out to huge numbers of people via display ads with the expectation that a certain percentage will click on the ads. Media buyers evaluate the return on investment through particular measurable activities that relate to their campaign goals—prospective customers reading parts of a minisite, asking for more information, providing e-mail addresses, and the like—that may encourage branding and move a customer toward a purchase. Increasingly, advertisers are erasing the traditional distinction between branding and direct response to assess instead various levels of engagement. General Motors' Chevrolet division conducted a survey to determine the relationship between clicking on any of hundreds of features of its site and visitors' interest in the brand and their intent to purchase a car. Chevrolet used these findings to create an index that assesses the return on investment it gets from people's click and mouse-over responses to different forms of Web advertising.[24]

For Web publishers, the existence of advertising networks has been at best a mixed blessing. Sites that have no ability to generate revenues independently use networks to make money. When costs are low (for example, if the sites carry mostly volunteer blogs and pay little in salaries), the revenues from advertising networks might help them get by. But for sites with major expenses—often legacy publishers with off-line newspapers and magazines—advertising networks bring in money at shockingly low CPM levels, prohibiting publishers who might otherwise consider a switch to an online-only model from having sufficient resources to do so. A 2008 survey of four anonymous companies by the Bain consulting firm found that while the Web advertising they sold directly to advertisers yielded between $12 and $18 average CPMs, they were getting around $1 CPM for advertising sold through networks. More than 80 percent of the revenues of those firms came from the 20 percent of their advertising.

The anonymous *New York Times* executive mentioned earlier also said that to try to leverage as much revenue as possible from its advertising opportunities his company discounts ad positions that it cannot sell at premium prices. In paying lower prices, the advertisers are not guaranteed an exact date or placement for their ad. The executive also acknowledged that nytimes.com has an agreement with Google's Display Advertising Network (DAN) to auction off the website's unsold positions. (Google therefore places cookies into the browsers of nytimes.com visitors and tracks their behavior there and across the Web.) In distinguishing Google from other advertising networks he noted that although a bidder can specifically request the nytimes.com website, the DAN's AdSense platform allows his company to exert control over the kinds of ads served to the site. In general, he said, nytimes.com and a few other major Web publishers such as NBCUniversal Interactive are wary of advertising networks because they might serve ads for products that would not fit the publisher's image—for example, diet pills or products that claim to enhance breasts or muscular physique. The *New York Times* official portrayed AdSense as a way to gather advertising from small companies—local restaurants, theaters, and the like—that mesh with the site's audience but that the *Times* ad-sales staff do not have the time to contact themselves. The amount and percentage of revenues that nytimes.com receives from ads sold this way are confidential, but the Google auction prices obviously will not come close to the rates that the nytimes.com sales force gets for the site's premium and even discounted ads.

The declining amounts of money publishers make as they move from print to selling their own ads on the Web and to accepting ad-network prices are startling. A source familiar with newspaper off-line and online pricing (and whose example was confirmed by others in the business), and who agreed to be interviewed on the condition of anonymity, described the situation using 2010 figures: The average CPM rate for a major print newspaper is approximately $50 (major advertisers may get a substantial discount). The CPM rate for direct sales for ads on a newspaper's website ranges from $25 to $40 (ads with videos typically fetch the highest amounts). But any given company sells only about 20 percent of its advertising positions through direct sales. The rest is sold through ad networks at a CPM rate ranging from $2 to $4. The ad network gets 50 percent of the amount earned, so a paper's website ends up with CPMs of $1 to $2 for 80 percent of its advertising space.

To improve these dismal numbers, firms such as Audience Science encourage publishers to enhance the knowledge of their audience that they bring to the ad networks; Audience Science contends that better profiling can make CPM values fifteen times higher. Yet while publishers are plumbing more and more about their audiences—and hiring companies to help them—they are being thrust further and further down a food chain that diminishes their value and power.

A relatively new ad-selling environment, the advertising exchange, does not materially improve the situation much for publishers even as it excites marketers. Advertising exchanges are centralized markets for buying and selling audience impressions. Instead of going to a few of the more than three hundred ad networks and buying the right to reach a certain number of individuals with certain characteristics on anonymous sites, ad exchanges provide a digital marketplace whereby any party—networks, publishers, and even advertising agencies—can buy and sell the right to reach anonymous individuals. Some in the industry predict that ad networks will eventually disappear as all parties move to exchanges to sell their ad positions. In early 2010 there were about a dozen ad exchanges, and the biggest were owned, not surprisingly, by Google (Ad Exchange 2.0), Yahoo! (Right Media), and Microsoft (AdECN). Advertising exchanges are more efficient than ad networks because all the buyers and sellers can come together in the same places. Moreover, unlike most ad networks, ad exchanges often let media buyers know the site on which the impression will be served. But the real benefit of ad exchanges at their most high-tech in the eyes of their proponents is the ability to make a decision to reach certain types of individuals on the fly, wherever they are. A growing number of exchanges offer this "real time bidding" (RTB) on individuals, at virtually the moment they load the page of the site they are visiting. One industry observer called "capturing the individual consumer" through RTB in exchanges "the holy grail of targeting."[25]

The rise of a market in impressions has naturally stimulated unprecedented data-collecting activity related to individuals. One investment firm's 2009 report noted that "contact information is now collected at virtually every step in a user's online experience (via registration pages, for example) and Web surfing behavior is tracked down to the millisecond—providing publishers and advertisers with the potential to create a reasonably complete profile of their audiences, and thus enabling the matching of a user with a user profile to enable robust, segmentation-based targeting."[26] For example:

- eXelate says it gathers online data from two hundred million unique individuals per month through deals with hundreds of websites that see an opportunity for revenue based on the firm's visitor analyses.[27] eXelate determines a consumer's age, sex, ethnicity, marital status, and profession by scouring website registration data. It also tracks consumer activities online to note, for example, which consumers are in the market to buy a car or which are fitness buffs, based on their internet searches and the sites they frequent. It gathers the information anonymously using tracking cookies placed on the hard drive of a consumer's computer when that individual visits a participating site. Through what eXelate calls its Targeting eXchange, advertisers bid on the right to target the consumers with those cookies (as well as those of other firms), and eXelate shares this revenue with the sites that provided access to the data.[28]

• BlueKai, an eXelate competitor, also strikes deals with thousands of websites to use cookies to collect anonymous data about visitors' activities. From that information, it makes inferences about the kinds of purchases that might interest those people—their "intent to purchase." The company also operates what it calls the BlueKai Exchange—"the world's largest data marketplace"—where it auctions its own cookies and those of other firms. BlueKai claims that it can target more than two hundred million users based on "actionable audience data" at "any stage of the purchase funnel."[29]

• The data firm Lotame tracks comments that visitors leave on websites and from these creates individual profiles based on what site visitors have written about movies, say, or about parenting and pregnancy. Lotame packages the data without determining individual names but attaches to them unique cookies, and then goes to exchanges to sell the profiles and access to these potential customers.[30]

Marketers often have cookies of their own that they've created for people who visit their product sites. Consider Procter and Gamble's Pampers diaper line, which has a "Pampers Village" website aimed at mothers. P&G scarfs up loads of information about visitors, from data requested at registration to be part of the site's "community" to behavioral data regarding what they look at or even write on the site, as well as to information from outside data providers about the individuals whose names it recognizes from registration.[31] To reach these people elsewhere on the Web, P&G might bid on an ad exchange to buy individuals who match its cookies. Cookie matching allows the cookie seller (for example, BlueKai) to detect in milliseconds whether the computer that has its cookie also has a cookie from Pampers. If there is a match, the company buying the impression not only obtains the information that the seller (such as BlueKai) has about the individual, it now can link that knowledge to information that it owns about the person. And there's more: data firms have found ways to link off-line data to e-mail addresses, registration information, and similar personal facts that people reveal about themselves online. For example, eXelate in 2009 began to offer advertisers the ability to append to eXelate cookies data from Nielsen that includes information from the Census Bureau, Nielsen's own research, and research by other consumer-research firms, such as Mediamark and Experian-Simmons.[32] P&G's Pampers is also involved in these online/off-line linkages. The firm's privacy policy says that it links information it gathers about visitors online to data "we collect about you from other sources, such as commercially available sources."[33]

So who are the winners in this digital selling-and-buying food chain? Clearly, the data-exchange firms are big winners. So are the major ad networks, even in the exchange world, because they have enormous amounts of data via cookies that they can sell to advertisers, sometimes merging their cookies with those of the data exchanges. Google presents an interesting case of the owner of data-exchange and ad networks that changed aggressively to meet the competition. In the early 2000s news surfaced that Google was gathering up huge amounts of information about its visitors' search activities and sometimes linking it to profiles gleaned through registration on its Gmail and other programs. Yet Google implied it was using all the data for a kind of actuarial research—to hone its ability to link search terms and website writings with search terms and ads that yielded lucrative clicks. Nevertheless, the revelations of the data capture resulted in calls by privacy advocates for short time limits for this type of storage. Google did, however, manage to avoid the privacy controversies that were roiling around its e-mail and Web-publishing counterparts, because for most of the decade the company insisted that it did not use personal or historical information about an individual either to influence that person's search results or in its AdSense network, where it served ads based on the context of a Web page.

The company changed course as part of its goal to become highly successful in the display market; these efforts accelerated after it purchased DoubleClick, an ad-serving company that also ran an advertising network.[34] It seemed clear that Google was adapting quickly to compete with, and to try and outstrip, its rivals with audience information. Although it kept its promise of not sharing users' personally identifiable information with its advertisers, Google increasingly ramped up its use of behavioral, demographic, and geographical data in serving its ads on the Google Display Network. The network also opened its tags (and therefore its cookies) to other online target marketers it "certified"—Turn, X+1, Data Xu, Rocket Fuel, and Appnexus, for example—as a way to get extra revenue. Significantly, Rocket Fuel presents itself as delivering audiences in ways that Google itself has never publicized, but for which Google's network and cookies are facilitators. "We build designer audiences for your campaign by buying individual impressions of the users," says a Rocket Fuel promotional document. "The Rocket Fuel platform is integrated with many of the leading third-party data providers—allowing us to leverage demographic, interest, lifestyle, past purchase, behavioral, in-market, social, purchase intent and search data. . . . We go beyond other audience targeting technologies by layering multiple unique data sources."[35]

Where do media-buying agencies stand in this hierarchy? In the face of the hundreds of millions of dollars made on display advertising by networks and exchanges owned by Google, Yahoo!, and Microsoft, declaring media-buying agencies winners should not imply they were in the same revenue league. Yet in view of the precipice on which large media-buying agencies and their owners—WPP, Publicis, Omnicom, and Interpublic—found themselves in the early 2000s, they remarkably have managed to find ways to remain relevant to clients. For a number of years, the Web's structure had threatened to make media-buying firms obsolete in the digital space. Their clients the advertisers could easily purchase blocks of search terms and banners directly and automatically from the networks selling them. WPP chairman Martin Sorrell famously called Google a "frenemy" amid worries that it had both the technology and the data to serve as the kind of guide to reaching audiences that had been the purview of WPP's media buyers. As a defensive measure, WPP and its counterparts began to invest in tools that would help their clients in ad targeting, buying, optimization, and measurement. A critical competitive advantage they enjoy is deep knowledge of their clients' target audiences. That includes information about what individual customers buy as well as access to the cookies of customers or potential customers who have visited client sites such as Pampers Village. While clients share such knowledge with their media-buying agencies, they would not want to reveal it to ad networks such as Google or to data providers such as BlueKai, because the networks and data firms might use the information in ways that could compete with the advertisers confiding in them.

Media-buying agencies' desire to help their clients use their cookies most effectively meshes with the agencies' interest in developing businesses that allow them to eke increasing revenues from their client relationships. The two goals have led media-buying agencies to join or create buyer-driven real-time ad exchanges aimed at efficiently auctioning cookies. Also called demand-side platforms (DSPs), they are controlled by the agencies even though on many platforms any publisher or network can submit a bid for a certain number of the cookies being offered. In a seller-driven—"supply-side"—ad exchange (for example, Google's DoubleClick Exchange) the owners (in this case Google) have the best views of the advertising space that exists in the online world and of the auctions that are taking place throughout. That means Google knows the difference between what the sellers of the ad space want to charge and what buyers will bid. Google has the advantage if it wants to get into the market, while media buyers have the disadvantage, as they see only the asking price from the publishers, the networks, and the exchanges. By contrast, with DSPs the agencies' media buyers know both numbers; the exchange is fully transparent to them. DSPs also give the media-buying firms control over unique identifiers in cookies that publishers and marketers set through the bidding process; they don't have that kind of power in seller-owned exchanges. They can consequently plant their own cookies in the computers of the people whom they have bought from publishers. All this makes the DSPs quite valuable to their marketing clients.

Web publishers, by contrast, continue to get pushed around, and down, the power ladder. Leaders representing the networks, data exchanges, advertising exchanges, and media-buying firms continually exhort the publishers to keep the system humming by giving up more and more information about their visitors. The chief operating officer at the digital agency Neo@ Ogilvy warned publishers that increasingly specific data was the only way to stop the downward spiral of Web ad prices. "The saviour of this commoditization [of advertising space] is data," he contended.[36] Other executives contend that publishers should marry such detailed information with real-time bidding (RTB) to get the most revenues from their visitors. Pubmatic, a firm that aims to help, puts the situation this way:

> Currently, most digital media buying is done based on assumptions about certain audiences. For example, audiences bought through ad networks and ad exchanges are often purchased in buckets [that is, simply in large numbers of uncategorized people] or by segment. How the audiences are categorized in certain segments depends on who is selling them. And while some audience sellers do a better job of segmenting users than others, so long as individual impressions are being

grouped into a bucket and sold at a pre-negotiated price, they are not being fairly valued and are often sold at under-valued prices.

In Example 1, a luxury car advertiser is looking for a very specific audience type and is willing to pay a premium price to reach a specific user that is highly qualified. The more qualified the user, the more the advertiser is willing to pay. On the right side of the example below, the advertiser (or rather the technology company placing bids on behalf of the advertiser) can see the unique characteristics about the user and therefore is willing to pay a $3.90 CPM to target that user. [A graphic notes that the user has visited multiple auto sites within the past few days, is currently—at 9:30 am—reading a vehicle financing page, and lives in Aspen, Colorado.] On the left side, the same user would have been bucketed into an auto-buying segment and priced according to the segment price, which [at $1.75 CPM] is far lower than what was paid via RTB for the individual.[37]

The reason for the higher price, Pubmatic explains, is that more information about users leads to improvement on click-through rates and conversion rates. Turn, a network that trades in real-time impressions, claims that its advertisers are seeing up to 135 percent improvement on the former and 150 percent improvement on the latter.[38]

All this sounds great, except that publishers face several dangers that are built into the process. The first is the CPM price. David Cohen, the head of digital resources at the Universal McCann subsidiary of Interpublic, noted that the average price a publisher receives on Google's DoubleClick exchange is under $1. He said he didn't know the amount that nytimes.com receives when it sells advertising space on the exchange, but he doubted that it was much different.[39] Yield-optimization firms such as Pubmatic and X+1 try to help publishers by serving as automatic bid gatekeepers that evaluate all bids for publishers' impressions (including non-real-time bids from networks and advertisers) in real time and select only the highest bids. Nevertheless, the increase in CPM that Pubmatic illustrates still doesn't come close to the more than $10 CPM that publishers make selling their premium ad positions by themselves. Publishers' yield is affected still further by the cut that Pubmatic takes in return for its services.

A second difficulty for website publishers is the danger of data theft. Some advertisers and networks have been known to try to place their own cookie tags or pixels on the publisher impressions they buy so that they can place cookies in the machines of the individuals who load the ads and then retarget them without having to pay the publisher.[40] "Your data is being stolen," eXelate warns in a PowerPoint slide show aimed at publishers.[41] Tom

Hespos, president of digital-marketing agency Underscore Marketing, has urged publishers to consider that demand-side platforms are pretty well set up to allow advertisers to drain value from Web publishers. He points out that "agency-side audience networks are leveraging the targeting data in which publishers have invested to target and segment audiences across the Web."[42] Interpublic's DSP, named Caedreon, has developed an ethics code that explicitly says it will not adopt such tactics to steal publishers' audiences.[43] Other DSPs have not announced this prohibition. Pubmatic, eXelate, and other firms claim they have technologies to protect publishers from audience theft if the publishers work through them instead of going into exchanges on their own. But the need to lean on these third parties further erodes the independence of publishers in the digital environment.

Perhaps the most significant danger for publishers is that selling individual impressions has resulted in a marketing perspective that the publishing sites on which they appear are unimportant; the goal is to reach people with particular characteristics wherever they show up. Agencies' decoupling of audiences from context is a profound change. Traditionally, advertising executives often tried to place ads where the "environment" of editorial matter or programming would fit with the tenor of the commercial message or the personality and status of the product.[44] So, for example, food ads in magazines would best be placed among recipes, while creators of television commercials generally want them to air on the types of shows that they believe draw attention and sales.[45] In the digital environment, this concern has narrowed to not wanting to have ads served near salacious content that might hurt the brand in the eyes of the audience. Apart from that concern, as an eXelate executive commented to ClickZ News, "who a user is is becoming more important than where [users] are."[46]

Publishing executives are beginning to recognize the exchange-driven devaluation of the website context as a danger to their websites' long-term health. Wenda Harris Millard made just that point in a keynote address at the Interactive Advertising Bureau's annual meeting in late February 2008. Millard, the incoming Bureau chair, was at the time the president of the media division at Martha Stewart Living Omnimedia. She was also a former high-level Yahoo! executive. Millard excoriated the new digital marketplace for harming online publishers. She noted that Madison Avenue was "repaving itself" as agency giants resurged to dominate many areas of digital advertising, including planning and buying. She added that DoubleClick,

Microsoft, Yahoo!, and other firms were fundamentally altering the media-buying landscape via their automated exchanges. Their bartering process will make sites that carry advertising interchangeable, she said. The result: a race to the lowest price without any concern for a site's personality, its history, or its credibility with visitors. Comparing the new marketplaces to commodities traders, she cautioned that publishers "must not trade our assets like pork bellies."[47]

The warning prompted a response at the meeting from Michael Rubinstein, who at the time led DoubleClick's ad exchange. He disputed Millard's contention that automated buying and selling would necessarily decrease the cost of advertising. The key to correctly understanding the situation, he said, is to change the metaphor. Forget pork bellies; think gems. Gems, he noted, are also traded in markets, yet each one has distinctive characteristics and therefore a particular value. "We [at DoubleClick] like to think of our publisher impressions as diamonds," he said, "not pork bellies."[48]

The exchange encapsulated anxieties swirling at the center of the advertising industry. Randall Rothenberg, executive director of the Interactive Advertising Bureau, tried to make peace between the publisher and the marketer, a role his organization (previously the Internet Advertising Bureau) had played since the time of Procter and Gamble's historic 1998 conference. He framed the tensions as long-standing; he said they went back to the recovery from the dot-com collapse in 2002. They involved, he noted, basic fights over audience measurement and the best ways to prove audience attention at a time of the enormous changes Millard had mentioned. He exhorted all the actors involved that they had "better stop marveling at all the creative destruction going on around us." Instead, he said, "It's time to write the constitution that will help us live in peaceful and profitable existence."[49]

Rothenberg undoubtedly knew this was easier said than done. He might also have understood that the gems metaphor didn't really change Millard's fundamental argument. Where gems appear is increasingly not as important to advertisers as getting the gems. Moreover, as the new advertising norm progresses, the pork-bellies-vs.-diamonds metaphor raises questions about the value of individuals. Are individuals like pork bellies, with their value and the value of sites delivering them pushed down incessantly? Or are there ways to make at least some of the people into diamonds, with a resulting rise in the price to reach them? As we will see in the next two chapters, the precarious position in which Web publishers have found themselves as a result of the new media-buying logic pushes them in three socially troubling directions: it leads them to pursue the kind of personalization toward useful targets or waste that database-driven media buyers demand; it causes publishers to create privacy policies to hide particulars of buyers' audience-tracking and targeting activities from visitors to their sites; and it encourages them to further retreat from longtime professional norms in the interest of packaging personalized advertising with personalized soft news or entertainment.

Chapter 4 Targets

or Waste

Marketers are increasingly using databases to determine whether to consider particular Americans to be targets or waste. Those considered waste are ignored or shunted to other products the marketers deem more relevant to their tastes or income. Those considered targets are further evaluated in the light of the information that companies store and trade about their demographic profiles, beliefs, and lifestyles. The targets receive different messages and possibly discounts depending on those profiles.

This work of creating reputations from profiles was at the heart of a 2010 PowerPoint presentation that Publicis, a French multinational advertising and communications company, made to some of its clients. Below the title "Why We Are Betting on Ad Exchanges" was a phrase that the agency offered as the basis for its decision to devote its energies to the new approach to advertising spending: "Key benefit: Buy only the impressions that match." To illustrate how the company would help its clients succeed, a slide displayed several concepts, linked with arrows, leading to the ultimate goal: Publicis would draw on its expertise in "Insight," "Media," and "Technology" to achieve "No Waste" advertising for its clients. In other words, the presentation suggested that marketers could finally direct their enormous investments to reach only those customers who mattered to them. Publicis would create target segments based on its clients' data about best customers. It would then bid in the exchanges for the right to reach people who fit those profiles. They would receive the client's messages, and the audience reached would be free of waste—consumers the client didn't care to reach.

This approach is by no means Publicis's alone. It is becoming standard among media buyers in the top firms as well as many of their smaller competitors. The system described in Chapter 3 is running on all cylinders. Wide-ranging data points indicating the social backgrounds, locations, activities, and social relationships of hundreds of millions of individuals are becoming the fundamental coins of exchange in the online world. Violation of privacy as the law defines it is not at issue here. The companies that deal in Americans' data know the rules and have learned to hew carefully to the letters of those rules, if not their spirit. Still, the personalized use of the data raises questions about the ways privacy is currently defined in the law and in the advertising industry.

Moreover, circumventing the spirit of privacy has led the advertising business to another social dilemma. The quiet use of databases that combine demographic information about individuals with widely circulated conclusions about what their clicks say about them presents to advertisers personalized views of hundreds of millions of Americans every day without their knowledge. Marketers justify these activities as encouraging *relevance.* But the unrequested nature of the new media-buying routines and the directions these activities are taking suggest that *narrowed options* and *social discrimination* might be better terms to describe what media buyers are actually casting. Despite qualms, publishers are warming to the idea of customizing news and information based on the characteristics of people that advertisers would want to approach. Their aim is to increase the number of clicklike activities on their sites and related engagement measures that will allow them to raise their prices at a time of plummeting CPMs.

Many cookies used for this purpose don't last more than a few months because individuals and browsers delete them. Some marketers that want to have control over the deletion process have been adopting ways beyond the standard cookie to keep persistent knowledge about people. Other marketers believe, though, that most of their cookies last long enough for them to engage target consumers with messages specifically tailored to what they know about them. Regardless of the life of a particular cookie or other anonymous identifier, much of the information about individuals endures and spreads beyond individual marketers, as this chapter will show. That is because a small number of data-collection companies continually and anonymously add basic personal information to the cookies they insert on the computers of hundreds of millions of people. Even with short-lived cookies, then, the media-buying system is laying the technology and philosophy for cultivating enduring characteristics of people across the Web. Replacements for the cookie that substantially extend the ability to identify people take this notion of enduring identities quite a bit further.

Advertisers have been way ahead of publishers when it comes to the interest and ability to personalize material for audiences. Publishers have been lagging partly because implementing personalized material with news and entertainment is more difficult than it is with advertising, and also because executives have worried about negative audience response to content personalization without their knowledge and the ability to control it. Important recent changes in the news-and-entertainment environment, however, have made content personalization based on data collection inevitable. But that story is for the next chapter. Here we will focus on how marketers have enforced the target-and-waste strategy on the Web. Publishers, eager for advertising revenues, are deeply involved in two ways. As we saw in Chapter 3, publishers provide marketers with much of the data used for targeting. And, as we'll see in this chapter, they also help keep the audience in the dark about what is actually taking place.

The social and consumer discrimination that defines personalized advertising results from three converging developments: advertising practitioners' infatuation with data about online audiences, the rise of companies that can provide that data in a readily accessible form, and the growth of technologies that can selectively serve advertising to individuals based on the data associated with them. Underpinning this massive enterprise is contemporary advertisers' belief that the best way to engage potential customers with a brand is to follow them with messages that are customized so as to be as relevant as possible to their behaviors, backgrounds, and relationships.

The notion that in the twenty-first century potential customers ought to be pursued with personalized blandishments and appeals represents a new twist on a late twentieth-century understanding of customer relationship management (CRM). In the 1980s and 1990s, CRM proponents preached that it was far more expensive to enlist new customers successfully than to retain and cultivate the best current customers. CRM gurus, notably Don Pepper and Martha Rogers, further argued that new media technologies would allow for mass customization—the efficient personalization of advertising and public-relations messages that would keep customers feeling good about the brand through their understanding of its utility for them.[1] The twenty-first-century version of this CRM philosophy holds that databases and other technologies allow for reaching even *potential* users of the product—individuals who will act like best customers once they are brought into the fold.

That is certainly the view of Acxiom, a firm that catapulted to the top of *Advertising Age*'s list of the largest marketing-communication agencies in 2009 largely because of its expertise in producing data for the purpose of targeted advertising. Based far from Madison Avenue, in Little Rock, Arkansas, Acxiom touts its ability to help "clients strengthen relationships with existing customers—and initiate the right new customer relationships."[2] The company offers a suite of digital marketing services involving strategy, creative, targeting, and measurement. These services are based on the premise that "expertise in building, maintaining and delivering the most accurate and valuable views of prospects and customers—also known as Customer Data Integration (CDI)—is the single most important ingredient in optimizing every buyer-seller interaction."[3] That activity, Acxiom insists, must take place across digital platforms. "Today," the company's website proclaims, "brands can gain better control of their advertising and marketing across multiple types of addressable media and concentrate on their 'best' prospects and customers through: Display ads, social media, interactive TV and websites."

Procter and Gamble, one of Acxiom's clients, adheres to this logic.[4] Challenged by competitors, concerned about economic downturns, and motivated by a long-standing interest in using digital media to maximize its return on media spending, the world's largest advertiser has in recent years been focusing on more efficient ways to cultivate customers and potential customers. As if following an Acxiom game plan, some of these activities represent an effort to strengthen ties to current customers, and some are attempts to find new ones. "Fan pages" for brands such as Tide on the Facebook social-media site are prime examples of the first category.[5] (Facebook encourages what it calls "Public Profiles" for just this purpose.) So are P&G's websites for specific products such as Pampers (PampersVillage.com) and Mr. Clean (MrClean.com). In seeking new customers, P&G sends bloggers free product samples with the understanding that they will write about them if they like them. The company also collaborates with NBC-Universal on websites that target lifestyle segments (Petside.com and DinnerTool.com) and age segments (Lifegoesstrong.com, for baby boomers).[6]

P&G lurks in the background of the NBC-Universal sites, perhaps suspecting that they will have greater credibility without the company's name featured visibly on it. In fact, it's hard to tell that P&G is connected to them at all. Ads for a first-time site visitor do not highlight P&G products. Moreover, although the Web pages note NBC-Universal's ownership quite prominently, disclosure of P&G's involvement turns up only on the privacy page. There visitors who click beyond the superficial privacy assurances to the more detailed version will learn that Procter and Gamble has an interest in personalizing its digital encounters with them. A preambles states that "we may collect information about you from a variety of sources, including information we collect from you directly; information we collect about you when you visit our sites, use our services, or view our online advertisements; and information we collect about you from other sources (where permitted by law)." Among the reasons it offers for collecting this information, P&G explains, is its desire to "develop and provide advertising tailored to your interests" and "where permitted by law, provide you with customized, unsolicited offers and information about P&G's products and services through postal mail."[7]

The amount of knowledge P&G reserves the right to glean about the customers it encounters online is stunning. Three sections lay out what it collects. The first refers to information P&G requests when people register for one of its sites or fan pages. The long list includes name, e-mail address, postal address, phone or cell phone number, age, demographic information, and "other information about you and your family such as gender or product use preferences and/or behaviors." The second section notes "information we collect when you visit our sites, use our services, or view online advertisements." Among the listed items are the links the visitor clicks, the visitor's IP address, the site the visitor went to before coming to the P&G site, P&G e-mails that the person opened or forwarded, and P&G offers or links that the person accessed via e-mails. The third section includes information the company "may obtain about you from other sources, including commercially available sources, such as data aggregators and public databases." Listed there are data that would have been obtained had the person registered on a P&G site (for example, name, address, age, marital status, and number of children) as well as information that people would not likely share or even know themselves—such as purchase behavior, the person's activities both online in blogs, videos, and discussion groups, and off-line, during in-store shopping.

An executive at an agency that markets some of P&G's brands suggested in a 2010 interview for this book that P&G isn't as aggressive at tailoring ads as the privacy policy might imply and that the disclosures were primarily "forward-looking" statements designed to protect the firm when it does want to use the data in that way. That executive doesn't work for Acxiom, however, and P&G's quiet ownership of the sites and its privacy policy seem right out of Acxiom's playbook. In 2008, *Advertising Age* reported that "Procter & Gamble, long accustomed to a bombard-the-masses-with-heavily-tested-ads strategy, has been working on better personalizing the consumer experience."[8] It seems evident that for P&G a primary purpose of these sites is to create opportunities for inserting cookies in visitors' computers to learn what they do on that particular site, on other NBC and P&G sites, and across the Web through cookie matching. In this way P&G can serve these visitors messages—ads, coupons, articles—that leverage the company's understanding of them to promote particular products. These exercises in online personalization may indeed pale in the face of P&G's huge expenditures on mass-audience vehicles such as network television. But with these relatively low-cost activities millions of people experience P&G's concept of them in ways that reflect the company's best interest. So, for example, a mother with a young baby who uses Pampers might receive ads reinforcing that use. She might also receive a series of online discount coupons for P&G products to parallel the growth of her child and Procter and Gamble's desire to guide her purchases related to child-rearing.

For the Ford Motor Company, too, targeted personalization is a central marketing strategy. Andy Pratkin, the digital director of WPP's "Team Detroit" media-buying agency, noted in an interview for this book that his fundamental concern when reaching customers is discovering how these prospective customers learn and how their perceptions are formed. Pratkin argued that the digital environment makes it possible to follow an individual across a gauntlet of brand-related mind-sets, from awareness to initial attitude to various attitude shifts. This sequence of activities reflects what marketing students learn to call "the funnel"—the different stages through which consumers move toward purchase (or not). Pratkin noted that his group could now track individuals as they lurch through these steps. He added, "If we can fit into that dynamic"—that is, if through serving personalized ads Ford could make itself a natural part of a person's car-search process—"we can fit into her." Success—the sale—would develop organically. "It's kind of like dating," he said.[9]

According to Pratkin's logic, then, carrying out a successful dating ritual between a person and a brand requires good matchmaking. That is what Publicis's announced commitment to "buying only impressions that match" means in practice. An extension of this logic points to marketers' creation of silos of messages surrounding individuals they want to target over time. Consider a few of the strategies that Team Detroit used to cultivate online audiences for the Ford Motor Company's advertisements during 2010:

- It purchased ads on many automotive sites that planted Ford cookies in the computers of visitors to the pages where the ads appeared. This "tagging" of computers by cookies allowed Ford to serve individuals different messages and photos depending on where their clicks positioned them in the car-purchase funnel. "We do a fair amount of tagging," said Pratkin during the interview. "If people are exposed to our ad, we study their behavior, and if they come to our site, then we retarget them and try to entice them back. . . . If you go to [the] Kelly Blue Book [website], we serve an ad. We'll know if you didn't do anything. Next time, we'll serve you a different ad. You go to our site, and if you do something and you go off our site [to one of Ford's advertising networks], we serve you other ads."[10] The technology often assembled the advertising automatically, on the fly, to match what the cookie data said about the person's car-searching routines and the previous commercial messages that had been served to the individual.

- In other internet buys, Team Detroit tailored its ads on the basis of people's ages, incomes, geographic locations, and specific social behaviors (soccer moms, for example) that suggested they would purchase particular vehicles or could be persuaded in certain ways. In addition to taking these differences into account, Ford's ad servers varied the messages depending on whether the person had or had not previously clicked on a Ford ad and on which Ford ads the person had been served previously. In addition, the agency presented ads to the friends of people on Facebook who seemed to be ideal targets insofar as they appeared to be in the market for particular types of cars. "On Facebook, you take friends into account," said creative executive vice president Scott Lang when interviewed for this book. "So-and-so liked this; you will too. People find that creepy in the beginning, but . . . they slowly get used to it."[11]

• Team Detroit was the first agency to use the Google Display Network of one million Web publishers to serve audiovisual commercials that matched the content of a publisher's site. It worked this way: The agency supplied Google with keywords that its research suggested would resonate with different types of individuals who might be inclined to buy automobiles. When a person went to a site containing one of the keywords, Google Display Network posted specific Ford display ads embedded with particular audiovisual commercials that were in turn designed to evoke those keywords. As *AdWeek* noted, "Depending on the context of the website, the most relevant Ford content is pulled and displayed in the ad unit, using video from the Ford YouTube channel and information from Ford websites thefordstory.com and fordvehicles.com."[12] So, for example, a site that discussed green issues highlighted Ford's hybrid models. A tech site might show a clip from Ford at the Consumer Electronics Show.

Andy Pratkin noted that these activities represent merely the tip of the iceberg. Ford, he said, has a wide-ranging capability to compile all of the demographic, social, and behavioral qualities it uses to define users' profiles and then to present them with views of Ford products designed to match these profiles as the users move through the Web. He acknowledged that the capability certainly exists in the Google Content Network. Its wide-ranging collection of sites provides companies with the technology needed to track people with cookies and then serve them commercials based on their personal characteristics, their web-searching history, and the nature of the particular site on which the commercial is being served. According to Pratkin, as of mid-2010 Ford had not yet taken that step because the company was still testing its new capacity to selectively serve audiovisual commercials based on a site's context. He suggested that Ford already leverages these capabilities when serving text-and-picture ads on the Google Display Network and that commercials could easily be integrated into this approach.[13]

But the blending of conclusions about consumers' online behavior with purchased information about them to tailor ads for them doesn't stop at particular brands. To the contrary, the business of discriminating digitally is leading many marketers to a small number of firms that sell a wide range of information about online customers and potential customers. These agencies, in turn, get their data from a small number of primary sources. From these cross-pollinating building blocks reputations are created as is, in turn, consumer discrimination in the form of narrowed options.

Acxiom, one of the top U.S. marketing-communication agencies, is a good place to begin exploring these building blocks and how they travel across advertisers. Established in 1969 to guide direct-mail firms with customer-relationship management, Acxiom has branched out to help clients "acquire, retain, and grow loyal (and profitable) relationships" in the digital media, especially via e-mail, banner ads, search engine optimization, website optimization, and cellular phones.[14] The company's cross-advertiser reach is prodigious; Acxiom says its client list includes some if not most of the leading companies in all these areas: credit card issuing, retail banking, telecom/media, retail sales, automotive manufacturing, brokering, pharmaceutical manufacturing, life/health insurance, property and casualty, lodging, and gaming.[15]

Acxiom's use and analysis of customer data is central in serving these clients. Not only does Acxiom help its clients analyze their own information regarding particular customers, it offers a great deal of additional data about these same people in order to help the client better determine the value of specific individuals and tailor their sales approach accordingly. A major part of its role, the company repeats throughout its website, is to help clients decide which consumers are *not* worth targeting. This segment is called "contact suppression," and it's based on making assessments of the "risk profile" of individuals for certain industries. Tom Mangan, the firm's senior vice president of consulting services, described Acxiom's contributions this way at a shareholders meeting:

> Should I continue to target people who are in fact going to default on their loans? Or, take, for example, a telecom industry where they're constantly flipping cell phones. I want to understand those characteristics and to say, is that a customer I really want to target? . . .
>
> So the opportunity here is, first, let us get an enterprise view of who your customer is. . . . That's the fundamental building block we have to have in place. Once we have that fundamental building block in place now, we can then enhance that with external information that we keep in our knowledge bases about every purchasing consumer across the country. And we can then use that to now start doing strategic segmentation, so we can break your customer base into each one of those strategic segments, from high value to low value.[16]

Acxiom's *Consumer Data Products Catalog* reflects the heart of this operation for the United States. The catalog promotes the agency's ability to sell "data enhancements" about individuals whom the client has identified by name and address or via some other unique convergence of information about them. Identification may have taken place through a website registration, a sweepstakes sign-up, or some other activity that explicitly or implicitly gave the marketer the right to use that identification for its own business purposes. The advertiser may want to know whether the person is worth pursuing or, if already a customer, how to best address him or her personally to achieve additional sales. The Acxiom catalog distributed in 2010 details what it offers about people in seventy-seven pages of single-spaced data codes, or "elements." It claims it can help marketers by selling demographic data such as age, gender, marital status, race, ethnicity, address, and income "covering over 126 million households and approximately 190 million individuals."[17] But that's just the start. Noting that everything it offers conforms with U.S. privacy laws, the booklet sells quite particular constructions of the interests, lifestyles, and life circumstances of the population, including dozens of specifics about individuals' online, catalog, and in-store purchases. For example, Acxiom places individuals into "interest buckets" that include such disparate categories as arts, celebrities, Christian families, and aviation. It divides people by their use of various credit cards and the recency, frequency, and dollar value of purchases from low-, mid-, and upscale catalogs. It sells health-related access to consumers whose purchases and self-reports indicate categories such as allergy-related, arthritis/mobility, cholesterol, diabetes, orthopedics, and senior needs. It can deliver individuals according to recent purchases organized into dozens of categories such as apparel/big and tall, donation/contribution, gardening, high-end appliances, and hunting. Acxiom assures marketers that "the freshness and accuracy of Buying Activity makes it . . . highly predictive in consumer models."[18]

Acxiom statisticians combine demographics and various behaviors into seventy colorfully named and artfully described clusters arranged on an income spectrum, from the affluent (for example, "Summit Estates," "Corporate Clout," "Hard Chargers," "Kids and Clout") to the upper-middle income earners ("Soccer and SUVs," "Acred Couples," "Clubs and Causes"), middle-income earners ("Urban Tenants," "Outward Bound"), lower-middle-income earners ("First Digs," "Home Cooking") and low-income earners ("Single City Strugglers," "Mortgage Woes," "On the Edge"). Here is where profiles get turned into reputations. To help its clients make sense of the data efficiently, Acxiom links many of the seventy clusters into twenty-one larger combinations, which it calls "LifeStage Groups." The "Taking Hold" group, for example, brings together the "Married Sophisticates," "Children First," "Career

Building," and "Spouses and Houses" clusters under the conclusion that all are "fueled by wealth, as these clusters have already made it into the middle and upper-middle income brackets."[19]

Probably the most useful frames for its clients, though, are packages of data that the firm customizes for particular industries. The agency's "enhancement data packages" bundle the kinds of details clients in particular industries typically use to make decisions about whether and how to pursue particular prospects. The number of elements about a person that each package includes varies by industry. Acxiom presents the auto industry with eighteen elements, for example, while auto insurance gets thirty-three; health care, forty; investments, thirty-one; travel and entertainment, thirty-six; and media, thirty-three. The company customizes its clusters for the insurance and financial-services industries—thirteen for the former and twelve for the latter. It also parses Hispanics in a separate cluster for companies seeking to sell to this fastest growing U.S. ethnic group.

These elements, clusters and grouping, are lenses through which many of the largest companies extend their understandings of their customers. They often include far more than the initial data that the client holds about a person. Speaking extemporaneously at a stockholders' meeting, Mangan, the firm's senior vice president of consulting services, put it this way:

> [W]hat we find today is [the utility of] breaking consumers into logical, strategic segments, understanding the attributes of those segments in terms of lifestyle, life stage, geo-demographic information, understanding the attitude of those particular segments, of the consumers and what they like to purchase and actually analyzing the behavioral information of the transaction data inside the company.
>
> So you understand what are they in market for. . . . What is their product preference, how loyal they are to specific brands and then what channel do they like to be communicated. Once we have those together, now we can start doing effective targeting to that particular segment and be much more effective into what they want to buy.[20]

Use of Acxiom data between and across industries is intrinsic to the process. The work, company president John Meyer noted in 2008, involves "continually figuring out how we take that information but [use] it in new forms, different industries, different capabilities, so that we can open new markets for ourselves." This repurposing of individuals' data, he said, involves applying "what we have in solutions and take the best of those solutions and package them, product-ize them, put a little box around them and say what value does a [client] see of being associated with this."[21] Corporate marketing strategies will vary. But in the large number of cases where an overlap might exist for current or future consumers for cars, financial firms, and insurance companies, Acxiom bases its presentations to advertisers within and across industries on the same data about individuals. It reports, for example, on the individuals' online shopping amounts, income levels, interest areas, discretionary-income score, and vehicle propensity. And it even brings those data together to tell the same stories about individuals to all clients. Think of a person Acxiom positions as an "outward bound," "married sophisticate" who is a "chiphead" (the company's catalog doesn't define this appellation) with a MasterCard and a "diabetic focus." That kind of profile—and the story about the person that is built into it—often travels far.

As if to illustrate the point, Acxiom turns out press releases touting its willingness to sell data about the same individuals to all comers in the auto industry. A 2009 self-promotion, for example, offered to "reveal consumer-centric insights across more than 130 million U.S. households [about] demographic and life stage portraits, shopping behaviors, attitudes, intentions and propensities toward vehicle purchase and ownership for 2009."[22] The company was selling its pinpointing of particular households and consumers who fit the various profiles to any interested advertiser. Buyers might use the data differently; Ford might decide that the individuals in certain of Acxiom's propensity segments ought to get its ads and attention, while Cadillac might prefer only some of those in addition to other prospects Ford didn't pick. Still, both would be making decisions about how to address Americans based on the basic stories that Acxiom has told about them.

What takes place within Acxiom also occurs in numerous other firms that provide data to media buyers for targeting. In presentations to clients during 2010, executives of the media-buying agency MediaVest listed Acxiom as one of five companies that it was negotiating with for targeting consumers on behalf of its clients, as well as noting thirteen other data-centric firms with which it already had such arrangements. Acxiom's expertise, according to MediaVest, is in providing "very granular data around demographics and psychographics within households, including segments such as education level, cars owned, and life stage." The other firms—for example, BlueKai, eXelate, Media6Degrees, and Mindset Marketing (now called Medicx)—have reputations for delivering particular types of prospects to marketers via cookies for online advertising campaigns.

Unlike Acxiom, which typically offers people who can be identified by name, these firms generally offer individuals who are anonymous because either they are tracked by cookies that are not tied to registration material, or the firms selling the cookies have stripped out personally identifiable information as a result of the privacy policy under which it was collected. Either way, marketers know that a certain percentage of those reached anonymously can be seduced into revealing who they are when they are offered a sweepstakes entry or information about a product sent to their e-mail address. The information gathered that way can then be used to purchase more information about the individuals from companies such as Acxiom so that interactions around products can be as "relevant" as possible. But even when marketers don't know the names of the people associated with the cookies, the data they hold can still be extremely valuable for making judgments about their interests and the most persuasive strategies to advertise to them.

Companies that sell access to individuals via networks or exchanges typically specialize in profiling people's lifestyles or buying intentions, which they determine by placing cookies on people's computers to track their visits to particular sites. The companies then analyze what those visits generally mean about an individual's interests. Not surprisingly, each company contends that the information it collects and analyzes is superior to that of its competitors. Some cookie providers insist, for example, that the act of clicking on products while visiting websites is the key to understanding a buyer's intent and therefore cookies that report such "in-market" behavior provide the best insight into the products that should be advertised to particular people. As discussed in Chapter 3, BlueKai and eXelate specialize in this domain. An eXelate "intent" segment called "auto buyers," for example, includes planting cookies on computers of individuals who have visited "leading auto research and auto dealer lead generation sites" and who, eXelate concludes, are "in-market car buyers that are actively searching to purchase a vehicle." For its sixteen "shoppers" categories (one of which is "babies and kids"), eXelate uses "comScore Top 10 shopping sites and vertical sites that track product interest and drive specific purchasing behavior." On these sites it tags people with cookies when they are "looking for pricing, ratings, and purchase information on specific products [for example, cribs] as well as enthusiasts commenting on and shopping for [the] niche-interest [that is, the baby and kids-related]-items." It then sells to media buyers the right to reach people via those cookies.[23]

Other cookie providers disagree that in-market behavior is necessary for understanding what a person will buy. They say that more can be learned from the terms people use on search engines such as Google and Yahoo!. A firm called Magnetic contends that "the integration of leading-edge search technology and advertising is the wave of the future."[24] The company inserts a Web beacon on sites serving Google and Yahoo! search ads, and the beacon creates a cookie that records the search words that led the person to the site. Magnetic then offers marketers access to those cookies as a way to "retarget" ads to individuals virtually anywhere on the Web based on the interest they expressed via the search term(s) they used.[25]

Yet another approach to finding people who are likely to buy certain products involves collecting data about individuals' off-line areas of interest and then providing this information to marketers so they can advertise to them online. Two areas of particular concern are health care and financial services; some advertisers will pay considerably for the chance to get the business of Americans who spend a lot of money in one or both of these areas. Medicx Media Solutions is one such "vertical" data provider. The company contends that its "Geo-Medical Targeting" "minimizes waste" by helping advertisers narrow the locations of individuals with specific "diagnosed medical conditions, prescribed treatments, both Rx and OTC, health styles, type of insurance coverage, co-pays, and medication compliance or consumption measures."[26] To facilitate its licensing of this information, Medicx obtains medical and pharmacy insurance claims data for tens of millions of Americans from third-party data providers that purportedly strip out personally identifiable information irreversibly in conformance with regulations set by the 1996 Health Insurance Portability and Accountability Act (HIPAA). Even though Medicx supposedly cannot tie the data to particular individuals, it has developed statistical techniques (which the company is attempting to patent) that it says can connect the medical and pharmaceutical findings to the U.S. Postal Service's ZIP+4 system. That scheme breaks down ZIP codes into areas as precise as a city block or an apartment complex, or even into a portion of a street comprising as few as three to eight homes. To enable advertisers to reach these patients online, Medicx licenses millions of cookies with ZIP+4 data and then serves its clients' display ads to individuals in the targeted ZIP+4 areas. The company states that this process has "turned the art of reaching audiences by medical condition across virtually any digital medium into a measurable and accurate science."[27] The people receiving the ads about specific medical concerns would have no clue as to how they were targeted.[28]

The companies discussed here are just a few of the choices ad agencies have when they are trying to decide whom to research and target. A particularly popular approach involves mapping interpersonal relationships and predicting the value of those relationships, as we will see when we explore social-media advertising in Chapter 6. Clearly, the notions that advertisers would have about their targets would vary depending on the data firm they choose, and perhaps even depending on the segments that they use for targeting. Advertisers also have the ability to adapt to the particular responses that consumers make to their offers. A training manual from Omniture, a company that helps firms make these modifications, states that "dynamic models automatically adjust to changes in propensity over time, both for individual visitors and the population as a whole. In other words [the Omniture system] constantly refines its understanding of 'who you are'/'your preferences.' And then automatically (i.e. in real time) serves you different content as it learns more."[29]

The transient nature of cookies is another factor that encourages variability in the ways individuals' profiles are constructed. A segment of the population routinely erases cookies; newer browsers sometimes help them do that. Moreover, some data providers consider cookies that identify people who are seeking particular products to be useless or of little use after a couple of weeks since by that time those people are likely to have made their particular purchase and have moved on to other things. But data executives largely do not seem to be troubled by the temporary nature of cookies. They simply note that a new cookie will be created in short order when the person returns to one of the many sites that their companies use for placing cookies on computers.

These chances for variations and change in peoples' profiles contribute to the varying approaches that advertisers use to market to an individual, and indeed sometimes perceptions of a person's interests and value may even be at odds among advertisers. Nevertheless, the evolving mechanisms for generating longer-lasting profiles and the increasingly broader sharing of them also need to be noted. For one thing, companies that want ongoing knowledge of visitors to their websites can certainly find ways to get around cookie deletion. For example, some firms have turned their third-party cookies—the kind that ride on ads and that people typically delete—into first-party cookies.[30] These are the "good" cookies that help websites remember who you are—for instance, based on the preferences you set on previous visits to a website, cookies will communicate to the site how you personalized the appearance of its home page. By hiding among the good cookies, the bad ones can stay active longer. Storing a computer's unique internet protocol

(IP) address to detect its return to a site is an alternative to cookies. Other approaches conceal cookielike identifiers that are difficult to detect and erase in places on a computer's hard drive. A less-direct approach to storing and preserving a person's data is to connect anonymous cookie-linked data to legally collected, personally identifiable data—for example, by encouraging a person using a computer on which a cookie has been placed to fill out a registration form or sweepstake entry that requires a name or e-mail address. Databases can hold on to this and other combined information even after the individual's cookies are lost. The stored data can be reconnected to the person when he or she again identifies herself and that identification is linked to a new cookie. Such a system violates no existing privacy law, and, judging by my conversations with industry personnel, it's an activity that is growing.

Just as significant as the persistence of people's profiles is the spread of consistent information about individuals across the digital universe. Despite what seems to be a segmented online world, the core elements that data packagers use for distinguishing and classifying consumers and discriminating among them are surprisingly extensive. Virtually all the companies in the business of describing consumers for advertisers rely on the same small number of providers. The three major agencies that keep tabs on people's creditworthiness—Experian, Equifax, and TransUnion—are particularly important sources of information. Experian, for example, offers marketers more than 1,200 pieces of lifestyle data on more than forty-seven million households; address verification; ways to reach individuals "at the precise time they are shopping for credit"; and more.[31] Reed Elsevier, another big information provider, positions itself as helping companies manage risks through such services as "Know Your Customer (KYC)," identity verification, fraud analytics, due diligence, and credit risk assessment solutions.[32] Most of the data packagers, in turn, start with public records such as U.S. Census data, county records, tax assessments, and telephone directories. Once data-exchange firms tie previously anonymous cookies to personal identities, they still need to conform to the anonymity requirements of various privacy policies before selling them on networks and exchanges, so they append the details about the individuals to the cookies and then make them anonymous again. The demographic and lifestyle categories of a person's profile may well appear across many of the cookies that different advertisers use, and these classifications often fall within segments that marketers and agencies such as Acxiom assign to consumers and that broadly guide decisions about whether and how to pursue specific individuals. These assessments include whether an individual should be considered a desirable or an undesirable customer, whether a person should receive an ad for a particular product, what the ad should look like, how much the product should cost, and even what the ad copy should say.

An area where these sorts of social discrimination have already become part of everyday thinking is the digital discount-coupon business. Despite the huge popularity of paper coupons, online coupons finally began to take off in the late 2000s. Gian Fulgoni, the head of the comScore internet ratings firm, was surprised when he noticed increasing enthusiasm for online discounts in October 2008. "Coupons had never been a big factor online the way they are offline. This is something new," he told the *New York Times*.[33] ComScore estimated that twenty-seven million people visited a coupon site during that month, up 33 percent from a year earlier. Coupon distributors assumed that the rise in digital coupon searches was a result of the dire economic downturn that was now facing the nation. The use of coupons clipped from newspapers and other places were enjoying a boost, too, after several years of nominal growth. The trade magazine *Progressive Grocer* reported in late 2009 that 90 percent of all coupons were still being distributed through freestanding inserts (FSIs) in newspapers. The real news, according to the magazine, was in the redemption rates. Only 50 percent of the coupons being redeemed were those from FSIs. The rest, and the fastest growth, was coming from online coupons delivered through the internet and mobile phones, and at booths in stores. According to the coupon-processing company Inmar, redemption increased 263 percent to about fifty million coupons in 2009. "Consumers can simply print the coupons at home or at a kiosk in the store, or download them to their cell phones, and redeem them at the checkout," *Progressive Grocer* noted.[34]

In 2008 many companies were irked by the spike in coupon use, because the technology made it easier for people who found coupons online to use them. "When the coupons get wider exposure," the *Times* noted, "retailers lose control potentially costing them more money than expected."[35] In spring 2008 Harry & David, a high-end seller of gift and fruit baskets, threatened legal action against the RetailMeNot coupon site for publishing its discounts. The online and catalog retailer Sierra Trading Post in 2006 had to sell $300,000 worth of merchandise at a very low margin because someone posted its unlimited-use catalog coupon code on the Web, and the company noted that it was looking for ways to control its allocation of discount offers. Adopting the apocalyptic, consumer-power rhetoric of the day, Fulgoni said that online coupons have "taken pricing power away from retailers and given it to the consumers, because the consumer is totally up to speed on what the prices are."[36]

More recently, a *New York Times* article took a wholly different approach in describing the coupon industry's efforts to create technologies to regain leverage over shoppers. The article's first line sums up its theme: "For decades, shoppers have taken advantage of coupons. Now, the coupons are taking advantage of the shoppers."[37] Part of this new advantage—a development the article doesn't discuss—are the methods that digital-coupon sites are using to protect a retailer's revenues by limiting the number of times a digital coupon can be used—"distribution control" is the industry phrase for it. The article focused on a related development in digital coupons: personalization, noting that the bar codes of coupons printed from the internet or sent to mobile phones "can be loaded with a startling amount of data, including identification about the customer, Internet address, Facebook page information and even the search terms the customer used to find the coupon in the first place."[38] All that information, the article continues, would follow the customer into the physical mall, which is where most consumers still make their retail purchases. Sometimes the coupon-holding shoppers are anonymous, other times they aren't. The co-founder of RevTrax, a company that facilitates the personalization process, gives an example of how it works with Facebook for the Filene's Basement clothing store:

> "When someone joins a fan club, the user's Facebook ID becomes visible to the merchandiser," Jonathan Treiber, RevTrax's co-founder, said. "We take that and embed it in a bar code or promotion code."
>
> "When the consumer redeems the offer in store, we can track it back, in this case . . . to the actual Facebook user ID that was signing up," he said. Although Facebook does not signal that Amy Smith responded to a given ad, Filene's could look up the user ID connected to the coupon and "do some more manual-type research—you could easily see your sex, your location and what you're interested in," Mr. Treiber said.[39]

The article goes on to specify that, according to an executive from Filene's digital agency, "Filene's [does] not do this at the moment."[40] But even if the retailer doesn't link the Facebook ID to the demographics in its database of store customers, it could still draw important conclusions about who would respond to what discount offers—which is the whole point of using RevTrax. Categorizing people simply by their registration answers on the company's Facebook "fan site"—a spot where people can sign up for more discounts and interact with others who share their interest in the company's products—would help the retailer maximize revenues from different current customers. It could also help the firm's media buyers decide on how best to pursue "lookalikes"—people whose profiles resemble individuals with certain amounts or types of Filene's Basement purchases. This group would receive coupons via display ads or e-mail with the media buyers' unique codes on them, while people with different profiles wouldn't get the coupons.

Filene's evident desire to distance itself from these activities reflects a discomfort by some retailers about talking publicly about their involvement in using data the customer hasn't knowingly presented to the retailer. This uneasiness is also reflected at the popular Coupons.com, which proclaims, "We enable digital coupon programs for the nation's top brands and advertisers."[41] The home page of Coupons.com invites people to join and shows examples of the sites' offers. It suggests a person might receive discounts for products based on where he or she lives; a "local" tab seems to be guided by the IP address, and the company asks for the registrant's ZIP code. Nowhere on the home page or in the description of the firm's activities in "About Coupons.com" is there a suggestion that offers will vary based on a person's social categories and activities on the site.

The only mention of this is buried in the firm's privacy policy. Several paragraphs after a preamble attesting to "the importance of protecting the privacy of all information provided to us [as well as] information we collect" in "our relationship with our users and consumers who use any of our websites, co-branded Microsites, services, or applications owned or provided by us (the 'Sites') (collectively or individually, 'Consumers')," the policy states that "when you visit the Sites, you may provide to us what is generally called 'personally identifiable' information (such as your name, email address, postal mailing address, and home/mobile telephone number, etc.) if you print a coupon from or otherwise participate in activities offered on the Sites. In addition, you may have the option of providing us with certain demographic information about yourself or your household (such as age, gender, household compensation, interests, zip code, and state)." Buried within the next section ("The Way We Use Information") the policy explicitly states that the firm uses cookie data to "provide custom, personalized coupon promotions, advertisements, content, and information." By way of explanation of its right to personalize based on information requested directly from consumers, the policy states that it uses such information "to understand the usage trends and preferences [as well as] to improve the way the Sites work and look."[42]

The company separates cookie-based findings from information consumers give the site directly in order to comply with its statement that "we do not link the information we store in cookies to any personally identifiable information you submit while on the Sites." Yet this statement must surely puzzle a visitor who continues reading, paragraphs later, that the company may well give its advertisers the ability to customize coupons from data yielded through linking cookie and personally identifiable information. The policy says, "We disclose both personally identifiable and automatically collected [cookie-based] information to our clients . . . to process such information on our behalf," and it adds, "We disclose automatically collected data (such as coupon print and redeem activity) to our Clients and third-party ad servers and advertisers. These third parties may match this data with information that they have previously collected under their own privacy policies, which you should consult on a regular basis."[43]

Clearly, Coupons.com acknowledges in this section only the possibility of tailored coupons by its sites and its advertisers while not saying what it actually does, who really does it, how extensively, and based on what information. Yet such coupon tailoring is an activity that happens frequently in various digital formats. In an interview for this book, Jonathan Treiber of RevTrax described a basic retargeting routine that inserts coupons on display ads, using as an example shopping for power tools at the Sears website. He said, "You don't have a Sears account. You go to check out and you abandon the shopping cart. A banner ad will show up on another site, saying 'Come back to Sears and we'll give you 20 percent off your power tools.' "[44]

Don Batsford, Jr., a partner at the digital agency 31 Media, agreed that data-driven coupon customization has become the norm. His clients are interested in direct response, and he works "at the bottom of the purchase funnel"—the point at which a customer is ready to be persuaded to buy one or another product brand. Batsford prefers to skip social networks and general display and focus instead on paid search, which involves an advertiser auction for words that individuals might type into the box of a search engine such as Google, Bing, or Yahoo! (which is powered by Bing). The highest bidder isn't necessarily the winner. The search engines use secret formulas to evaluate the relevancy of a proposed ad to the keywords the advertiser is bidding. The tighter the connection between the two, the more likely that advertiser will win the bid. Search engines also consider past successes of the firm's ads in getting people to click on them; a history of clicked ads weighs in a bidder's favor.[45]

Ads for the winning bids show up to one side of the organic search results as well as above them. To Batsford, paid search is "Zeus" because, he says, keywords indicate people's interests at the moment of searching, as opposed to tracking past behavior on websites or comments on Facebook. "They confess to the search engine [and] are very open about what they want." Because of the ads competing on the page, "you have to have the neon sign to get people to pay attention, so you need the coupon." Batsford uses data from the search engines as well as the RevTrax system to determine the characteristics of the best responders so that he can know whom he will offer the best deals in the future, as well as to correlate keywords with spending habits.[46]

The hottest, and perhaps thorniest, issue regarding coupon tailoring involves customizing the prices. "This is really the holy grail in a sense, pricing to the individual," noted Willard Bishop, a retail consultant in suburban Chicago who focuses primarily on supermarkets.[47] Batsford agreed, but he insisted that certain forms of coupon discrimination online could backfire. Sending people offers for different products based on keywords and background characteristics is fine, he said, but varying the discount amount for the same product can work only if a company carries it out very carefully. His concern is not about ethics; using data in this way falls squarely within privacy regulations, he said. Rather, he said, building distinctions based on demographics, search, or behavior won't work if simply presented to different consumers on the same website. People would find out about the various discount levels and figure out ways to game the system and always get the biggest reduction. He said he did feel comfortable giving new customers higher discounts than those given to existing customers because the website would be able to identify the existing customer and not give that person the higher discount. Similarly, "friends and family club" members for some of his clients could realistically be separated out for special treatment.

This idea of selectively presenting differently priced offers while precluding nontargeted consumers from taking advantage of them seems to be the evolving norm in the business. Jonathan Treiber of RevTrax noted that although his company doesn't approve of the ethics of evaluating people based on their movements through the Web, he knows of many firms—including his clients—that carry it out to decide who should get their coupons. He argued, though, that going further and giving chosen people different discount prices without tying it specifically to them won't work because "internet information gets shared rampantly," and the coupon deliverer cannot be absolutely sure a discount coupon will be redeemed by the intended shopper. A company *can* be assured that a specific consumer will get a coupon, Treiber continued, if its site has log-ins—or cookies that do the signing-in for the customer. In this way, "Coupons can only be redeemed by Joe. If you get the coupon, you can only get it once," he said. "That may piss other people off; that's neither here nor there. People get different coupons. The client is not concerned because it's clear as day that it's exclusive to Joe."[48]

Other Web coupon practitioners agree. They say the aim of price and product personalization is often to lure a potential or actual customer who has particular buying patterns by giving him or her a particularly attractive (and often low-margin) offer that will ignite or reinforce a lucrative relationship. From their perspective, the trick to achieving successful product-and-price personalization involves exploiting as much data as possible about consumers without violating privacy regulations while also making sure that the separation of consumers is secure so that unintended people won't be offered these precious deals. Omniture is one of several firms that provides websites and e-mail servers with the capability to carry out these activities. The company's training manual says that, for visitors arriving at a client's site from an e-mail campaign, Omniture will "make sure that only those visitors are served promotions that align with the special offer they were given in the email, thus ensuring consistent messaging throughout your site."[49]

If any company has taken this data-driven online separation of targets and waste to its logical conclusion, Next Jump has. The company has been unknown to all but close observers of retailing even though it runs employee discount and reward programs on behalf of ninety thousand corporations, organizations, and clublike associations (often called affinity groups) that reach more than one hundred million consumers. Its low profile reflects Next Jump's desire to remain in the background in order to broker or facilitate deals. On its website it depicts itself as giving "over 28,000 merchant partners, both retailers and manufacturers," the technology "to create the most targeted, cost-effective and measurable campaigns to reach more than 100 million users."[50] The capability it offers prospective clients on its website is certainly familiar in the digital age: "Simply created targeted ads that are promoted by free emails. Gain insights to your marketing performance to improve future campaigns. Target your most profitable customers."

Next Jump's ability to target the most profitable customers depends on a trade secret that, according to founder and CEO Charlie Kim, augers a new future for advertising. The business is based on the proposition that the best way to advertise is to present lower prices specifically to individuals whom statistical calculations suggest are the best customers to reach with a deal. According to Kim, Next Jump's conversion rate on product offers is 11 to 1, compared to 1000 to 1 or worse for typical internet ad-conversion rates. But not every advertiser can get the data to target individuals so carefully. What Next Jump has done is insinuate itself directly into the fabrics of Fortune 500 companies and other larger firms by running the online purchasing programs those firms set up as perks for their employees. Those firms pay Next Jump for its work on a per-employee basis, but the company seems to derive a lot more income from the fees merchants pay every time someone buys a product. Next Jump therefore has a vested interest in increasing the purchases. Because Next Jump operates discount programs for roughly one-third of all U.S. corporate employees, "it is considered a non-traditional benefits provider and gets updated weekly on the employment status of 30 million workers (who also happen to be consumers). It gets part of the employee record, including things like name, address, employment status, home and work address, marital status, and sometimes even job title or salary grade."[51] To that information and inferences about it (such as salary grade), Next Jump adds transactional data from the firms it deals with as well as from credit companies. It then overlays all that with information it collects through the firms' human relations departments and employees to determine not only what people want but what they will pay for. With all that knowledge, Next Jump can create predictions of who should get what product e-mail offer at what price. It also generates what it terms a "UserRank" score for every employee based on how many purchases a person has made and how much he or she has spent.

"Shopping and advertising has always been the same to us," Kim noted in 2010. His goal is to separate consumers to the extent that the conversion rate (which in 2008 was 100 to 1) will get down to 3 to 1. He sees his mission as a statistical challenge. Of his 225 employees, 150 are engineers. One industry analyst noted, "If Kim keeps perfecting his shopping algorithms, you may never shop the same way again—and you won't even know that you are doing anything differently."[52]

The mining of data, its circulation, and its use for personalization doesn't stop with commercial messages and discount offers. As the next chapter shows, publishers, eager for advertising revenues, are likewise deeply involved in trying to carry out targeted personalization of their content. And in the process they help the advertisers keep what they're doing hidden from public view.

Chapter 5 Their
Masters' Voices

"Marketers haven't ever wanted to underwrite the content industry," Rishad Tobaccowala says bluntly when interviewed for this book in 2010. "They've been forced."[1] Tobaccowala is chief strategy and innovation officer of the Publicis subsidiary VivaKi. Publicis is the fourth largest marketing communications holding company in the world (behind Omnicom, WPP, and Interpublic). Publicis is also the world's second largest media planning and buying group, second only to WPP. VivaKi functions as a hub of innovation for Publicis, creating structures that subsidiaries don't have the resources to put together on their own. At one point Tobaccowala was the entire company's chief innovation officer.

The cold, rather unsympathetic eye Tobaccowala casts on large twentieth-century corporations that create and distribute content is therefore telling. He predicts that media firms such as Condé Nast, CBS, the *New York Times,* and Time Warner will no longer be able to compel marketers to support their print, electronic, or digital publishing edifices in the twenty-first century. For many decades, he notes, these and a few other media powerhouses have been able to set steep prices for advertising in their industries, generating revenue that has enabled them to create and own expensive content. But in the fragmented digital environment, he says, advertisers are increasingly able to encourage and exploit competition among media firms. Ultimately, the cost of advertising will shrink to the point that the prices reflect only the actual cost of delivering an ad onto a physical page, a website, a radio stream, or a television time slot. In other words, Tobaccowala says, no longer will the cost advertisers pay also support the news, information, or entertainment that surround the ads—and this change will wreak havoc on the practices the media system developed in earlier decades. If publishers of all sorts—print, electronic, digital—want to survive on advertising, he implies, they will have to adapt to their advertising masters' new demands.

The advertiser pressures that Tobaccowala notes are already at work throughout the media system. Taking advantage of the withering competition among media creators and distributors, media buyers are eroding the power of Web publishers and causing them to play by advertisers' new rules to survive. The process is only beginning, but its logic and trajectory are clear. Increasingly, these publishers are channeling their masters' voices in ways that will culminate in customized content. In other words, the principle of personalization will no longer be applied just to advertisements but will shape news, information, and entertainment as well.

According to Tobaccowala, in this new media world major advertisers are releasing long-held, pent-up resentment. "The backbone of the old content system," he explains, "had three features." First, distribution of the editorial content was integrated with its creation. For example, the magazine company Condé Nast both created and distributed the fashion periodical *Vogue.* Second, editors determined what the editorial items would be and how they would be integrated into overall issue—*Vogue* appeared to readers as an integrated single product composed of a collection of articles. And third, advertisers underwrote it; *Vogue* readers typically paid less than 50 percent of Condé Nast's cost to create and distribute an issue.

In the twentieth century this three-pronged approach not only led to the sales success of many products, it also enabled the products' parent firms—marketing behemoths such as Procter and Gamble, Colgate Palmolive, and General Motors—and the advertising agencies that worked with them to reap great rewards as well. While undoubtedly aware of the success that the media-advertiser relationships of the twentieth century brought for his industry and clients, Tobaccowala says that throughout that period many marketers were aghast that a significant portion of their media expenditures were supporting the aggrandizement of media behemoths rather than the direct persuasion of their audiences. He implies that one of the unintended and problematic consequences of helping to build such massive media legends as Hearst Publishing, *Los Angeles Times,* Time Inc., NBC, CBS, and ABC is that their dominance allowed them to turn their power against advertisers when the financial or political moment warranted.

Certainly, throughout the twentieth century even the biggest media firms continued to help their sponsors. They delivered attractive audiences, who saw the advertisements within content environments designed to encourage them to pay attention to the commercial messages. Some examples: at the turn of the 1900s magazines introduced color to their pages, and this made products stand out; beginning in the 1920s, radio networks allowed advertising agencies to create programs that best fit sponsors' self-images; and starting in the late 1950s television networks avoided programs about the poor and other downbeat topics that would clash with optimistic visions presented by commercials.[2] Nevertheless, media firms often saw value in maintaining credibility with audiences, advocacy groups, and government regulators by adopting policies and principles that sometimes conflicted with the advertisers' direct interest in getting the most for their money.

The newspaper and magazine industries, for instance, endorsed something akin to a separation of church and state, whereby the editorial side of the company should not be influenced by the advertising part of the business. Henry Luce, founder and publisher of *Time* in the 1930s, first used the term *church* to refer to the editorial process and *state* to indicate the business side of publishing. Flush with a successful newsmagazine built on advertising, he wanted to make sure that everyone knew that his writers hewed to the journalism codes established by reporting organizations and universities. According to these media overseers, good journalism consisted of resisting publicity sources and being loyal to the "objective" ideals of reporting. It also meant pushing back if and when the advertising department pressured writers and editors to support sponsors' interests. Luce proudly trumpeted the clear separation of his organization's church activities from its state work.[3] The irony, of course, is that Luce himself, serving as both head of business operations and of content, violated the separation principle from the start. Moreover, reporters quickly learned they often had to get along with publicists and flacks if they wanted to get good stories and exclusives.

Still, the norm did have force, for example, by ensuring that marketers were not allowed to demand a story about its product in return for buying an ad.

These values migrated to television in the 1960s. Public anger at sponsors that rigged quiz shows in the mid- to late 1950s alarmed the three broadcast networks. Moreover, executives at CBS, NBC, and ABC saw profit in controlling the programming they aired and selling time to various advertisers in program breaks. It was a major change from the heyday of network radio of the 1940s through the early 1950s, as well as early television. During that time advertisers owned individual shows, and their agencies produced them. Yet advertisers went along with the change willingly, recognizing the value of scattering their commercials across the schedule to reach large audiences at different times rather than mounting just one or two expensive shows with the hope of big ratings.

In the wake of the quiz-show scandals and congressional hearings about excessive TV violence, the broadcast television industry went even further to appease government authorities and advocacy groups regarding the commercials it aired. Led by the three networks, it tightened a self-regulatory regime that began in the late 1940s and lasted through much of the 1970s. Among other things, this regime limited the number of advertising minutes per hour and monitored the content of commercials to block exaggerations and deceptions. The policing sometimes gave agency personnel headaches because they weren't allowed to make certain claims. And the commercial limits reduced the potential number of spots available and so raised ad prices. It also inhibited product placement—the manipulation of sets and story lines in the interest of particular products. Even the biggest marketers and their agencies had trouble pushing against these dicta. Advertising monies pouring into the big content-production and distribution firms had helped them grow to the point that they could dictate terms to their sponsors. The decline in sponsor power, Tobaccowala suggests, bred resentment among advertisers and their agencies. Today, he notes, the power balance is shifting; advertisers may now have more power than ever.[4]

The starkest reflection of this change is the eroding utility of printed periodicals for advertisers. Brian Wieser, an analyst at Interpublic's Magna Global media agency during the 2000s, calculated that consumer magazines' ad revenue totaled $20.3 billion in 2006 and rose to $20.9 billion in 2007, but in 2008 it dropped to $19.5 billion and then plummeted to $15.6 billion in 2009. Newspapers suffered much worse: $46.6 billion in 2006, $42.2 billion in 2007, $34.7 billion in 2008, and $24.8 billion in 2009. The downturn in newspaper ad revenues paralleled a downturn in circulation, though that drop was not nearly as steep. In the magazine industry, circulation figures were pretty well flat in the late 2000s, despite a drop in single-copy sales.[5] Both industries garner substantially over 50 percent of their total revenue from advertising, so Wieser's numbers essentially reflect the withdrawal of advertiser support.

Wieser himself does not attribute most of the decline in ad revenue to advertisers' movement toward digital media. He notes that the shift from newspapers was to other forms of paper media—circulars, for example. The decline also reflected the severe recession from the end of 2008 through 2009, and magazine ad revenues improved a bit during 2010.[6] Nevertheless, data gathered by the Price Waterhouse Cooper consulting firm suggested something more basic was taking place. The company found that magazine growth rates were, until recently, usually more buoyant than the economy in general. From 1970 to 1999, the growth rate in magazine ad pages matched or exceeded the growth rate of gross domestic product in nineteen of those years, or 63 percent of the time. From 2000 to 2009, they surpassed gross domestic product in only one year—2004—and equaled it just 10 percent of the time. Similarly, from 1970 to 1989, newspaper ad revenues matched, exceeded, or came within two percentage points of the overall growth rate in ad spending in fifteen out of twenty years, or 75 percent of the time. The dynamic has begun to change in the past two decades. From 1990 to 1999, newspapers managed to do this in only four out of ten years (40 percent of the time). From 2000 to 2009 it happened only twice, in 2003 and 2005 (20 percent of the time).

Analysts agree that the internet is the main factor driving long-term revenue downturns in the magazine and newspaper industries. The Veronis Suhler Stevenson consulting firm forecast in 2009, for example, that "total spending on consumer magazines" would decline "as advertisers continue to slash traditional media ad budgets and shift spending to alternative media, such as online advertising and word-of-mouth advertising."[7] Similarly, regarding newspapers the firm predicted that "advertising in all three major categories—retail, classified, and national—will continue to shift spending to digital platforms to target audiences and achieve more reasonable return on investment (ROI)."[8] Brian Wieser made the same prediction numerically. In 2010 he projected a further decline of magazine revenues through at least 2015, with the result that the industry would be about $1.5 billion poorer. As for the newspaper industry, Wieser projected an even worse drop. From a starting point of $22.5 billion in ad revenues in 2010, he saw the business ending up with $19.3 billion by 2015.[9] Price Waterhouse Cooper's projections for the magazine and newspaper businesses, while a bit higher, were still fundamentally downbeat.

The real problem for newspapers and magazines, though, lies in adapting to the digital realm. The huge availability of content on the Web and media buyers' emphasis on picking up impressions at the lowest possible cost-per-thousand impressions (CPMs) meant that advertising in a digital environment could not possibly support their organizations the way it did in the print sphere. As Chapter 4 noted, because of fierce competition online the CPMs newspapers were able to charge their Web advertisers was miniscule compared to what they received for delivering a thousand readers to their print products. To make matters worse, in most cases readers paid no money to read the periodicals online. The upshot was that, in 2007, the amount of money newspaper websites were bringing in from annual unique visitors was less than one-tenth the annual revenue they were generating from an average subscriber to a print newspaper.[10]

Industry prognosticators are sure that newspapers and magazines will continue to get more revenues through print than digital for years to come. They are equally sure that the magazine and newspaper businesses in general are on the decline because they won't be able to make their economics work in the digital realm. Executives from what analysts call the "legacy" periodical firms (those that originated in the print world) are working hard to reverse the negative trends and prove the analysts wrong. Part of their strategy involves charging readers more for the print editions; magazine subscriptions and newspaper prices have risen in many cases. Legacy periodicals are also struggling to figure out ways to charge readers for digital products. Some pin their hopes specifically on paid applications for lightweight tablets, such as the iPad, that show off the gorgeous editorial and advertising displays that were the hallmark of print editions for readers and advertisers. (Applications—"apps"—are downloadable software bundles designed to encapsulate a particular set of content and activities, from news stories to games.) The possibility of starting over on a portable, interactive device capable of gathering data about users intrigues traditional newspaper as well as magazine executives. Many agree with News Corporation chairman Rupert Murdoch, who said that in the initial rush to get on the World Wide Web they had squandered the opportunity to charge consumers fees that would make up the shortfall from advertisers.[11] Yet while these firms experimented with paid apps for individual magazines, search engines and news-aggregation businesses such as Huffington Post and Flipboard were coming up with free apps that create customized magazines from articles gathered for individuals from around the Web based on their preferences. Murdoch branded them scavengers, but they survived, and some thrived.

As Tobaccowala tells it, the advertising establishment sees two key irreversible changes to the old publishing system. The first is that content production and distribution are no longer integrated but rather performed by two different entities. Think of a Yahoo! politics site distributing a video created by the *Washington Post* and Google pointing to a *New York Times* article. Separate production and distribution was in existence before the rise of digital, Tobaccowala says, but now it has become the norm. The other difference is that consumers no longer typically confront media products as unified branded products or programming flows. Many read individual newspaper articles, listen to individual songs, and view individual program episodes unmoored from a "channel" that has been constructed by the content-creating firms.

Tobaccowala says advertisers believe their sponsorship of content should reflect these realities in ways that benefit them. Their eyes are no longer so much on supporting the original creators and distributors of the content. The focus, instead, is on pushing the price for advertising down so they are really just paying to reach the individual target wherever that person may see the content. He puts it this way:

> Now you've got this explosion of content flying around: Distribution is disaggregated from content, and everything is moving fast. Everything is flying about. So [media firms are] trying to re-aggregate their ability to reach audiences, but now with mass customization. Google and ad networks do this. And advertisers want to pay to reach the target audiences. They don't want to pay for the creation of content. . . . The amount of money advertisers are willing to spend with media firms reached a high in real monetary terms in 2007. Now advertisers have so many ways to reach people. They ask, "Why am I spending so much money to help create big media firms such as ESPN?" Advertisers resent that.[12]

That is why, as Tobaccowala says, even big media firms such as Disney's ESPN now have to scramble to point advertisers their way. Many Web publishers cozy up to advertisers not just by helping them track, label, and target their audience members, an activity noted in Chapter 3. They also assist them in masking these behaviors so that their audiences won't know about them. What's more, in the process an increasing number of publishers saddle visitors with profiles that result in combining personalized news and entertainment with personalized commercial messages pitched to calculations of the individuals' value. And more alarmingly still, much of the packaging of personalized editorial matter and advertisements is likely to be determined by relationships between Web publishers and a new class of content producers. Perhaps more than anything else, these relationships have made the violation of church-state norms routine, by forcing content producers to meet marketers' twenty-first century needs. Together, these developments encourage reputation silos: automated packaging of commercial messages and editorial matter that present individuals with content—advertising, information, entertainment, and news—that has been customized to reflect the data mining's profiles of them.

Advertising networks run by Yahoo!, Google, Microsoft, AOL, and other firms already model this behavior. They routinely place ads next to content based on the perceived congruence between the ads, the content, and the visitors' characteristics. Consider the Google Display Network, an enormous world of advertising offerings—"text, image, rich media, and video advertising on Google properties, YouTube, and millions of web, domain, video, gaming, and mobile partner sites." Citing comScore numbers in late 2009, Google asserted that its network reaches over 76 percent of U.S. online audiences and 73 percent of global online audiences.[13] At its beginning, in the early 2000s, Google's display approach aimed to attract advertisers by making sure the ad fit well with its environment (the content on the Web page where Google sent it). However, Google did nothing to target individuals. Its display placements at the time were based solely on making the best thematic fit between ads and websites, as determined by Google's analysis of the themes on the thousands of websites with which the search engine had made deals to serve ads. Like its paid-search operation, the company also served an advertisement tied to the winning bidder of the relevant keyword.

Now both Google's paid-search operation and its display network target individuals based on information gathered about them. Google Display Network has become a gold mine for advertisers looking to connect their own information, third-party information, and Google's categories about individuals with the aim of persuading them across the Web.[14] The company's less-exalted competitive position in the display advertising business compared to its position as search engine undoubtedly has played a large part. Lagging behind Yahoo!, Microsoft, Facebook, and others in display, and still drawing only a small fraction of its revenue from it, Google Display Network by 2010 became increasingly pliable about tagging and following members of the public than it is on its search-marketing engine.[15] Like Yahoo!, Google Display Network mandates certain requirements of advertisers regarding ad layout and format, the pages on which the advertisements land, and content acceptability; the last condition can vary by country (for ads regarding abortion, for example).[16] But the firm has also followed Yahoo! in the other direction, trying to give the Google Display Network collection of display technologies a reputation for being superfriendly to advertisers. Many observers believe that Google's Display Network will not rule in its realm of advertising as completely as the company has done in search.[17] Nevertheless, Google has stated that "display is the next advertising frontier for the firm," if only because it expects advertisers' expenditures on display to rocket from $20 billion to $40 billion in the next few years.[18] Susan Wojcicki, the firm's vice president of product management, acknowledged in a 2010 blog post that the Google Display Network platform had been a sometimes-feeble work in progress. Recent "improvements," she said, "will make it far easier to buy ads across the web at scale, create engaging ad formats, measure the impact of ad campaigns in innovative and insightful ways, deliver relevant ads to precisely the right audiences in real-time and maximize the value of publishers' online content."[19]

Following the custom of other networks and exchanges, Google Display Network asserts that personal data present no social problems, as no personally identifiable information guides the serving of ads without the person's permission. Moreover, consumers can opt out of the firm's tailored advertising.[20] At the same time, this firm that can reach over 70 percent of Americans individually has assembled an armamentarium with virtually all the advertiser targeting and personalization products that, as Chapter 4 noted, marketers want.

- On the most basic level, Google allows advertisers to bid by gender, age, geography, and language.
- To this Google Display Network adds a form of behavioral targeting it calls "interest-based advertising." It categorizes people's behavior across a firmament of sites (including its heavily visited YouTube video destination) and

stores these tags on their browsers via a cookie from the ad-serving firm DoubleClick, which Google owns.

- In addition to the demographic and behavioral designations, Google allows an advertiser to show individuals messages based on the advertiser's previous interactions with them, as stored in their Web histories.
- Further enhancing its Display Network's attractiveness to advertisers, Google allows certain ad-serving firms to place tags on Google's ad sites to both note the individuals they have tracked in the past and place cookies on the computers of individuals whom Google believes match their clients' interests. This allows advertisers to accomplish most, if not all, of the desired data-matching activities of individuals described in Chapter 4. BridgeTrack, one of those third-party ad servers, generally proclaims its ability to "integrate data from different sources on a real-time, daily or weekly basis" as well as "segment and target your offers using a complete view of all customer interactions."[21] Google lets the third-party ad server do this on the Display Network.
- To cap it off, Google offers the services of its Teracent subsidiary, which can tailor literally thousands of creative elements of a display ad in real time based on database information about the categories that define the person to be targeted.

Competition from powerful display-advertising networks such as Google's as well as from the hundreds of thousands of websites the networks represent profoundly influences publishers' content decisions. The reason for this has to do with the basic perspective of media agencies, which chase target audiences and low prices, particularly low CPMs for the targets. When a site offers both, they buy. If the prices are relatively high, advertisers need a sufficient reason to pay. As Tobaccowala suggests, in many cases providing a prestigious context in which to show an ad no longer justifies a higher price. This view has dire consequences for websites that spend a lot of money on content.

Let's say, for example, that hypothetical sites HenryFootball.com, GoFootball.com, and GeorgeFootball.com offer via exchanges several million people they and their data providers label as male football fans between twenty and twenty-five years old who are in the market for a new car. Let's say that ESPN.com also offers via exchanges and through its sales staff millions of impressions that also reflect those types of individuals. HenryFootball, GoFootball, and GeorgeFootball are primarily fan-blog sites where visitors come to fight it out about their favorite teams as well as to learn about the latest trades, opinions, and player statistics. ESPN places many professionally created football game segments online, has deep profiles about each one, and uses its on-air personalities in features about the upcoming weekend's games. ESPN's cost structure reflects its high reputation, and so one might expect that advertisers would pay a higher CPM to buy impressions there than on the cheaply run other sites. The logic of bidding that doesn't take context into account says that this is not necessarily the case. Other than certain key positions on a site—the home page, for example, or a sponsored section—where advertisers will pay above the going rate for certain impressions, it's a hard sell.

Some sites are set up to handle bargain-basement pricing. Dictionary.com, owned by InterActive Corporation, is one such site. Essentially a cross between a publisher and a vertical search engine, Dictionary.com is like many made-for-Web platforms with cost structures suitable for CPMs of about $2—the $4 average minus the amount that the ad networks and various data providers might take in the transaction. The site follows the common route of relying on advertising networks that use beacons to follow an individual's activities on the Web page as well as tracking cookies to trace and store other information about the visit to that site as well as to others. In 2010, a *Wall Street Journal* consultant found that a visit to the online dictionary site resulted in 223 files for tracking Web users being downloaded into the *Wall Street Journal*'s test computer. That was enough to keep the site afloat without an extensive ad-sales team.[22]

As explained in Chapter 3, legacy firms such as local newspapers, national dailies such as the *New York Times* and *USA Today,* and major magazine publishers such as Time Inc., Condé Nast, Meredith, and Hearst can't survive on $2 CPMs. They have large staffs and expenses based on CPMs that often hover around $40. Increasingly they see their off-line advertising pages dropping while their online traffic often surges. For several years they expected that advertisers online would want to associate with their stellar media brands (for example, the *New York Times, People, Ladies Home Journal*) in the digital era as they have done in the analog world. That would allow them to charge a substantial premium for ads appearing on their sites compared to sites without their reputations. They have found, instead, that many digital-media buyers share Tobaccowala's contention that agencies should no longer pay a premium for a media firm's status when they place ads. Media buyers agreed in interviews for this book that if they had to

choose between an ad on ESPN and reaching people with the same characteristics (or even the same people) on lesser-known sites for far less money,
they would often choose the latter.

The buyers justify positioning their ads on so-called down-market sites by
arguing that a quality location is in the eye of the consumer. If a person
enjoys viewing material on a site, they contend, then the site is fine for that
person, and the advertiser shouldn't have a problem with that. The media
buyers do offer caveats. Sponsorship of a high-profile section of a major
media brand's website deserves consideration, they said, because of the pres-
tige that connection implies. So does a medium's ability to associate with a
big sporting event linked to the brand. Executives representing major
marketers also want to make sure that the less-expensive sites that carry their
ads will not place them next to editorial content that could embarrass them.
Although such situations have happened on domains as large as YouTube,
websites are increasingly sensitive to the issue and have been devising ways to
assure advertisers that their placements will not harm their reputations. The
rise of huge, inexpensive advertising networks that do not always reveal
exactly where an ad is displayed increases the potential for infelicitous ad
placement. One alternative is to advertise on a collection of sites deemed
safe; the comScore research firm suggests such a grouping, often tagged as
the comScore 500. At the same time, however, the appearance of exchanges
that allow media buyers to bid for particular (anonymous) individuals, often
with cookie matches, across a galaxy of sites, makes the purchasing of
impressions without attention to the media brand even more alluring.
Consequently, even elite brands such as the *Washington Post* have to sell a
high percentage of their ads on low-cost exchanges rather than through its
premium-priced sales force. For brand-conscious firms with expensive business models, the context-free trading of impressions has underscored a need
to persuade media buyers that purchasing ads specifically on their sites at
premium CPMs offers more value than purchasing ads elsewhere.

One such strategy the websites are exploring is content personalization. As
expressed in interviews, trade-magazine articles, and industry meetings,
digital ad practitioners tend to appreciate the utility of content personalization for bringing in advertising revenues. Some believe that consumers are
more responsive to commercial messages in an editorial environment that is
closely related to their interests. Another view is that personalization is
needed in the escalating competition to draw audiences because people
pursue material most relevant to them; websites that don't personalize would

therefore lose visitors. Edwin Wong, Director of Market Research at Yahoo!, sees the importance of content personalization somewhat differently. He notes that research conducted for Yahoo! by Publicis found that an ad customized to a person's interest tends to work as well on a Web page unrelated to that interest as it does on one related to it. He argues that encouraging media personalization is nevertheless still useful, because it allows publishers and their advertisers to learn increasing amounts about individuals' interests and their responses to those interests. That information, in turn, can help create profiles that advertisers would want to target.[23]

Whatever the reasoning behind it, the surge in personalization is clear. Wong himself said in 2010 that "content optimization is where things are happening."[24] And in the same year Lisa Donohue, CEO of Publicis's Starcom media-buying subsidiary, confirmed her clients' interest in all sorts of tailored content. She rooted its cause in audience interest. "Content has taken a center stage in how we go to market for clients, and consumers are demanding more from entertainment in the world of digitization, personalization and interactivity," she said of the goals of her "branded entertainment" division.[25]

The actual meaning of *content personalization*, however, varies. The term covers a broad spectrum of genres. At one end is material that is created for an individual based on the person's profile and value—that is, the person's reputation. On the other end the content does not change at all, but news, entertainment, and information pieces are sent automatically to people whose data suggest they have found their topics interesting in the past. In between are hybrid strategies that alter aspects of the content to a greater or lesser extent. A headline and lead paragraph might change, for example, but the content would otherwise remain the same.

It is quite possible today to change aspects of audiovisual programming and games based on the social background of an individual whose data suggest that he or she will purchase a product. Yet altering character and plot elements based on individual audience members' attributes can be expensive and require faster computer processing than most people have available to them.

Audio and audiovisual entertainment targeting nowadays therefore tends to be of the most basic type. People with particular attributes and media habits receive certain links, articles, videos, or audio streams; people with other attributes confront different rosters of content. When it comes to text-based news and news photos, the technology and current processing power

certainly exist to tailor headlines and lead paragraphs, as well as to tailor articles on the fly based on knowledge of the audience member. Yet when it
comes to news—current events as well as human interest stories—even the
most basic form of current-events personalization did not take off until
recently. News providers had limited their activities to visitor customization:
allowing them to choose the kinds of stories they want to receive rather than
making the decisions for them.

A large part of the reason, executives say, was the philosophical-ethical problems that they and their colleagues had with personalization. In mid-2010,
when he was president of digital efforts at Time Inc., Kirk McDonald reflected
that one reason editorial divisions at his firm have been loath to personalize
their presentations for audiences is a belief that "content is based on serendipity. We want to tell you what you don't know." He also suggested that
personalization can harm the company by startling people about the knowledge firms have about them. "If I saw that the magazine editor said, 'Kirk, we
know you're in debt up to your eyeballs. Here are articles that can help you,' I
might well freak out."[26]

Imran Aziz, the group program manager for Microsoft's Bing News,
voiced a similar view about news firms' reluctance to pursue sophisticated
machine-driven personalization. "There have been experiments [highlighting
the problem of] making it 'too apparent,'" he said. "You can sort of determine what a person is by their search, so there may be ethical issues. To use it
in a visible way would be creepy, many believe." In distinguishing the
genuine news and entertainment parts of Microsoft sites from commercial
forays, Aziz noted that in the current situation "ads, by contrast, are a lot
more personalized. Commerce is a lot more focused on it. And the feeling is
that people accept that [kind of] personalization. . . . Travel, local, finance,
people—commercial search personalization in these areas are accepted."[27]

And yet everyone who spoke to me about content personalization for this
book acknowledged that increasingly competitive times required new attitudes. Both Microsoft's Aziz and Time's McDonald agreed that times were
changing and that the trend toward personalizing editorial content for individuals is unmistakable. The challenge for their companies, they noted, was
trying to figure out how to carry out editorial personalization in a manner
that wouldn't cause audiences to freak out. McDonald, with a strong background in digital ad sales, believed that just as "technology platforms move
ads around quickly" to match the audience, so "content firms" should learn
to do the same with editorial matter. He noted that "lots of firms are

beginning to create content for specific audiences." The goal for a firm such as his was to learn how to connect audiences and content—to "be nimble in the use of data when creating content." He described what he saw as his legacy magazine firm's competitive advantage vis-à-vis Google, Microsoft, and Yahoo! when it came to personalization in terms of the audience's relatively high degree of trust in the publisher:

> The keys to navigating this area are access, authenticity, and authority. "Who are the editorial sources I truly trust and what do I trust them to tell me about it?" If what I notice [is] that by giving some permissions the site has begun to serve things that are relevant, I would find this relevant. You have to have an authentic brand with real authority, with access to real information and authority to say it. So I think we're going to see a time where the brands will cut through the material. When they take on and adopt tech and make sure [they have] the authenticity to bear for the user experience, that will work. Google, Yahoo or MS brand service value are too vague to do this with authenticity and authority. We're beginning to think out the requirements at Time Inc. about how that would work.[28]

Microsoft's Aziz clearly believes that his firm has as much credibility as a legacy news firm such as *Time.* Preferring to think of the issue from the standpoint of Microsoft's global footprint, he stressed the need to understand the subtleties of cultural lines where personalization would not be noticed as an intrusion. "Lately," he said, "Microsoft has been using a lot of crowd information—[noting] how people are interacting with one another over the news—to improve relevance. [Microsoft] could implement this [personalization for relevance] by market; could be U.S. English, for example." He has also thought about how to get users to give permission for seamless personalization. If the user opts in to tailor his or her own content, "then it's easy"—and implicitly acceptable, he reasoned—to follow up with more automated personalization.[29]

While big firms such as Microsoft and Time are in the throes of thinking about how to implement content personalization in the service of advertising revenues, a far smaller firm, The Daily Me, is already implementing a version of content personalization on the online sites of more than a dozen newspapers with print origins. The Daily Me started as an attempt to encourage people to customize news on its own website. The company quickly found, however, that people didn't want to list their preferred news agenda. Moreover, the site had very few visitors. As a result, in November 2009 its executives changed their business model. They kept the website and visitors' ability to personalize news there. But they turned much of their attention to providing online newspapers with the ability to serve visitors to the site— even those who hadn't been there before—news that they would want to read based on what they had read elsewhere, along with ads that also reflect those reading interests.

Gerald Hauser, The Daily Me founder and CEO, offers the example of someone who typically reads the *Boston Globe* visiting the *Dallas Morning News* site because of a link to an article encountered on a blog or search engine. Both the *Globe* and *Morning News* are The Daily Me clients, and a cookie notes the anonymous individual at the *Morning News* site. Because The Daily Me's cookie indicates that the person reads a lot about soccer on the *Globe* sports section, it tells the *Dallas Morning News* to serve him soccer stories as well. Moreover, when an ad is served along with the story, its text and photos are arranged instantly to include soccer terminology and photos as part of the advertising pitch. A basketball fan receiving an ad for the same product will get language and photos familiar to people with hoop interests.[30]

Hauser states that with this approach the paper gets a 98 percent higher click-through rate than it does with regular headlines. He also claims that people viewed 35 percent more pages on the site. He also reports that his firm's ad serving is facilitated by third-party advertising networks. Depending on the revenue agreement, The Daily Me, the news site, and the ad network might share in the revenue. Note that bringing the ad network into the picture also means that the site visitor is fodder for targeting based on his or her online news or sports-reading throughout the Web. Add some cookie-matching and data-appending activities along the way, and the information picked up by a small number of firms on a small number of sites now becomes part of a roster of information about individuals whose names are not known but who have provided lots of other information that can be used to evaluate their worth and to determine whether and how to address them.

In spinning out the implications of these activities it is not hard to see how they could cultivate the creation of wide-ranging reputation silos. Consider a news site that uses its registration data and tracking abilities, as well as income and employment information that it purchases from the credit reporting company Experian, to label a person named Karen as a visitor worth cultivating. The site's data-analytics firm determines topics that seem to lead Karen to stay longer on the site pages and therefore increase the chance that she will notice the site's ads. The news site has also learned that Karen has shared certain types of health articles from the site numerous times, which is of particular interest to related businesses, because they regard people who engage in this sharing activity as "health influencers," both online and in off-line life as well. Karen's habit of sharing, combined with her valuable reputation, prompt the site to make sure that articles fitting her interests appear in important areas of the news site's home page. Types of articles on which she has never clicked or on which she spends short amounts of time either no longer make it to the home page or are pushed further down the screen. Every time she returns to the site, the personalization technology reevaluates Karen based on her actions as well as on new information received from other sources.

The personalization of news takes place in tandem with the personalization of ads. The website shares its anonymous profile of Karen, selling the right to reach her, along with millions of others, on networks and exchanges. Some advertisers may have created their own reputation for Karen via cookie matches or similar actions; data firms may have had a hand in supplying elements of that profile. In concert with the Web publisher, they may decide that they want to reach her when she is reading certain types of editorial matter or viewing certain topics from among the news site's videos. Because of her high income and professional status, a high-end retail advertiser decides to serve her an ad for an exclusive shopping spree. Only women under age thirty-five and earning annual salaries of more than $100,000 receive that particular ad. Other advertisers, using similar profiles, also surround her with blandishments befitting a high reputation.

Karen's value, in fact, leads marketers to find ways to identify her elsewhere on the Web and surround her with similar commercial messages there. The publisher, too, sees value in her record and decides to sell her interest profile anonymously to data firms that can find ways to follow her elsewhere on the Web and turn this tracking into commercial value. Eventually, too, one of the news website's sponsors figures out how to interest Karen and others like her to click on an ad and sign up for a special deal based on her interests. The advertisers now have her name and e-mail address, which provide an additional way to find out even more about her and spread her characteristics around the Web so that she can receive yet more personalized advertisements, discounts, news, and maybe even entertainment. Over time, consistent shared notions of this now not so anonymous person by publishers and advertisers will lead them to place her in a reputation silo simply through their regular activities. Some people will see more elaborate silo packages than others; some might evade consistent profiling; and some may elicit enough interest to have content routines associated with them. And Karen, like tens of millions of others who have profiles more or less attractive to media and marketing firms, will have only a vague idea that this is taking place.

Karen's story is actually one of two imminent scenarios. The principle behind Karen's silo is that news, entertainment, information, discounts, and advertising is to be automatically personalized according to an individual's reputation. In the other version, the silos have an even more commercial flavor. Websites work with media buyers to personalize news, information, and entertainment in ways designed to enhance the value of the ads. In these cases, websites send Karen collections of news that both reflect her interests and reflect well on the advertisements that surround it. The connections are typically subtle, though product placements in entertainment videos some-times echo the commercials that interrupt them. Overall, the agenda of worldviews that make up a fair amount of Karen's day is consistently inflected by commercial intent.

This hypercommercial version of reputation silos will probably prevail—and it will do so precisely because of the slow disintegration of the church-state separation discussed earlier. The disintegration is taking place just as many websites reveal a ravenous need for both inexpensive content and lots of advertising (sold cheaply) to survive. The situation has opened the door for a new breed of public-relations practitioners, whether acting alone or with a new class of content creators, to flood the Web with news and enter-tainment subtly shaped by marketers' interests. In one version of the activity, publishers looking to personalize content will choose the free or inexpensive articles and coincidentally place them alongside personalized ads from those same marketers. In another version, the marketers will pay the publishers to do it. Both approaches will present individuals with differently tailored worldviews.

The battle to weaken the barrier between advertisers and editorial stan-dards began early in the twenty-first century as the new media world unrav-eled stable traditional approaches. Marketers increasingly wanted to "cross borders," as Randall Rothenberg put it in a 2001 *Advertising Age* article, meaning that they increasingly wanted their advertising messages to show up in regular editorial matter precisely because audiences were likely to believe the nonadvertising pieces more readily. Rothenberg knew that such border crossings had taken place despite news and entertainment companies adopting the church-state doctrine as part of their work ethic. He pointed out, however, that in the new century marketers were putting greater pressure than ever on publishers to blur the boundaries between the editorial and the commercial. And publishers, wanting the additional advertising purchases that would typically accompany these deals, were agreeing in greater numbers than ever. "What should be . . . frightening to executives in media and marketing . . . is that such border crossings are becoming entirely unexceptional," he wrote. "Combine audience and media fragmentation and throw in a dose of market maturity. You've got a recipe for desperation— among brand marketers who, for some 70 years, have had the ability to reach 80% of their audience via a handful of media vehicles using ads that were stamped out by factories."[31]

If Rothenberg didn't note that publishers were also becoming desperate, it was because that situation wasn't so clear in 2001, when big newspaper and magazine firms were still raking in advertising money. A permanent downturn in the traditional money sources had already begun to affect television program producers, though, as they chafed under the lower license fees the broadcast television networks were paying them now that they competed with cable television for advertising. Consequently, the producers cheered a 1996 U.S. Supreme Court ruling that invalidated an industry code dictating maximum hourly commercial minutes. That ruling gave producers, and later the networks themselves, the opportunity to begin charging marketers for mixing commercial components into programming.[32]

Print-industry writers remained nervous about the willingness of some media firms to allow advertisers into their content as a matter of course. Under pressure in 2005 to loosen its guidelines about labeling when items are sponsored, the American Society of Magazine Editors (ASME) held fairly firm in keeping church and state separate. As with the old rules, the new ones called for periodicals to tag advertising that imitated editorial copy in a way that clearly differentiated it—though the new rules did allow the option of labeling such pages *promotion* instead of *advertisement*. ASME also accepted the idea that companies could be the sole sponsors of nonrecurring editorial features like special issues and inserts as long as mentions of the sponsors were marked clearly as advertising. The guidelines continued to forbid the same sponsor from supporting *regularly* occurring editorial features. They insisted that companies and products "should appear on covers only in an editorial context, and not in a way that suggests advertisement." And they asserted that "advertisements should not be placed or sold for placement immediately before or after editorial pages that discuss, show, or promote the advertised products." They also stipulated that "advertisers should not pay to place their products in editorial pages nor should they demand placement in return for advertising."[33]

ASME's rationale for these prohibitions was the "core conviction" that "for magazines to be trusted by consumers and to endure as brands, readers must be assured of their editorial integrity." Yet even as it promulgated the guidelines, some member consumer magazines flouted them or their spirit. *Sporting News,* for example, regularly touted advertisers' support of specific types of items. And *Inside TV* ignored ASME's prohibition of sponsored content since its debut in 2004. By 2009, heavy-hitter periodicals *ESPN, Entertainment Weekly,* and *Scholastic Parent & Child* were selling advertisements on their covers. *Dwell* and *Scholastic Parent & Child* allowed commercial messages to flow through editorial matter. Just a year later, *Parent & Child* had its editorial staff compose a page for one of its advertisers.[34]

"Personally speaking, this crap may be groovy, but it still stinks," exclaimed ASME CEO Sid Holt when an *Advertising Age* reporter asked him about the developments during 2010.[35] In the resulting brouhahas with ASME over such activities, advertisers, publishers, and editors argued that readers had grown savvier, that they could distinguish sponsorship from editorial even when not told explicitly. In October 2010, ASME allowed for more advertising on covers and editorial work with sponsors but still insisted that "editorial integrity must not be compromised by advertiser influence." It prohibited "advertising that disrupts editorial" and "editorial staff and frequent contributors" that "appear in the creation or production of, advertising that appears in their own magazine."[36] A *Scholastic Parent & Child* executive said the company's research concluded that its readers were not confused by the blending of editorial writing and advertising. *Entertainment Weekly* publisher Scott Donaton also contended that "we would never do anything to confuse our audience, but we seek fun and innovative ways to engage our readers and work with our [advertising] partners."[37]

Media buyers supported the changes. At WPP's Mediaedge:cia agency one buyer remarked that "advertisers and agencies are starting to demand the same types of integration found in TV and online. The big watch-out is that once you compromise reader trust or your integrity, it's hard to get it back. None of the [marketing activities] I've seen seem to do that."[38] Robin Steinberg, a senior vice president and head of what Publicis's MediaVest

Worldwide called "print investment and activation," crossed ASME's church-state line by arranging for a Walmart ad in Time Inc.'s *Real Simple* that reflected the theme of the editorial matter preceding it. (The Walmart ad was titled "Decorating with Walmart," and the article was titled "Decorating with Yellow.") To Steinberg, the opportunity was worth it. "If it's relevant and appropriate and engaging to the consumer," she asked rhetorically, "why not?"[39] As if to buttress her comment, Scholastic also argued it was worth it monetarily. The publishers trotted out a poll of readers showing that the cover ads led other ad placements in key measures of engagement such as recall of the commercial message, saving an ad for future reference, visiting a website or store, and buying the product or service.

Newspaper companies were beginning to ask the same question Steinberg asked. By 2010, a few, including the *Los Angeles Times,* had started accepting ads for their front pages. This form of commercial placement had traditionally been off-limits for U.S. daily newspapers. In the tough financial environment, editors were increasingly open to discussing the potential for generating stories that prospective advertisers would find compatible with their messages. The director of the Executive News Media Leadership Program at Columbia University noted that "the boundaries of what's permissible and not permissible are going to be explored." The editor of the *Christian Science Monitor,* which began as a print publication but has now evolved into a completely online product, noted that the changed financial environment required breaking the church-state taboo. "What we're doing," he told *Advertising Age*'s Nat Ives, "is trying to remove the taboo about having a conversation across the wall and put various people—not just the editor and publisher, but deputy editors and national editors—and put them in conversation with the business people, and say rather than never talk, go and talk." The *Dallas Morning News* assigned editors to report to general managers on the business side. Many of these moves related to funding soft news and sports and not the still-sacrosanct hard-news beat. Nevertheless, the change was profound. "I don't think we have the luxury any more of being isolated," said Bob Yates, deputy managing editor for sports at the *Dallas Morning News.* Having covered the attrition of the church-state boundary for several years, Nat Ives concluded in 2010 that "the wall was almost a privilege of simpler times, more editors and publishers seem to agree."[40]

To the publishers and editors of some consumer magazines, the erasure of these boundaries has become a necessary part of their professional lives. At a panel discussion at the 2010 American Magazine Conference, Nancy Weber, chief marketing officer at Meredith Corporation, said that her company's approach to inserting brands into magazine editorial matter is based on "how authentic it is; we don't want it to feel forced or disturb the consumer. We want it to feel editorial and we want it to feel authentic."[41]

Weber had no qualms about the importance of product integration into content. Her firm distills the mandate into what the corporate website calls "our 360° approach," a "strategic marketing unit providing clients and their agencies with unparalleled access to the vast portfolio of media products and services Meredith has to offer."[42] That includes Meredith "content," the website continues, and the company is not shy about promulgating it to the trade press.[43] The company cites as one such success *The Broadroom,* a Web-based series collaboration between Meredith's *MORE* magazine and Maybelline. Each episode, which lasts just a few minutes, centers on women in the workplace. The drawing card is creator Candace Bushnell, who generated HBO's hit series *Sex and the City.* Her *Broadroom* contract required Bushnell to integrate plugs for Maybelline cosmetics into each episode. Initially she balked. "Candace Bushnell was a real puritan for church and state," Weber recalled, "but she came around."[44]

Some magazine and newspaper officials are less willing to admit that the walls between advertising and editorial have been so worn away. They say they accept advertiser influence with respect to only marginal issues of content. That might mean placing ads systematically near articles on the same topic. It might mean writing articles on a specific topic if advertisers promise to sponsor it. It might also mean allowing an advertiser to produce a website page that looks like editorial matter but that carries the somewhat ambiguous disclaimer "Sponsored Content." It does not mean the wholesale throwing away of autonomy and integrity for advertising. Their caution seems to be the result of a sense of professional ethics mixed with a worry that their credibility would plummet if readers were to find out what they were doing.

Yet as publishers begin to redefine the once sacred church-state separation at the margins, the concept that advertisers can exert direct influence on at least certain elements of an editorial package gains mainstream acceptance. When it comes to Web publishing, this represents a major win for *marketers* at a time when elements of content are precisely those editorial units that digital consumers encounter regularly—that is, digital audiences now commonly come across individual articles from periodicals via vehicles such as search engines, Facebook, Twitter, and e-mail. (*Snacking* is a popular term for these bursts of online consumption of information, news, and entertainment from various sources.) The website to which a reader is directed to access such an article might well have no concern about placing it next to an ad on the same general topic if its database says the person's profile fits. These types of "harmonized," or integrated, placements benefit advertisers in passive ways, as advertisers exert no direct control over the personalized placements. Marketers, however, do want to be more actively involved in pairing editorial matter and advertisements. Some publicly deny this, arguing that they have an interest in maintaining the public's belief in editorial integrity precisely because that belief draws people to media where commercial messages appear. Yet the denials do not stand up to marketers' long-standing awareness that it is useful to intrude on editorial if they can get away with it *and* also ensure that consumers aren't aware of this activity.

Marketers and their agencies try to carry out these two goals by sparking media and interpersonal buzz around a product. To do that, they use any of three means, which they call *earned media, owned media,* and *paid media.* Paid media involves traditional advertising, in which advertisers purchase specific space or time. Neither earned media nor owned media explicitly involves advertising. Owned media refers to vehicles that the marketers themselves create and populate with materials relating to their products and services. For example, in the analog world custom periodicals such as American Airlines' *American Way* flight magazine fit the bill, while their counterpart's in the digital domain include product websites such as Pampers.com. *Earned media* involves mention or discussion of brands in situations that don't involve the purchase of specific advertising space or time. Rather, products are named because the media practitioners involved think it useful to discuss them. As two *Advertising Age* reporters put it, earned media include "everything from the reportage of professional journalists to the patter of blogs and social networks."[45] Marketers believe that favorable comments are more beneficial for sales than an ad because people trust editorial matter more than they trust the ads.

Earned media practitioners believe that getting products mentioned in outlets as varied as news programs, how-to videos, and blogs ought to be far from accidental. Consequently, they use a range of marketing-communication firepower to place favorable items on their clients across various platforms used by their target audiences. They also encourage those audiences to respond to these mentions and interact with each other about the products. Ben & Jerry's global digital marketing manager emphasized this approach when explaining her choice of public relations agency

Edelman for the ice cream company's campaign beginning in 2010. "What Edelman brought back was extremely strategic," she said. "It told a story and took into consideration all the different spaces—earned, owned, paid and social. It hit on everything. I felt like they got our voice and maybe because their roots are in PR it was never just about buying banner ads."[46] Note that three of the four activities did not involve paying directly for advertising space or time. The focus on earned and owned media reflected the fact that marketers were putting the responsibility of reaching their targets into their own hands even as they continued to buy advertisements. The mention of *social* (as in the use of social-media sites) underscores Edelman's understanding of the two-way, trackable nature of the new media environment.

The logic behind a publisher's use of a marketer's earned media offering is simple: it makes sense to save time and money by using an attractive idea, or even a completed piece, that is offered free from a marketer—as long as the audience believes the publisher created it.[47] For example, publicists or public relations agencies are responsible for many of the guests who appear on broadcast television's *Good Morning, America* and *Today Show.* The shows don't announce how their guests are procured, however, and viewers may be more or less savvy about why, say, an actor or an inventor is appearing for a segment. Clearly an actor is there to pitch his or her new movie, while the reason behind the other is more ambiguous. Was the inventor approached because of his news value, or was his selection the result of a press release from a manufacturer he has begun to represent? The program host won't say.

While many traditional articles and videos are still widely circulated, people searching for information or visiting particular websites are increasingly likely to encounter articles written by a new type of production firm, the *content farm.* Associated Content, Demand Media, and Answers.com are among the firms that pump thousands of articles every day into the internet, written by freelancers who are told what subjects to choose based on trending topics: the popularity of words searched on Google, Twitter, and other search and social-media platforms. Peter Berger, CEO of one such company, Suite101, notes that the goal is search-engine optimization—that is, the firms try to ensure that the articles are written so that they appear to Google and Bing robots to be the kind of material the "search engines want to present their users." In 2010 Roger Rosenblatt, CEO of Demand Media, the biggest of these operations, said that his firm's output of more than four thousand articles and videos per day, written by thousands of freelancers, "helps fill the pages" of newspapers, magazines, and other digital media properties.[48] Demand Media had been a large content production factory for Yahoo! until it bought competitor Associated Content.[49] On its website Demand says it focuses on helping "the world's leading publishers and media companies tell the best story possible."[50] Rosenblatt said that the articles the company generates should be compared with Associated Press lifestyle or soft news content.

Rosenblatt has also stated that he does not consider Demand Media's staff to be "reporters," a point that he may believe absolves him of church-state considerations. In fact, unlike the Associated Press, Demand Media has embraced the attrition of the church-state boundary and turned it into a business model. According to the trade website ReadWriteWeb, Demand purposefully produces articles on subjects that, according to its computer algorithms, have strong advertiser interest and target audience plus the potential for drawing large numbers of people to the material (for example, through search). As an example of advertiser interest, a ReadWriteWeb article highlighted a Demand Media video called "How to Make Cornbread," which it placed on YouTube during the Christmas season. Demand recognized that YouTube would find it conducive for ads targeting those concerned about holiday preparations. In fact, YouTube placed the video into an advertising program with the retail giant Target, which highlighted the store's solutions to Christmas party and gift-giving dilemmas.[51] As ReadWriteWeb made clear, when multiplied thousands of times per day with articles circulated to millions of people, this approach makes lifestyle content a handmaiden of advertisers' interests.

Moreover, although Demand Media may not have colluded with YouTube to craft editorials that precisely match ads, ReadWriteWeb notes that packaging ads and editorial is not a philosophically tough step to take when church-state distinctions are fading: "An example might be something like this: Demand Media produces a how-to article on playing tennis; then sells it to a Yahoo! sports site accompanied by tennis equipment adverts placed around it."[52] A third step logically follows: an earned media firm pays Demand Media or one of its freelancers to mention its client's racquet in the midst of the how-to article about tennis. Demand Media then sells the article—or gives it free—to a Yahoo! sports site, accompanied by tennis-equipment advertisements from that firm. Yahoo! serves the packaged editorial-ad product to millions of individuals throughout the Web who fit the advertiser's profile.

Journalists were outraged that Demand Media, Associated Content, and other firms were pushing good articles down the organic search results by paying low rates to create superficial articles according to search-engine-friendly formulas. Consequently, Google altered its search algorithm in February 2011 to reduce rankings for sites with low-quality or unoriginal content.[53] Google anticipated that this move would affect roughly 12 percent of search results overall, but some sites blamed a 50 percent decline in traffic on their new search positions. Rosenblatt disputed reports by measurement companies that Demand Media had seen a huge decline in search-driven traffic, though he did note a moderate decline in the number of people coming to some of his firm's sites.[54] He pointed out that Google executives were not targeting particular companies and, in a May 2011 earnings conference call, added that Demand Media had decided to turn out stories that were longer and that had more substance to make them worthy of attention and a high ranking by search engines.[55]

As content farms evolve to serve the needs of personalization on a large scale, it will make sense for them to create articles not only for trending topics on search engines, websites, and social media, but also for trends in the characteristics of individuals whom advertisers want to reach. In this manner the packaging of editorial and advertising matter will get closer and closer to the needs of data miners. Publishers may well share anonymous data about their most desirable audiences in the hope that the content farms will pitch more articles in their direction. Data-mining firms such as eXelate and Lotame may find "inclination to read or view" to be useful variables for advertisers interested in buying profiles of individuals who will receive editorial items that reflect well on the advertisers' business at the same time that they also receive the company's ad. As this process develops, the data flowing about visitors from media firms to advertisers and data suppliers and back will optimize the opportunities to create reputation profiles with text, video, and audio offerings that reflect individuals' profiles and that are often shared broadly across the Web.

Content farms help websites without writing staffs or journalistic commitments to survive even while charging advertisers low prices for impressions. Legacy firms from the print, radio, and television industries, suffering under higher costs, may syndicate content-farm material for the same reason. Yet the fear of losing brand distinctiveness for marketers and audiences in such an environment may simultaneously lead them to spend money to personalize news and entertainment offerings as well as advertising. Although the labels the legacy firms use may come from their own information storehouse, they may also derive from the information that advertising and database companies share across the Web. They may mix these targeting decisions with decisions visitors themselves make when they ask for customized topics and feeds. Reputation silos may therefore evolve from the editorial matter and advertisements that come to individuals as a result of the personalization choices that they make, that publishers make for them with an eye toward advertisers, and that advertisers send to them. If the receivers of these customized mosaics of the world do notice consistent patterns in their worldviews, they will have no way of figuring out why the specific tiles were presented to them.

Contemporary industry logistics are pushing these ideas far beyond the traditional Web. According to hard-nosed practitioners, social, mobile, and television technologies will extend these developments into digital spaces far beyond the Web with the ability to connect with target customers up to the point of sale. In these environments, linking the appropriate material with the appropriate person in the appropriate place and time becomes paramount. And, as the next chapter demonstrates, it's already beginning to happen.

Chapter 6 The Long Click

Two digital-agency executives whom I interviewed separately for this book in 2010 both described Facebook as a "black hole." This is an ironic description of a social-media vehicle that has been criticized for shedding *too much* light on the bodies, boasts, and other personal affairs of some of the approximately half a billion people worldwide who use it. Yet the two officials, Rishad Tobaccowala of Publicis and Michael Stich of Bridge Worldwide, were echoing media buyers' complaints that Facebook interferes with their ability to follow individuals across the Web. Facebook, they noted, is a walled garden where only Facebook itself can drop the cookies that make it possible to trace members' clicks around the internet.

At the same time, both Tobaccowala and Stich acknowledged that advertising in Facebook and relying on its knowledge of its audience have become indispensible to many marketers. With well over one hundred million members in the United States, Facebook is the standard-bearer for a crucial new form of media outlet that explicitly links gossip, mobility, and social relationships. Facebook CEO Mark Zuckerberg coined the term "social graph" to describe the networks of relationships that Facebook could detect among its users.[1] Many marketers accept that describing individuals in terms of what their relationships suggest about them provides powerful knowledge for selling to them and others. For that reason they see Facebook as complementing the demographics, buying interests, Web behaviors, and lifestyles that paid search, websites, display networks, and impression exchanges yield for marketers. The website's facilities for sharing photos, activity updates, videos, and comments among friends—and, importantly, with companies they "like" on so-called fan pages, which companies establish as a marketing tool for specific products—allow marketers to link people's names to what they say about their lives and the products they do and don't like. Facebook's "like" feature also offers advertisers the chance to tap into social networks of like-minded people who may well share interests in certain products. And with its "Places" and other mobile-phone applications, Facebook provides the opportunity for advertisers to reach "fans" and likely customers in the physical world by featuring products that are in close proximity to them.

Facebook is by no means the only company involved in opening up the social and mobile worlds to target advertising. Apart from many direct competitors (including Microsoft, Google, Foursquare, and Twitter), a mini-industry of companies exists to swoop into social-media sites and gather social-relationship data at levels of detail that Facebook and its ilk will not divulge. These companies pursue two broad activities: first, they use the social graph together with other information to identify those individuals they conclude are worth pursuing for specific products and using a particular set of incentives; and second, they follow the targeted individuals across as many geographical locations and devices as possible. This process can be defined as the ultimate "long click," which includes the following capacities: identify likely customers; use databases to encourage them to click on personalized content and relevant ads; reinforce their responses across a variety of websites and mobile devices; serve these customers personalized commercial messages at the moment of sale, what Procter and Gamble calls the "moment of truth"; and convince them to swipe their frequent-shopper card, credit card, or debit card to complete the gauntlet—and offer up more data.

Publishers don't want to be marginalized in this social-media environment. They increasingly have to prove their targeting value in a highly competitive atmosphere in which marketers have the ability to reach people through tweets, friendship messages (brief salutations via Facebook), e-mails, and discount coupons. And the competitive atmosphere provides advertising agencies with the leverage to push publishers to meet their long-click goals. Advertisers and their media agencies reward publishers who help them pursue and expand the logic of individual tracking, targeting, and tailoring. The competition for digital dominance in a social-media world is even affecting the biggest medium of all, the home television set.

The number of social-media outlets is mind-boggling, and most of them have their roots in the traditional Web, not in the mobile space. Andreas Kaplan and Michael Haenlein of the ESCP-EAP European School of Management in Paris list six different types of social-media channels: collaborative projects, blogs and microblogs, content communities, social-networking sites, virtual game worlds, and virtual communities.[2] They note that these channels often include technologies that facilitate writing and responding, picture-sharing, video, wall postings (that is, messages left on a person's main Facebook page, including the time and date of the message), e-mail, instant messaging, music sharing, crowd sourcing (carrying out a task through an open digital call for help), and voice conversations. Many internet analysts point to the important political and economic benefits that derive from the collaborative nature of these activities. But what they often fail to mention is that in many cases the platforms need to generate great economic value for the conglomerates and venture-capital firms that own them. That's especially true of U.S. social media such as Facebook, MySpace, LinkedIn and Twitter (and Orkut, Bebo, Hi5, and others outside the United States) that bring together many of those services into one place. They have become hubs of communication and sharing for hundreds of millions of people.

The companies that own the social sites find value in primarily two sources of revenue, most of it derived from advertising, but also from members' micropayments when they buy things such as virtual gifts and game items from companies doing business on the site.[3] For advertisers as well as the agencies and data firms that serve them, the benefits from social media are focused on three linked opportunities: the chance to shape target audiences' visions of their brands through both earned media and owned media; access to information regarding what specific types of people say and do regarding their products; and the opportunity to identify likely customers and target them with ads as well as with yet more earned and paid media.

Reaching out to bloggers represents the most basic version of the first opportunity—attempts to shape brand visions through earned media. Many marketers covet blogger mentions because they believe that, when it comes to product advice, people place more trust in friends and individuals who appear to be like them than they do in the companies themselves. To help marketers make the talk look earned when it's really paid for, companies have been created to generate and control buzz that, to the general public, appears to be spontaneous. BzzAgent, which conducts word-of-mouth campaigns online and off, charges marketers but recruits volunteers to do the job. "We have 700,000 passionate advocates who love to talk about brands throughout social media and off-line," noted its website in 2010. "And when they talk, people love to listen."[4]

Although it describes its agents as "volunteers," BzzAgent rewards them with discounts, a special rewards website, and, most importantly, the free products they receive to generate their posts. Izea, which confines its work to the online world, is another such company, but it pays its representatives (it calls them publishers) to blog or tweet about a client's product on a per-post and per-tweet basis. Some might question the ethics of passing off blogs or tweets as personal opinions when individuals are getting compensated. The Federal Trade Commission (FTC) wondered about that too, and in 2010 began requiring marketers to comply with its updated guidelines defining an endorsement as any advertising message that consumers are likely to believe reflects the opinions, beliefs, or experiences of a party other than the marketer that sponsors the endorser. To BzzAgent, "this means that companies involved in blogger and networked marketing programs must take steps to ensure participants disclose their involvement and avoid making atypical claims"— that is, claims about the product the marketer can't justify. The company describes an elaborate process to make sure its agents "let people know you're involved with BzzAgent."[5] Izea's website, by contrast, includes nothing about such transparency (through 2010, at least). Its mission, it says, is "to empower everyone to value and exchange content, creativity and influence."[6]

The websites of both companies parade the names of clients huge and small. The sites also make claims for the pervasiveness and effectiveness of their work in seeding the environment with brand claims. "A mature diet soda got 136,000 new purchases through its BzzAgent program," says one BzzAgent note. "84% of BzzAgents are on Facebook vs. 41% of the rest of the US adult population," says another.[7] Izea asserts that it "is the only company that can execute large scale, multi-faceted SMS [short message service] campaigns through proprietary marketplaces. Our publishers' blog posts, tweets, check-ins and tasks are distributed throughout the social web and propagated to the blogosphere, Twitter, Facebook, Foursquare, Google,

Bing, Yahoo! and countless others. Advertisers can reach the publishers' immediate peer group and beyond in a measurable and meaningful way."[8]

The number of online and off-line conversations started by those sparks may be large. They are also uncontrollable, potentially quite negative as well as positive. The fear that these unmonitored references may lead marketers to lose control over their ability to define their brands has sparked yet another set of businesses eking out money from advertisers. Established firms such as Nielsen and Dow Jones are vying with new names such as Visible Technologies and Radian6 to evaluate and further influence the digital conversations occurring among millions of bloggers—as well as on Facebook, Twitter, and other incarnations of the social-media landscape—on behalf of their clients. A report from the Forrester Research consulting firm concluded that "as more businesses build out their strategies, listening platforms—technology and analytics infrastructures that mine and analyze social media to deliver insight—become essential tools within the enterprise."[9]

One aim is to sift through the seemingly chaotic streams of text and talk to create what is referred to as "Social Intelligence"—that is, "the concept of informing marketing and business decisions with insights found in social media data."[10] Another goal is to influence that stream of conversations themselves by hiring people to inject the companies' viewpoints into the flow. The FTC edict that the company's voice be identified is hard to enforce when anonymous interactions are taking place. These conversation starters and the responses to them may themselves become part of the flow of messages tracked by an evolving group of "listening platforms," which employ various methods to evaluate the success of attempts at influencing brand discussions online. Among the metrics companies use are likelihood-to-recommend measures. Once such metric, for example, called the "Net-Promoter Score," uses listening platforms "to track and measure year-over-year improvement in customer advocacy."[11] Firms evaluate their returns on investment through such criteria as traffic to a website or a Facebook page, the number of "friends" a brand has on Facebook, and brand awareness. A key is the impact on social relations. One analyst notes, "A good measure of influence is whether people are willing to talk broadly about a brand experience and inspire others to take action not only in terms of a buying decision but also in terms of engaging their own personal networks. The 'network effect' of word of mouth can deliver ever-increasing value at little or no incremental cost."[12]

Much of this social intelligence becomes grist for advertising agencies that create their clients' commercial messages. Their goal is to figure out where to find likely targets for their clients' products, how to identify them, and how and to what extent the messages they send succeed in bringing back a return on their investment. Agencies want to have access to as much information as possible about their target audiences when they create earned-, owned-, and paid-media materials to steer them toward fan pages, websites, or purchases. Media planners and buyers warm to the conclusions of the listening platforms when the findings suggest the best earned- or paid-media outlets on which to place their messages.

By 2010, Facebook had the reputation as the strongest social-media outpost from which to mine data and find prospects. Marketers were further attracted to the site because companies can set up pages on Facebook in the same way that individuals can. Rohit Thawani, the Publicis social-media expert, noted that in the late 2000s companies "having a Facebook profile went from being socially savvy to having a mandate. Not having a Facebook page is like not having an 800 number."[13]

The fan page is especially important as a way to distill what listening platforms convey about people's attitudes toward a brand into articles, videos, games, and contests that leverage the brand's personality. Facebook tells the builder of a fan page the name and profile characteristics of every person visiting the page. What individuals say and do on the fan page might further add to their profile. The information can be used to glean additional knowledge from various off-line and online databases. That, in turn, can fuel a customer relationship management (CRM) campaign via e-mail or on the Web and elsewhere, tailored to specific individual profiles.

To attract people to a fan page, firms often announce the availability of coupons on it via ads throughout Facebook, on websites, and on other social-media vehicles, including Twitter. Marketers have also treated Facebook's *like* feature as a way fans can encourage others to visit fan sites. When people click that they "like" a fan site or a page on a website related to a product, the Facebook News Feed sends a message about that to their friends, hoping that this will lead them to visit the advertiser's Facebook site, thereby gaining more fans. The new fans' interactions with the brand then lead to more news feeds, which in turn might mean additional fans, and so on.

But this sort of friending on social-media sites—Facebook is only the most popular of the many such sites—is just the beginning of a new approach to identifying potential customers via online social networks. Facebook, Twitter, and even Google and Bing now accommodate social searching. While the results of traditional searches are based on noting how Web pages are linked to one another (see chapter 3), the outcomes of social search are based on what friends say to one another. Only 2.7 percent of searches were of the social type in 2010, and most were conducted to find people mentioned on Facebook, Twitter, and other social-media sites. Nevertheless, social-media experts are betting that over time the trend will shift toward social search as people conclude that their acquaintances' opinions can help them get better advice about products or anything else than they can get from search engines that link to websites that may or may not be trustworthy.

The results that tumble out of social searches do certainly reflect a much more active world of discussion than does traditional search. Type the words "mad men" into the Facebook search box and the resulting links reflect a cavalcade of interactions about the AMC cable television show. Results array around what Facebook members say about the show (on their so-called walls), Facebook members' discussion threads about it, and upcoming events connected to *Mad Men,* among other information. For each result, you can see how many people clicked that they "liked" it and view their comments. Gigya, a consulting firm that integrates businesses with online social networks, analyzes the logic of the search: the search results first display items pertaining to the search that the user has previously noted that he or she *liked* both on Facebook and on the Web. If the individual had already noted, for example, that he or she liked the website imdb.com (Internet Movie Database, which also lists TV series), then its discussion about *Mad Men* would be among these results. Next the results display relevant items the searcher's friends have *liked.* Then it displays relevant items other Facebook users have *liked.* If the user doesn't click on any of those results, Facebook also offers popular Facebook pages containing the searched term; posts by the searcher's friends that contain the search term; and Web results from Microsoft's Bing.com search engine on the search term "mad men."[14]

This approach to search places a new kind of importance on the click by relating it to the purposeful spread of information. Individuals must actively "*like*" or tweet, or click in some other way to indicate their desire to spread news about a person, place, or thing to social networks such as Twitter, Google Buzz, Facebook, StumbleUpon, Reddit, Delicious, Digg, and sphinn. The social search links the clickers and, by extension, their friends to personally vetted news. Gigya exhorts marketers to see this type of search as a crucial strategy for earned media work. It urges them to ensure that their products and activities wend their way into people's discussions in social media (the "semantic stream") and as *liked* places and things. In that way friends will point friends to the marketers' products, sites, and fan pages through social search without even knowing it.

Success in social search means urging visitors to share, Gigya advises in a report. It suggests that marketers set up connections to social networks on their Web pages and "content streams" (feeds of continually updated brand-related information sent to individuals on request via Web browsers). They should then encourage visitors to click on icons that start the social-media process. "Be sure," the report advises, "to give your visitors multiple options for sharing, as well as the ability to share to multiple feeds at once." This applies "to image, copy, links and more for every item shared. Be sure that each of these elements is optimized to drive the maximum number of return clicks whenever someone views it in a feed." Not only is this an opportunity to spread owned media to attract fans, it also is a way to spread earned media for that purpose. "Comments, reviews and forums are the most popular type of user-contributed content, and most of the platforms that offer these features are built with SEO [search engine optimization] in mind, but check that you are taking advantage of all of the tools available to structure the content. Also, be sure you are incorporating all of your content opportunities; for example if users can contribute recipes, photos or other rich content, ensure that it is also accessible and well-structured."[15]

The social-media sites on which people often end up as a result of things such as searches, friends' suggestions, discount coupons, or news/information articles also present special data-collection challenges to marketers. Facebook is a good example. Because it is a private preserve, cookies and the knowledge of firms such as BlueKai and eXelate are not helpful to marketers for learning about what people do on the social network. Instead, the data provider is primarily Facebook, which gathers an enormous amount of information about what everyone on its site does and then turns around and sells the ability to reach them anonymously with advertising based on the profiles that Facebook members have created for themselves. As Facebook members construct their profiles and then hide behind privacy settings, they probably don't know that these lockouts are irrelevant when it comes to advertisers. In offering the data anonymously, Facebook claims the right to use even aspects of profiles that members have chosen not to make public.

The targeting Facebook sells is therefore fairly robust, with the important caveat that the information is only as accurate as those who post it want it to be. The Facebook advertising engine lets any buyer choose individuals by exact age (or age range), geographical location, gender, relationship (single, engaged, in a relationship, married), and education level (college graduate, college student, high school student). It lets advertisers send messages to people on their birthday. It offers the marketer the ability to search profiles for, say, a specific workplace and an interest, and then to reach this group. For marketers working with agencies, Facebook opens up even more of its data storehouse. It allows them to target people when they are visiting their Facebook "home" pages, Facebook event pages, group pages, or applications such as the online game Farmville. Facebook also offers the option of reaching people who never go to applications or to fan, event, or group pages. It even provides the opportunity of connecting to friends of the targeted users.

Advertisers complain that despite such hearty targeting and discovery options, the actual kinds of ads Facebook allows on member pages are fairly small boxes that are not likely to jump out at visitors. One agency executive suggested that Facebook mandates the small ads because the company doesn't want to alienate members. It does allow videos and dramatic display ads—the kind that expand—but only on fan pages. It also charges marketers for helping to create fan pages so that the fan pages themselves will become advertisements that welcome targeted visitors with versions that reflect the marketer's impression of them. When individuals come to a fan page, the company hosting it automatically gets to see the person's profile data, which forms the basis of a dossier about him or her and which the advertiser may be able to connect with other information sources or Web registration data. What the person does and says on the fan page can add to the profile. One challenge for marketers is the situation in which individuals who are initially drawn to particular fan pages, often by coupons, might return to the pages only infrequently. Marketers therefore offer them attractive applications ("apps") from the fan page to place on their own Facebook pages. The aim of Facebook apps is to encourage fans to be in touch with, and click *like* on, new offers, contests, or other owned media activities at their own Facebook page. The applications have the additional benefit of being outside Facebook's control and therefore are able to track what people do in the app and report back to the marketing company's servers, further extending their profiles.

John Nitti, digital director at Publicis's media agency, ZenithOptimedia, notes that enticing people to download apps from a fan page is difficult.[16] Rather than being concerned about the lack of extensive tracking and profiling capabilities on Facebook, he tells his clients it is "best to think of a fan page as an ECRM [electronic customer relationship management] database"—a list of people who care about the marketer's product and whom you want to cultivate. "What you're seeing more and more," he explained, "is the desire to get people to like your brand and have them identify themselves. On Facebook, when they come to your fan page, they are automatically identified based on the profile, so that is a useful thing for marketers."

Despite these possibilities, the control the social network keeps over most of its truly social data has frustrated marketers, who want to know more about what people are doing there. That knowledge hole has created space for firms that have found ways to gather information about member relationships from Facebook and other social networks without their help. Called "social targeting" by some, the activity adds yet another set of data points for trying to identify people's potential and value as customers for particular products. The guiding proposition is, as the *Wall Street Journal* put it, "in the Internet age, a customer's friend is a potential customer."[17]

The offerings of Media6Degrees sit in the bull's-eye of this trend. The company collects social-graph information by mining ad-serving data. Each month it places Web beacons in ten billion display ads bought on social-networking sites such as Facebook. When one of those ads appears on a person's social-networking page, the beacon causes a cookie to be inserted in that person's browser. Let's call one of these individuals Lisa. The Media6Degrees cookie connected to Lisa's browser records the URLs of the people who visit Lisa's social-media page. It calculates the history and frequency of their visits as well as how often Lisa's visits to their pages prompted a return visit to Lisa's. These calculations create Lisa's "micro-affinity group"—those who are connected within Lisa's social network.

This kind of tracking lays the groundwork for cookie-driven, tailored advertising across all sorts of internet outlets away from Facebook. Let's say Lisa goes to the Avon cosmetics, perfume, and toy site and that her visit is recorded by a beacon placed on the website by Media6Degrees, which we'll say has been hired by Avon's media-buying firm. After Lisa leaves the website, Media6Degrees retargets her on other websites that she visits. But, Media6Degrees states, "That's just the beginning. Media6Degrees then delivers targeted Avon ads to Lisa's micro-affinity group on [a network of websites] across the web." Moreover, this process can continue with Lisa's friends. Some of them (usually ten for every one lead) will click on the Avon site and so will receive the Media6Degrees cookie. That, in turn, will lead Media6Degrees to track *her* social-media friends and send them Avon ads. All this is "massively scalable," the company says. "If Avon gets 2 million unique [visitors] a month to the home page[, and if] we find a 40% match rate in our social graph databases, [that will equal] 800,000 seed customers to retarget [multiplied by 10 to equal] 8 million customers to target from our social graph database. . . . [A]nd the cycle continues."[18]

While Media6Degrees begins its cookie distribution at social-networking sites, other firms track individuals from a wide variety of starting points. The social-network company 33Across, for example, "follows how consumers interact with one another—commenting on posts or sharing messages, for instance—across about 20 sites, online networks and third-party application companies, which build software like games and quizzes for social-networking sites."[19] 33Across says those sites reach a total of one hundred million unique U.S. visitors monthly; it also says it tracks five billion connections, then investigates them to determine the closest ties. That claim has to be taken on faith; 33Across and other social-network firms are not transparent with buying agencies (let alone with the public at large) about the technology they use to analyze connections. They also don't disclose the specific sites, that for a fee, agree to let the firms place cookies into consumers' browsers in order to track them. (Clearly, the sites don't want it known that they're permitting this.) Nevertheless, companies such as eBay and Sprint found that online sales exceeded their standard yields when they accepted 33Across's strategy of pursuing friends of customers. Joe Migliozzi, managing director of digital at WPP's Mindshare media-buying agency, noted that the use of social targeting is generally now assumed. "A lot of what goes into a purchase comes from a general conversation between you and your group," he told the *Wall Street Journal.* "We're identifying links between people."[20]

Media buyers are well aware that the emerging system won't be perfected for decades. They understand, too, that contemporary marketing logic points toward applying these developments in data collection, exchange, and use on the Web to individuals when they are on the go, engaging in such activities as taking a walk, driving around, or shopping. Local businesses—cleaners, haircutters, and restaurants—have an interest in opportunistic advertising to people who venture near their locations. Moreover, brick-and-mortar stores also have begun to realize the utility of personalized communication while shoppers are strolling their aisles. Consumer packaged-goods marketers particularly consider the retail environment to be the place where most of the final decisions about product purchases are made. Procter and Gamble CEO A. G. Lafley says that the "first moment of truth" for his firm takes place when the consumer stands in the supermarket or department store staring at a shelf holding P&G products.[21] In the past ten years Lafley has shifted the packaged-goods giant away from an almost singular focus on advertising outside the store toward the display and promotion of products in the retail environment itself. Retailers and other marketers have followed, and stores consequently have become cavalcades of print, billboard, shelf-card, and television outlets, all angling to woo the customer at those selection points.

In the past few years marketing executives increasingly say they want to carry out tracking, targeting, and personalization activities in as many venues as possible. As Seth Kaufman, director of media strategy for Pepsico North America, notes, "We are always looking for new technologies and emerging platforms."[22] Of all the emerging digital media, mobile media is now best positioned for advertising; one estimate of mobile internet users in the United States puts the figure at 91.4 million in April 2011, a 46 percent increase from 2009, and by 2013 that number is estimated to rise to 115.1 million—representing more than a third of the U.S. population.[23] More than phones, these devices are becoming multipurpose instruments. The Pew Internet & American Life Project found that, as of May 2010, nearly 38 percent of cellular telephone users in the United States—a total of 85.5 million people overall—said they had accessed the internet on their mobile device.[24] A year earlier this number was just one in four (25 percent—or 68.6 million people), and the rise reflected the growing popularity of so-called smart phones powered by Apple, Google (Android), and RIM (BlackBerry) operating systems. An eMarketer online industry newsletter headline concluded pithily that "mobile content soars thanks to device and network advances."[25] At the start of 2011, the actual amount of money spent on mobile-phone advertising—estimated at several hundred million dollars—is minor compared with the almost $25 billion dropped on a variety of banner, rich-media, and video ads on the Web. Those numbers don't include owned or earned media, but even if they were included the Web numbers are still likely to be far higher than the mobile figures. Nevertheless, the logic of mobile's ad growth is inescapable—a major reason being the sheer ubiquity of the connected device and people's apparent dependence on it. As eMarketer noted, "Mobile phones have become a staple of daily life, so much so that most consumers can hardly imagine going through the day without one by their side. The reliance on mobile devices for just about everything makes mobile a platform that content publishers and marketers cannot afford to ignore."[26]

As a result of the surge in mobile devices, publishers that have been taking in advertising on the Web have been streaming in this new direction. Until the mid-2000s, the major mobile carriers—Verizon, AT&T, Sprint, and T-Mobile—made it difficult for advertisers to reach customers on their phones without the carriers' consent. With the rise of sophisticated mobile Web browsers that could accommodate cookies and rich-text ads, the carriers had to accede that targeted advertising would be a fact of mobile life. Advertising networks that serve ads specifically to publishers on mobile devices offer a variety of banner, rich-text, and video ads that mimic Web ads in their capability. Google's AdMob, for example, touts its advantages for both brand advertisers ("the ability to reach the addressable mobile audiences . . . onto the top mobile sites") and direct marketers ("we offer performance advertisers sophisticated targeting capabilities and low-cost customer acquisition with measurable return on investment"). "Sophisticated targeting capabilities" and "addressab[ility]" imply sophisticated data collection, and a case study on the AdMob website about the way the network helped Universal Pictures and its agency Ignite promote the movie *Wolfman* suggests a mirror of Web-world enticements to click, including banners, text ads, a variety of screen coverings hot-linked to the movie's website.[27]

What makes mobile devices especially tantalizing for advertisers is that the devices can transmit their owner's location. In 2010 and 2011, two such models received considerable attention. One involved a person walking near a restaurant that had contracted with a publisher whose app the person has on his phone. An instant phone message appears, informing the individual of the restaurant and offering a discount coupon for dining there. The other model involves a social-network publisher such as Foursquare. When Foursquare users "check in" at a participating location (such as a bar, a park, or a museum) via an iPhone app, SMS, or mobile site—that is, inform Foursquare that the user is at a particular location—the service tells friends on Foursquare that you are there. You also accumulate points that eventually enable you to become "mayor" of that location (awarded to those with the most days checked at a particular venue over the past sixty days) or get other badges that reinforce the use of the service. The company also has partnerships with activity-oriented firms such as Runkeeper, a mobile application for tracking your running and jogging activity. When users connect their accounts, they can earn Foursquare badges for running a marathon, among other activities. And, in the manner of Facebook, Foursquare has also created a button that will add any location in the app to the user's to-do list, and it will serve a reminder when the user is near to-do items. The company has extended this effort beyond the app so that publishers can include an "Add to Foursquare" button on their websites.

This means that if you're reading on a website about a restaurant that appeals to you, you can click on this button, and the restaurant will be added to your to-do list.[28]

Foursquare's revenue model and the sharing of individual data that comes from it won't be a surprise to anyone who has been reading this book:

- Foursquare centers on discreetly gathering up enormous amounts of information about the travels of its members. It explores the interconnections of friends on the network and their implications for actions, creates categories out of those data that will attract marketers, and sells to businesses the ability to send advertisements to anonymous people linked to those categories. The longer of Foursquare's two privacy policies states that "we receive and store any information you enter on our Service or provide to us in any other way."[29]

- To increase the Foursquare population, tie into what all those people are doing, and analyze members' social networks as part of its data mining, the company encourages members to "add friends." It exhorts new members that "Foursquare is more fun when you connect with your friends. Your friends can see the email address and phone number you gave us when so signed up, so choose wisely." The service then encourages joiners to "scan my address book," "find Twitter friends," and "Find Facebook friends." Of course, by giving Foursquare access to your Facebook profile, you're giving it still more data about you. You've also added a stream of new data for the Facebook and/or Twitter computers to ponder. Moreover, the encouragement to check in at participating locations does not remind you that this and other Foursquare actions can be viewed by subscribers to those services—plus, in the case of Twitter they may be discoverable by search engines. That bit of information shows up only in one of Foursquare's privacy policies.[30]

- Foursquare's attempts to gain advertisements involve more than just selling marketers the opportunity to reach particular types of individuals at locations near their establishments. To its members Foursquare trumpets the fact that advertisers offer discounts or other rewards for people who click on their ads or present them at the establishment. But the blandishments are a clear prelude to data mining. When a person connects to Foursquare via a browser on either a computer or a mobile device, the advertiser's cookies are served onto your device to collect information about you during return visits to the site. Many of those cookies are served by ad networks that then have the ability to connect the information to other information they accumulate about you, match it with offline data, and sell it on exchanges.

Although Foursquare, its advertisers, and its ad networks can drop cookies into visitors' mobile browsers, they cannot track people on their mobile devices through technologies such as apps, which do not accept cookies. Apps do allow for storing an individual's ID, log-in information, or MAC address (a unique identifier stored in the device's hardware) so that the server of the company that created the app will recognize the person when he or she returns. Apps also allow for the presentation of personalized advertising, discounts, news, and other tailored information a publisher wants to convey. Consequently, if Foursquare used a mobile ad network to serve advertisements in its website, the company likely would do the same thing in its apps. An important difference between Web browsers and mobile browsers is that most mobile browsers prohibit access to third-party advertising firms such as BlueKai and eXelate. At present, at least, publishers are on their own when data collecting in the mobile space.

To overcome these limits, a few startup firms have begun pushing a startling idea: get rid of cookies and completely overhaul the way devices are targeted and tracked. The notion was just beginning to percolate in 2011 as BlueCava, Ringleader Digital, and a few other firms announced techniques called "device fingerprinting," in which a mobile phone or desktop PC transmits bits of information about its properties and settings when it connects to the internet. According to the online marketing publication ClickZ, "These individual signals can be collected and pieced together to form a unique, persistent 'fingerprint' for that specific device. That fingerprint can then be assigned an identifying number, and used for similar purposes as a cookie."[31] Creators contend that the technology applies not only to mobile devices but to any device with a data connection. David Norris, BlueCava's chairman, says that his firm's "ultimate goal is to replace the cookie. Cookies are temporary tattoos that fade away, but [fingerprints] don't fade away. Cookies had their point in time, but we've moved far enough along for a more sophisticated system now."[32]

But no matter whether tracking is done with fingerprinting in the future or with cookies today, mobile presents another drawback from a publisher's standpoint: the dilemma of identifying people who connect to networks with different devices. That problem typically doesn't affect Foursquare because it requires you to log on with an identity that reflects your name, so whether you log on to Foursquare on your laptop, your iPad, or your Blackberry, it will know you and collect your data based on what you do on any of these devices. But sites that do not require registration and that rely on cookies to note identities can't do this. They may well collect data about you continuously from the browsers and applications of your mobile devices, but the sites' servers would have no idea whether information about you also resides in their databases of materials collected when you use your personal computer's browser.

As you might imagine, the major Web-portal publishers—Google, Facebook, Yahoo!, Microsoft—would like advertisers to know that they will tap into their databases of individuals and their activities on as many networked devices as possible to locate likely customers and determine the arguments that will persuade them at a particular moment and location. To do this they need consumers to identity themselves on every machine they use—and this is a major reason that these publishers create services that require exactly that. For example, if you register for one of Google's many products, such as Gmail Buzz or maps, and you log in to Google at least once on each of your devices, Google can chart your cross-machine trail every time you connect with any of the millions of publishers that affiliate with Google for display-advertising purposes. Depending on the networked device, it notes your existence by dropping a cookie in the browser or creating an ID in an app. (This sort of matching would take place with fingerprinting, too.)

With megapublishers Google, Microsoft, Yahoo!, and Facebook doing brisk advertising business across devices, smaller Web publishers, advertising networks, and exchanges will consider cross-media connections with consumers a major competitive threat. Firms such as Foursquare have built-in reasons for getting you to identify yourself. Major Web publishers that haven't required registration—CBS, CNN, and Indystar, for example—will be trying more than ever to persuade you to self-identify, sometimes enticing you with the offer of points or coupons. Firms that don't have the audience clout or engagement to encourage registration will have to settle for dealing with populations on each device separately, with only rare knowledge of cross-platform connections. To stand out from their cross-device competitors, these firms will offer media buyers information about individuals that Google, Microsoft, Yahoo!, and Facebook won't give them. Recall, for example, that Facebook currently does not allow sponsors to follow their targets around the social network. This restriction irks some marketers. They will therefore also flock to publishers and publisher networks that can give them device-by-device knowledge of audiences but in more flexible ways than those offered by the portals and major publishers.

One journey that even the megapublishers can't take with their members at this point involves the end point of the long click, the final purchase of a product. Facebook typically cannot tell whether you ultimately bought a TV—and, if so, which TV—after the queries, searches, explorations, discussions, and comparisons you pursued on any of your mobile or other devices. Advertisers typically are unable to determine whether an ad for a television set that you received on your computer or mobile device led you either to use any of these devices or to travel to a brick-and-mortar store to purchase the product. One way marketers and publishers have tried to resolve this question is by offering an electronic coupon. Although its tracking capabilities are currently limited, the lowly coupon is undergoing developments that may result in its becoming a routine vehicle for tracing individuals backward from their purchases through many of their earlier media encounters.

As the *New York Times* noted in 2010, the coupons' bar codes "can be loaded with a startling amount of data, including identification about the customer, internet address, Facebook page information and even the search terms the customer used to find the coupon in the first place."[33] Sending you a digital coupon at a moment when you appear interested does more than stimulate a sale. It can help the marketer, which has been accruing lots of information about you, decide how to target you in the future. Of course, tracking via coupons has its limits; you don't often present coupons when you buy a dresser, for example, or a car. This could change for individuals identified as valued consumers, however, if the model currently developing in supermarkets and other mass retailers gets traction throughout the retail world.

Historically, these types of retail operations have already accumulated loads of data about their customers through frequent shopper cards. Supermarkets are a particularly interesting case because Americans probably shop there more regularly than at any other type of outlet. Moreover, the discounts for customers who use frequent shopper cards (all the major chains offer these cards) are so substantial that 90 percent of those retailers' customers use them. But while these chains have amassed huge amounts of information, they have not applied them in sophisticated ways to parse customers into different shopping reputations, even though executives have long talked about doing exactly that. Furthermore, supermarkets that have engaged in personalized discounting activities mostly have not drawn on data about individuals beyond their relationships with those stores. Stop & Shop and Albertson's have, for example, experimented for years with electronic kiosks that link to prior buying behavior as a way of offering information and discounts. They have used cart-based and handheld devices to track shoppers as they move through the store and offer them different discounts based on their buying histories. Most chains have websites from which people can order online, choose discount coupons, and produce shopping lists.[34]

Only quite recently, though, have supermarket chains made systematic attempts to trace customers and their attributes beyond the supermarkets' own orbits. Coupons and discount information lie at the core of these activities. Some chains engage with customers on Twitter, Facebook, and Foursquare. Some participate in mobile electronic coupon schemes (Kroeger works with the Cellfire firm, for example), which drop cookies and other identifiers into devices to supply information to the retailers. But the most far-reaching attempt to extend beyond their own sites and into the larger internet is being driven by a company that is not a supermarket but an umbrella provider of couponing to supermarkets as well as to other firms: Catalina Marketing.

Catalina runs a kind of Google Adsense for supermarkets, pharmacies, and mass merchandisers in that it serves ads to people based on keywords (that is, the names of purchased products) along with lots of statistical analyses of anonymous background information about them. It works this way: Using revenue-sharing deals, Catalina has placed printers that issue coupons at the checkouts of forty-two thousand outlets throughout the United States. Major retailers such as Safeway, Kroeger's, K-Mart, Acme, Winn/Dixie, and Walgreens dispense the Catalina promotions. (They are the long coupons separate from your receipt you may receive as you leave the checkout stand.) The stores provide Catalina with demographic and other data about every customer, stripped of any personally identifying characteristics; Catalina's identifying vehicle is the number on the frequent shopper card. In this way, Catalina claims, it follows the purchases of people in ninety million households.[35] Manufacturers buy exclusive twenty-seven-day chunks for promotions in their product categories on the Catalina network. Catalina sells the coupon positions to advertisers, and customers receive the coupons based on predictive models encompassing billions of transactions. As a result, two people who are purchasing the same over-the-counter pharmacy item may receive promotions for different products, or the same promotions with different discounts.

In explaining its approach, Catalina adopts a truism retailers use (often dubbed Pareto's Principle) that 20 percent of shoppers account for

80 percent of a product's sales. The goal is to carry out statistically based targeting to determine who fits into the 20 percent group for any particular product and to serve them tailored advertisements and discounts to attract them. As the company website suggests, the driving force behind its operation reflects the same desire to sift out profitable customers that motivates marketing in the wider digital environment:

> The effectiveness of traditional (mass) advertising has been reduced by channel proliferation and technology (user-generated content, DVRs, podcasting etc.). Additionally, a greater emphasis is now placed on accountability and attaining a justifiable return on investment (ROI) for each promotional endeavor. Shopper-driven marketing allows you to make decisions based on actual shopper purchase insights, linking the effectiveness of precision marketing with cost per performance to provide marketers with a measurability that previously never existed.
>
> Prioritizing the 20% of shoppers that account for 80% of a product's (or category's) volume is the key to minimizing promotional waste. Specific promotions and advertising communicated to the most profitable shoppers (the 20% or less), ultimately increases your efficiency and delivers a higher ROI for your efforts. . . . Catalina Marketing is the ONLY solution that can provide you with the actionable insight to effectively reach your best shoppers. The times have changed—primitive methods of reaching your shoppers have been replaced with a sophisticated measurable medium.[36]

The company offers a range of options aimed at helping marketers and stores, including the ability to advertise on its coupons and the ability to "reach specific households based on 65 weeks of past purchases insights. By accessing category and brand-level data, you can segment households based on product usage (brand loyals, switchers, competitive users and category never-buys) as well by lifestyle segments. Brands and retailers can then deliver customized offers to influence shoppers' future purchases." Catalina claims that its coupon redemption rates fall in the 6–10 percent range, which, it says, "corresponds to eight times that of traditional mass couponing methods."[37] It also states its coupons advertisements yield "proven shopper-driven advertising results—increasing awareness by 16% points, recall by 24% points and volume lift up to 35%."[38]

Despite these impressive claims, Catalina's management seems to be well aware of the long-term flaw in the firm's model: it identifies people and gives them coupons after they have been through the store, anticipating that they will redeem them on a return visit. By that time, however, many "best customers" will have lost the coupons or forgotten them at home. Another drawback is that Catalina has focused on only one electronic device: the customer checkout. Recently the company's leaders have recognized that, with modeling and computing power that rival those of Facebook, they should know more about what their clients' best customers are doing digitally outside the stores to help them better predict their buying habits.

The company's strategic remedy to both problems, begun in earnest during 2010, was to initiate what a press release called its "expansion into the growing digital space."[39] As part of this move the company hired its first digital-centered executive, Chris Henger, and embarked on a test of mobile coupons with ShopRite and other stores. In various press releases the company stressed that Henger had been an executive with the Google Affiliate Network, which, as this Google site notes, "connects advertisers and publishers who want to increase sales and drive leads through affiliate marketing."[40] Clearly his ability to deal with different parties in marketing relationships was a key to Catalina's interest in him. But knowledge of Web marketing and perhaps marketing on other devices seems also to have been crucial.

In view of Google's cross-device ambitions, it may not be much of a stretch to infer that Catalina's hiring of a Google executive may even have been a way into an allegiance with Google to work together on personalized advertisements, promotions, and data mining. The strategy would bring additional revenues to both companies without subjecting them to the withering regulatory scrutiny that would ensue if Google tried to buy Catalina. A joint venture between the two conjures up a marketer's dream: following signed-in customers from their movements on the Web, the iPad, the phone, and other digital technologies through to their physical presence in supermarkets, mass-retailers, pharmacies, and, ultimately, at checkout. To conform to its privacy policy, Google would not pass along customer names without their permission, and Catalina would undoubtedly try to persuade the individuals accordingly.

This specific linkup may or may not come to pass, but clearly the industry logic supporting the interaction of store information tied to individuals with specific data about them gathered broadly is very much the next step in implementing the long click. Google CEO Eric Schmidt suggested this direction in an interview with the *Wall Street Journal* in 2010. The information Google has collected about virtually every individual, he said, means that "we know roughly who you are, roughly what you care about, roughly who your friends are." And, as the article goes on to note, Google also knows, to a foot, where you are. "Mr. Schmidt leaves it to a listener to imagine the possibilities: If you need milk and there's a place nearby to get milk, Google will remind you to get milk. It will tell you a store ahead has a collection of horse-racing posters, that a 19th century murder you've been reading about took place on the next block. Says Mr. Schmidt, a generation of powerful handheld devices is just around the corner that will be adept at surprising you with information that you didn't know you wanted to know." Schmidt goes on in the article to say that individual targeting "will be so good it will be very hard for people to watch or consume something that has not in some sense been tailored for them. . . . As you go from the search box [to the next stage of Google], you really want to go from syntax to semantics, from what you typed to what you meant."[41]

To Schmidt, the message for marketers is that Google will know a lot about what a particular person needs at any given time. As a result, likely the advertisements it serves up next to content on its display network will increasingly be the most suitable ones and so will lead to the clicks the marketers want. For society, a more important message is that the profiles Google intends to create about us will ultimately augment what we say and do with profiles based on statistical inferences. Google will create statistical probabilities about attributes we have, beliefs we espouse, and actions we will take at particular times. This approach is not totally new; predicting a person's mortgage-payment reliability based on the reliability of that individual's Web friends is one example (see discussion of the tracking company Rapleaf in the Introduction). But the enormity of Google's mission to make social inferences a major part of its business means that the labels people receive will affect the commercial messages and offers that increasingly surround them across a variety of digital devices. Google may share with partners (such as Catalina, if that alliance takes place) the inferences it makes about the people to whom it shows display ads in its contextual advertising network. If so, this information may affect the inferences those partners use in spawning their own ads for those individuals—in turn broadening the reach of Google's labeling process.

What is more, when Schmidt told the *Wall Street Journal* his company would remind people to buy milk, he was indicating to marketers that Google wants to have the ability to infer what products people want to buy and to serve them ads and prices for products that suit those needs. "I actually think most people don't want Google to answer their questions," Schmidt elaborated. "They want Google to tell them what they should be doing next."[42] By stressing the trust implied in letting Google tell people what they should be doing next, Schmidt was also implying that his firm would have their trust in using their data to assess their future interests, friendships and activities. In so doing, Google will be turning profiles into reputations for marketers. That is, Google will help them decide that certain demographic, lifestyle, friendship, and personality markers make people targets for particular types of businesses—or that an individual is not considered useful for any of them. This, too, is not a new impulse. The data-management company Lotame has already been rating individuals on their potential interest in particular products. But Google's movement into defining reputations will probably ratchet up the attractiveness that publishers and data firms find in adding individuals' predictive value directly into their profile. At the same time, these people will receive increasingly consistent reputations as targets or waste across many devices and retail categories.

Schmidt's preoccupation with retail data analysis, discount coupons, and friending in the mobile as well as the PC space may suggest that disseminators of news, information, and entertainment are being marginalized in the social-mobile world. These sorts of publishers certainly don't believe they should be marginalized, and they also want to be involved in reaching out to likely customers through selling advertising in as many devices as possible. But publishers of professionally produced materials likely will have to try harder and harder to prove the value of their sites for targeting. They face stiff competition from the many opportunities marketers have to reach people among the blizzard of tweets, friendship messages, e-mails, and discount coupons. At the very least, publishers will try to serve tailored ads with articles or videos that they have found lead particular individuals to stay longer on the site—so they will see yet more ads. YouTube's decision to place Demand Media stories that support the commercial messages next to them will become a model for certain publishers. For some, an unabashed erosion of the church-state wall will lead them to work with marketers to serve advertisements together with packages of information, entertainment, soft news, and maybe even hard news that fit individuals' profiles, predict attention to the ad, and may even reflect the content of the ad. Advertisers with clout might be able to get one of those publishers to place articles or videos that are actually public-relations plants for the advertiser (earned media) next to its ads.

This emerging trajectory suggests that apart from a relatively few elite-oriented publishers (*New York Times, Atlantic,* and the like), the pressure to bring personalization synced to marketing goals will be difficult for companies to avoid if they want to survive. As reputations of individuals and niche groups get distributed widely around the Web and across devices, people will increasingly note that the offers, ads, and soft news they receive seem to reflect a particular view of them. Some may find the juxtaposition of similar ad and editorial topics startling at first, and they may wonder why certain themes keep recurring in the text and video soft news pieces that a number of their favorite publishers send to them. If they ask, the publishers will assure them that it's another step in making their media experiences relevant to their daily lives and that it's all OK because it's done anonymously. They might hear, too, that, as the CEO of the Arbitron research firm told the *New York Times Magazine* in 2005, "Every age group, every cultural group and every demographic group . . . is in the process of getting media packaged expressly for its members."[43] As we have seen, industry logic suggests that publishers will learn that to compete they must create advertiser-driven packages.

Now imagine your television set getting into this act. Such a development will extend the advertising system's new power profoundly. "TV matters in a way that nothing else does," James McQuivey of Forrester Research wrote in 2010. "Each year in the US alone, the TV drives roughly $70 billion in advertising. . . . Plus, viewers spend as many as 4.5 hours a day with TV." Google is well aware that, although media buying on the Web and on mobile devices is growing strong, these endeavors will for the foreseeable future represent a small percentage of the advertising pie compared with the big screen at home. Consequently, McQuivey concluded, "if you're Google and you want to know where the next advertising dollars you'll appropriate are, you need look no further than the TV."[44]

McQuivey was referring to a recently announced initiative in which Google had joined with technology firms such as Sony and Logitech to create easy links from television sets to the internet. A specially designed Google search engine would be the organizing mechanism that helps people decide what to watch: "Some have asked," McQuivey said, "why Google, which takes nearly $7 billion into its coffers each quarter from that little old search engine it sports, would care about the old-world TV technology in the living room." His response, which points to $70 billion advertisers currently pay annually to air their ads, explains not only why the Google advertising engine has invaded the television industry. It also suggests why several firms with digital expertise have been working to turn the traditional television viewing environment into an interactive domain built around their technologies and business models. At this point in the competition, it's impossible to be sure which parties will control "living room" television—that is, large-screen, home-based sets—in the coming decades. As McQuivey notes, though, it's clear that whoever is in charge will share the same basic goal that marketers have long championed for the internet: "the ability to put the right ad in front of the right person and then have them click on it if they want to know more."[45]

Consider, then, that the online advertising developments as they unfolded from 1994 through 2011 represented a kind of Spanish Civil War—that is, an armament testing ground—for marketers. It was the place where fundamental components for future engagements across new territories were introduced, tested, altered, honed, and put into regular use on the Web. Now marketers and publishers are trying to ensure that they can apply marketing strategies, tactics, and technologies used for the Web and mobile devices to the home television screen. The coming decades will involve improving and extending the tools of personalization for advertising and editorial matter, and television will inevitably be at the center.

The transformation of the living-room television set into an outlet for the new media-planning-and-buying system will amplify what advertisers, their agencies, and their data providers are already doing in their moves to colonize the Web and mobile spaces. In fact, contemporary activities suggest there eventually will be little difference between the "internet" and "television" in terms of advertisers' approach to people and their data. Two different groups of industry actors, logics, and technologies are pushing in that direction. One aims to directly connect the internet to the television set, perhaps linked to a search engine as an organizing mechanism. The other involves turning traditional cable and satellite services into channels that are "addressable"—that is, open to targeting and interactivity based on knowledge about the household. It's not hard to see that the two sets of developments can eventually converge.

Adding addressability to cable and satellite services is the older of the two ideas. Technology to allow interaction with subscription-TV transmissions to get viewing information, download streams of text, and make purchases goes back a few decades. It is only during the past few years, however, that technology firms, cable companies, and marketers have begun work on systems that would allow the selective targeting of commercials to narrow geographic areas and even to individual households based on what the cable firm and marketers know about the recipients.

Media buyers and their clients who historically have bought TV time have mixed views about these developments. On the down side, they voice concern about their declining ability to reach the mass audience. Since the 1950s television has been the greatest crowd catcher in history. It has been the place where marketers of appliances, packaged goods, financial services, and automobiles—the Frigidaires, Krafts, Charles Schwabs, and Fords of the world—could turn when they wanted to speak efficiently to almost every U.S. household. And that's not hyperbole. From the mid-1960s through the mid-1980s it was possible to place commercials on CBS, NBC, and ABC in the evening—prime time—and reach around 90 percent of all the households in America with their sets on. That typically translated to more than 60 percent of all homes. Moreover, despite the high prices the networks charged, the cost-per-thousand viewers for this mass marketing was still highly competitive with other media because of the huge numbers reached.

As the spread of cable and satellite subscriptions accelerated in the late 1980s and into the 1990s the fragmentation of audiences followed the fragmentation of channels. The rise of broadband internet further splintered the audience. Now commercials on those three still-major networks reach only about 30 percent of households during a typical prime-time period. Added to TV buyers' concerns was viewers' rising use of the digital video recorder (DVR) to watch programs during periods convenient for them (an activity called *time-shifting*) that often led to commercial-skipping. By 2010 the DVR could be found in approximately 20 percent of U.S. homes, and media buyers worried that their careful decisions to buy TV slots on particular dates were being derailed by viewing on other days and fast-forwarding or changing channels during their commercials. In response, Nielsen Research worked with networks and agency buyers to change the measurement for evaluating TV away from viewing programs to viewing commercials. National ratings today are reported on a "C3" basis, meaning that Nielsen reports viewing numbers for commercial spots within and around shows. It also reports the viewing of those commercials on DVRs up to three days beyond the recording of the program. Media buyers see the approach as a compromise with network executives, who worried about the effect rating commercials rather than programs would have on their revenues. But buyers note the rise of DVRs, and especially viewing commercials beyond three days of their original airing, as potentially weakening the precision of the advertising plans. Commercials viewed "late" have often lost their relevance to an advertising campaign and are difficult to track against sales results. A 2008 Forrester Research report noted, "As television loses control of its own viewing, it loses the power to deliver the impact that advertisers want."[46]

One response by marketers to the splintering of TV and the rise of the internet has been to use increasing amounts of their advertising money to press various forms of targeting in the digital world. Although just a few years ago the money spent on digital media ads was no more than 5 percent of the advertising budget, by the early 2010s some major marketers were spending around 15 percent, and the numbers were inching upward.[47] Some observers point to the relatively small percentage of money spent on advertising with major publishers as a mark of digital media's relative marginalization from mainstream media buying. Others respond that 15 percent of billions of dollars goes a long way in still-inexpensive environments such as the Web and mobile devices. Nevertheless, the consensus is that constituencies in major marketing firms and their agencies are quite conservative and that the impulse to continue mass marketing is strong. The tension has been evident since the 1990s. As Clay Shirky noted back in 1999, "Broadcast TV can charge higher prices for fewer households because the mass marketers simply have nowhere else to go. Despite the increasingly anemic performance of the most popular TV shows, there isn't another medium that offers the option of reaching 10 million households at the same time with a single ad—even giant portal sites fragment their reach across a number of offerings." He added: "It is obvious that both the networks and their advertisers are soon going to have to adapt to a fragmented media market where nothing regularly reaches 20 million people, and the only way to get mass will be niche plus niche plus niche. In the meantime, though, old habits die hard, and it is these old habits of looking for mass that are driving ad rates up for hit shows even as those shows lose the very audience that makes them valuable."[48]

The need to "soon" adopt to a fragmented media took more than a decade. A vocal though uneven push came from the cable television industry. In 2008 a powerful group of multisystem operators including Comcast, Time Warner Cable, Cox Communications, and Cablevision joined together to form what they called the Project Canoe consortium. The name referred to the notion that the companies must work together to achieve a common goal: create technologies that would allow the partners and eventually other cable firms to implement *addressability*. The *New York Times* saw Canoe's creation as "an effort to slow Google's siphoning of advertising dollars away from television." The article quoted industry analyst Craig Moffett, who said that "the investment community has been waiting for addressability for a generation. . . . But it was never going to happen without a coalition of the cable operators." The *Times* explained: "Here is what is at stake. Combined, the nation's cable operators generate about $5 billion in revenue from selling local advertising in markets where they own the infrastructure to people's homes, a small slice of the $70 billion television advertising pot. They largely compete with local newspapers and radio stations. But Project Canoe will allow the industry to sell ads on a nationwide basis through a joint platform." The article also noted that marketers and their buying agencies had a major role in pushing the consortium forward. It took "prodding from media buyers for General Motors and Procter & Gamble" as well as Publicis's Starcom media agency for the cable executives to get into gear about setting up a separate company with a mandate to change the industry.[49]

To pilot Canoe, the consortium chose David Verklin, an advertising executive who had done much to redefine the nature and importance of media buying during the 1980s and 1990s. Verklin was the head of U.S. operations for the media-buying agency Carat as it grew from $600 million in annual billings to $5 billion, demonstrating to the ad industry that stand-alone media agencies were viable. In addition, Verklin was an early believer among media buyers that digital technologies were fundamentally going to change the ways consumers interacted with advertising and other content. Now the cable consortium was anticipating that he could bring that knowledge to the other side with the hope of convincing buyers to pay more than they had previously for cable advertising. The reason: targeting—"delivering dog-food ads to dog-food owners," as he famously put it.[50]

The enthusiasm for personalized cable advertising echoed what many were saying about the Web, ratcheted up by a belief that two-way, set-top boxes installed by cable firms could beat internet companies in knowledge about households and even individuals. "Addressable advertising on television is in many ways the holy grail, because it can offer ever more targeting ability than Google," said Craig Moffett, a senior analyst at Sanford C. Bernstein & Company.[51] Others invoked the internet's utility for cordoning off audiences based on their value. Kris Magel, director of national broadcast at Interpublic's Initiative agency, compared the possibilities of Canoe to contextual and behavioral targeting on the Web. "The goal of the entire effort is raise the value and effectiveness of inventory for advertisers." The problem with the current mass-media model, he said, is all "the waste built into it." He noted that even targeted cable channels such as the Food Network could benefit financially from being able to change ads based upon who is watching.[52]

While Canoe is the most heavily financed targeting operation in the cable business, it isn't the only one. Cablevision has also experimented with targeting via its own technology outside the consortium. Two addressable technology companies are Invidi, owned by WPP, and Visible World, an independent operation. The logic of the Web permeates the firms' activities and rhetoric. A partnership between Visible World and Interpublic's Cadreon advertising exchange seems to be preparing for the possibility of bringing Web information about audiences to the cable environment. In 2010 Cadreon was able to track individuals who appeared to be researching new car purchases on the Web and then use Visible World's personalization platform on cable TV systems to place appropriate commercials in front of those same individuals. The partnership's goal is to increase the ability to personalize commercials based on inferences from more and more data. Cadreon CEO Brendan Moorcroft told *AdWeek* that Visible World "brings an infrastructure for ad serving to TV not unlike what Atlas or Doubleclick do [online]. It allows us to apply intelligence for TV buying like you do for the Internet." And if it were unclear to observers that people's reputations behind the screen would be the drivers of commercial messages, he added: "For the first time you'll see real scale [in the targeted space] with hundreds of ads seen by millions of people, all determined by algorithms and data as opposed to human instinct."[53]

Although personalized cable advertising had made progress by 2010, it had yet to catch the imagination or the pocketbooks of the cable and marketing industry. "The technology is here and we're doing [addressable ad deals] today," said Visible World president Tara Walpert Levy, though she acknowledged that it was not being done on a mass scale.[54] Both economical and technical factors are behind the reasons why the pieces haven't quite come together. Serving personalized ads across different cable systems that use a variety of set-top boxes means that the targeting hardware has to adapt to a variety of speed and memory requirements. For Canoe, with the largest ambition to personalize ads across systems, that has proven particularly frustrating. Another difficulty involves sorting out who gets the money from the ads when the technology serves them. Canoe, for example, provides the means to serve household-related commercials, but local cable systems control the activity. Each cable system would have to get permission for the ad to be placed on the cable network the advertiser has chosen. Those networks do allow local systems to sell a couple of minutes per hour without getting permission, but, for large-scale targeting to take place, the networks would have to give their consent. They would also probably demand a part of the revenue, as would Canoe. It is quite a job to sort out these economic issues in ways that satisfy many networks as well as many cable systems across the country. Nevertheless, it seems likely that marketers' increasing desire for targeting as well as competition from internet advertising on feeds streaming to the home set will push the parties to find ways around the financial and technical logjams.

Internet feeds streaming to the home set has also been a work in progress for several years. Even though they provide broadband service to millions of their subscribers, cable systems have not invited the broadband feed into the big TV's set-top box. The reluctance has involved turf battles and fears by producers, networks, and advertisers that Web streams would overwhelm traditional television and that they need to protect it. As late as 2010, Tom Cuniff, an executive at the marketing firm Combe Interactive Communications, wrote that "there is a long and fairly pointless war" being fought between the forces of "old" television and the new interactive, social media. He believes that advertisers, producers, and networks should see both as involved in a symbiotic "feedback loop," where they "not only can co-exist, they are now utterly interdependent. People Twitter about what they saw on TV. Hollywood makes a TV series from Twitter sensation *Sh*t My Dad Says*. The future isn't one side wins and the other loses. The future is a feedback loop."[55]

Fitting into this loop is one of the goals of Google Television, which is actually one of a number of developments from firms outside the cable industry that aim to link the internet to the living-room TV. A major difference among these participants is along hardware and software lines. While firms such as Microsoft, Apple, and various television set manufacturers focus mostly on physical devices (Xbox, Apple TV, Samsung TV) that will bring Web streams as well as Web-related applications into the big set, Google's interest is its open-source software that invites hardware partners that link TVs to the Web to add Google Television to their products. Google's aim here is much like its goal on the Web: to organize television via search so that people will use Google Television instead of individual channels as a starting point for viewing.

Despite the infighting and the reluctance among key actors, most observers were sure that the question was not whether most television sets would accept the internet, but when. In part they reached this conclusion because so much of "television" had already moved online that people wanted to watch it on their big screens. By 2011 many people were already downloading broadcast and cable network entertainment and news shows from iTunes, streaming them to their laptops and desktops via websites such as Hulu.com and

MySpace, illegally downloading them via the peer-to-peer file sharing protocol BitTorrent, and viewing them on their mobile devices through applications such as Mobi-TV. A number of manufacturers were already selling Web-enabled television sets. And many people without the newest sets were plugging their laptops into their televisions and watching the internet on the bigger screen that way.

For the large segment of the U.S. population involved in at least some of these internet-to-TV activities, it is no longer clear what *watching television* means. Asking the question, Have you watched any TV in the past day? has become complicated: it's not clear whether the answer should reflect all the alternate paths to network programming. It also isn't apparent whether an affirmative response should include programs specifically made for the Web. The headline of a September 2010 article by the Web magazine *Fast Company* declared, "Television on the Web Is Redefining Must-See Viewing."[56] The article argued acerbically that network TV is a "yawn," while "on the Web, new media networks like Funny or Die and performers such as Felicia Day are producing imaginative shows that redefine must-see viewing—whether you watch on an iPad or a Web-enabled TV." *Fast Company* went on to highlight a variety of businesses, such as Funny or Die and NextNewNetworks, that distribute their professionally produced programs across a variety of Web nodes, including iTunes, MSN, Hulu.com, and Boxee. Particular programs typically reach comparatively small audiences; for example, one episode of NextNewNetworks's *Freezer Burns* series received 135,000 views.[57] Overall, however, the numbers can be huge. In late 2010, NextNewNetworks, which describes itself as "TV for the Internet," claimed that its programming had been viewed more than 750 million times.[58] Internet-TV expert Aymar Jean Christian pointed to "the hundreds of millions of views web series garner every month . . ., the major advertisers supporting them (IKEA, Sprint, CoverGirl, and on and on), the major TV networks producing them (MTV, ABC, NBC, SyFy, and on and on), the thousands of dollars independents shell out to finance them, the millions the aforementioned networks and advertisers spend, the fascinating new online networks coming out to distribute them (from Atom and CollegeHumor, MyDamnChannel to Babelgum, RowdyOrbit to OneMoreLesbian)." His conclusion: "A lot is going on. Web series are serious business."[59]

Google's movement into this space has taken three forms. One is its heavily subsidized YouTube video subsidiary and the work of trying to sell ads on it so it can at least break even. A second involves expanding the computer-driven

Google ad-display business from the Web and mobile devices to include cable television. Google sells commercials to place on Direct TV and various cable television networks in a way that aims to duplicate the Google Display Network. (In the course of this activity, Google collects second-by-second set-top box data of anonymous Direct TV and TiVo users with the possible long-term aim of complementing or substituting for standard Nielsen ratings.) The third form is the more public-facing Google Television, with its goal of helping people find the programs they will like, wherever they are. Given Google's heritage, its marketing imperative is to become a hub for data-rich personalized advertising. If that information is linked to widely cast demographics and lifestyle categories, it can be yet another way for broadly sharing your profile and the specific offers that ought to be presented to you. When Google Television was launched, Intel CEO Paul Otellini, who sits on Google's board, said that it would become the "the biggest single change in television" since the introduction of color.[60]

A number of observers scoffed at Otellini's assertion, responding that both Apple and Microsoft were already operating in the "internet television" space, through boxlike technologies that aimed to bring the near-infinite choices of the internet, along with its apps and online bill-paying technologies, to the lean-back environment of the home television. Part of what Otellini sensed, however, are the unprecedented changes in advertising that would come with people's use of Google as a navigator to help them choose programs before they watch. Google can also bring its deep cross-device knowledge of logged-in individuals' demographics, lifestyles, purchase habits, and current interests—as well as the predictions of future interests that CEO Eric Schmidt mentioned—into viewers' searches for things to watch. When it comes to advertising, Google can make these profiles available to third parties, much as it already does on its Web display network. Google clearly aims to help advertisers identify desirable potential customers and then personalize their commercials based on individual or household members viewing the TV screen.[61] Teracent is a subsidiary that can help Google do that. In addition, the search engine owns part of Invidi, a firm offering technology that enables the distribution of television commercials to select groups of viewers, down to the individual household level. Among the other major investors in the company are WPP's GroupM media-buying subsidiary and set-top box maker Motorola. Both Group M and Google have executives on Invidi's board of directors, a clear indication of all three firms' common understanding that data personalization lies at the core of advertising trends.

"Google and GroupM share our vision that addressability will transform television advertising by increasing effectiveness and eliminating wasted reach,"
said Invidi CEO David Downey. "They want to play an active role in
shaping this revolution."[62]

Clearly, Google has a lot of skills and data to bring to the TV set environment to help it succeed. It also brings with it a lot of negative baggage. In
2011, the major broadcast networks and other content providers declared that
they would not cooperate with Google Television. They feared that the
search engine would find pirated programming, and they feared losing
control of the main ways people receive their programming on their television sets. They also may have been worried that Google was becoming too
powerful across too many media. The main point here, however, is not to
pick winners among Google, Canoe, or other players. It is to demonstrate
that the concept of data-mining, profiling, and personalization, which developed on the Web and which has been migrating to the mobile and brick-
and-mortar stores, is also moving to the TV. That direction is irrefutable,
and its momentum appears unstoppable. Competition will likely emerge
both with Canoe-like technology, which enables targeted commercials to
reach at least the household level, and with Google Television–like search
engines that present commercials at the side of the search results.

Expect to see television-marketing activities that address you based on
information gathered from tracing you across a variety of media and
nonmedia locations. The demographic, lifestyle, semantic, and social-graph
pictures created about your household will be core factors generating search
results about what these sources think you should watch. Eventually,
marketers will want to go further than just the household. They will
persuade you to log on to your TV set and its browser (via clicked buttons,
voice identifiers, fingerprint analyzers, or even face detectors) in order to get
special discounts for products as well as programs aimed not just at your
family but specifically at you. Search engines will then individualize their
results so that your suggested television agenda will depend on the search
company's understanding of you. And when you start a viewing session,
Google Television, Comcast, or another entity will take advantage of that by
watching you. It will use software that will have what Google calls a "content
aware interactivity layer," which can determine what is being shown
on-screen and then offer additional related information; it allows the viewer
to ask Google questions.[63] The software probably will treat TV-related questions as opportunities for contextual advertising, meaning that it will serve

ads that harmonize with the content of the show or the nature of the question as well as with what it knows about you and your family.

TV sets and cable/satellite box processors will develop to the point that program exhibitors—that is, cable systems, satellite companies, and even set manufacturers—can present households and individuals with modular program segments depending on the needs of advertisers. Expect these exhibitors, along with television producers and networks—including content farms—to work with media-buying agencies to stream different stories or parts of stories to match what they know, and share, about households and individuals. Parts of the packages will move freely from the TV set to the Web to a variety of mobile devices, and back again. Digital text articles that have been personalized by using many of the same profiles and reputations will ride alongside the audiovisual material. Cable firms and other companies seeing new revenue streams in (anonymous) TV viewers' profiles will sell the labels they have created about us to many advertisers. Over time, each of us will see larger and larger packages of audiovisual entertainment, news, information, and advertising personalized for ourselves and our households. Increasingly, decisions about whom to value will come from the same basic pools of data—often anonymous—that central data firms, media firms, and agencies share.

That doesn't mean that you and your family members will always be treated the same way by all marketers. Some marketers may find value in people who don't count to other marketers. The differences among you and people you know when it comes to offers, prices, and program suggestions may leave you mystified, annoyed that you're not getting the best deals, or worried that your reputation is not as good with A-list networks and sponsors as you think it should be. You will probably suspect that you have certain profiles with marketers and media firms—your neighbor received a Tiffany commercial when you saw a Ford ad—but you won't know quite why. Even if you try to find out, you'll be out of luck. Most of the calculations are carried out behind the scenes, and it is often impossible to know what leads to the different treatments. There are no toll-free phone numbers for reputation questions. Are you waste? And to which companies or political campaigns? What is the reasoning behind it, and what, if anything, can you do about it?

Chapter 7 Beyond the
"Creep" Factor

"Queasy," "Icky," "Creepy"—it's not unusual for people to use these words when expressing their concerns about companies tracking them online. These labels have even reached the halls of the U.S. Senate during a 2010 privacy hearing convened by Senator Claire McCaskill (D-Mo.), who said she found behavioral targeting troubling. "I understand that advertising supports the Internet, but I am a little spooked out," McCaskill said. "This is creepy."[1] Joanna O'Connell of the consulting firm Forrester Research spoke similarly in a National Public Radio interview that discussed marketers' tracking of consumers. In describing marketers' attempts to determine at which point negative reactions will start, "There's sort of the human element, the sort of ick factor," O'Connell said. "And marketers are aware of that. Depending on the marketer, there are some that are very reticent about using certain types of targeting."[2]

When lawmakers and analysts confront an issue by invoking an "ick" or "creep" factor as a reason for their distaste, society has a problem. Executives in the new advertising system counter that public and private officials' use of such terms merely demonstrates their lack of understanding of audience tracking and labeling, and in response they have adopted the position that the issue is basically psychological. The problem, they say, is rooted in consumers' negative emotional reactions rather than in any widespread or genuine threats to society or its members. Indeed, supporters of the emerging advertising world argue that the real threats have already been tackled. They contend that concerns about health information and the use and sale of personal financial data are addressed by the Health Insurance Portability & Accountability Act (HIPAA) and the Gramm-Leach-Bliley Act, respectively. Rules limiting the collection of information from children under the age of thirteen are covered by the Children's Online Privacy Protection Act. Identity theft, they note, is clearly illegal. Bad actors using deceptive advertising practices are being warned and even pursued by an increasingly activist Federal Trade Commission as well as by a new Consumer Protection Agency. They say that the rest—the recording of individuals' everyday actions and attributes for the purpose of selling them products and serving them material they are likely to enjoy—is really quite harmless and may even be useful for the people who are targeted. It's particularly nonthreatening, marketers note, when the individuals are anonymous, as they often are in this process.

At the same time, marketing executives allow that many contemporary audiences dislike the thought of being followed. Because people dislike it and because the marketers who are doing it may be tarred and feathered by public ire, advertisers agree they must be careful. The antidote, they argue, is self-regulation. But a look at what self-regulation means in practice, and what the public gains and doesn't gain by it, shows that we have to move beyond the oft-cited creep factor to discuss what's actually taking place. We have to broaden social discussion, and action, about the meaning of the advertising system's unprecedented tracing and labeling activities.

In a *USA Today* opinion piece in August 2010, Randall Rothenberg added a twist, *conspiracy*, to the industry line that the public's negative reactions to being followed and targeted online are misguided. Rothenberg had been an *Advertising Age* columnist and a strategist at Booz Allen Hamilton consulting; when he wrote the opinion piece he was the president and chair of the Interactive Advertising Bureau (IAB). Since the mid-1990s the IAB had helped bring order to Web advertising by creating technical standards that made it possible for publishers, media agencies, and technology firms to work together efficiently. Those standards would be irrelevant, Rothenberg implied, if determined attacks on internet-industry marketing activities continued. "A wild debate is on," he began, "about websites using 'tracking tools' to 'spy' on American Internet users. Don't fall for it. The controversy is led by activists who want to obstruct essential Internet technologies and return the U.S. to a world of limited consumer choice in news, entertainment, products and services." Rothenberg stated that the activists "have rebranded as 'surveillance technology' various devices—cookies, beacons and IP addresses—that fuel the Internet." He then asserted that "without them, Web programming and advertising can't make its way to your laptop, phone or PC. At risk are $300 billion in U.S. economic activity and 3.1 million jobs generated by the advertising-supported Internet, according to [an IAB-funded study by] Harvard professors John Deighton and John Quelch."[3]

Rothenberg went on to note that "thousands of small retailers and sites" depend on the Web for a living. After giving a few examples of regular folks' ad-supported sites, he concluded that the tracking activities that sustain them should raise no alarms because anonymity is the rule. "The information they use to deliver content is impersonal. Unlike newspaper and cable-TV subscription data, it doesn't contain your name or address." Besides, he said, "you already have what you need to control your privacy, by eliminating cookies from your browser. Major websites offer highly visible tools that put consumers in charge of their data."[4]

Privacy activists disagreed fiercely with Rothenberg's assertion regarding consumer power over their data, pointing to his claim about cookies as being especially disingenuous. Certainly, Web users can eliminate cookies (about a quarter of them say do that regularly), but marketers keep putting them back. There are ways to block the insertion of browser cookies—Ghostery.com is a site that helps with that—but there is little evidence that a substantial percentage of the internet population does it. Rothenberg undoubtedly is also aware that companies have been addressing threats to the traditional tracking cookie by figuring out new online ways to maintain the identities of people. One tack is to make a third-party "tracking cookie," which is typically the kind that browsers erase, look like a "first-party" cookie so that it won't be zapped. Another involves the use of locally shared objects (LSOs), also called Flash cookies, which perform the function of cookies but are harder to erase. Rothenberg must also have been aware that the need for continuous identification would push companies in his industry toward new ways to track people without erasure. Two months after his piece appeared, for example, a startup company called BlueCava announced that it had begun to provide original equipment manufacturers with technology that would provide a digital device "with the ability to identify itself" and that a website could associate with particular information it would store. Online Media Daily reported that the company "has put together a data exchange where businesses can contribute information they know about a device that should make targeting ads more accurate."[5] Also around this time the *New York Times* reported on a technology company called Ringleader Digital, which had created a product called Media Stamp that, according to critics, could surreptitiously acquire information from a mobile device and assign it a unique ID.[6]

Rothenberg was clearly exaggerating about individual controls, but the opinion piece's main purpose was to be a salvo on behalf of what Rothenberg called "the nation's largest media and marketing trade associations" to counter rising ire at the federal and state level about the tracking and targeting of individual consumers. The larger battle took place over a number of years, going into high gear in 2007 when the Federal Trade Commission (FTC) released a report that urged the industry to follow a set of principles for self-regulation regarding online behavioral advertising. Intentionally defining the activity broadly, the FTC said that "behavioral advertising means the tracking of a consumer's activities online—including the searches the consumer has conducted, the web pages visited, and the content viewed—in order to deliver advertising targeted to the individual consumer's interests."[7] "Town hall" meetings and petitions from industry groups as well as activists led the FTC to release a 2009 staff report in which it laid out a suggested regulatory framework that fundamentally supported marketers' needs. When the dust settled, it was clear the staff had written their document in a way that meshed with the views of industry lobbyists.

The new regulatory framework did respond to concerns nonbusiness interests raised in town hall meetings. It proposed that firms engaging in tracking and targeting explain, outside the site's formal privacy policy, about the information they gather. The staff report also encouraged firms to give audiences the choice of whether to receive targeted ads. It enjoined firms to inform consumers when privacy policies change, to receive consent to use the old data in new ways, and to make sure the data are secure and not retained indefinitely. It urged that use of so-called sensitive data—data about finance, health, or sexual preferences—be handled with great care to the point that consumers should consent, or affirmatively opt in, to their use. And it accepted privacy advocates' contentions that, because of sophisticated linking techniques and data accidents, distinguishing between the online collection of personally identifiable information (for example, a person's name, postal address, e-mail address) and information that was supposedly not clearly identifiable—an anonymous person's health condition, for example—made no sense from a privacy standpoint. Firms should treat all data in the same way.

Most prominently, though, the FTC staff accepted that tracking and targeting had become part of the digital landscape, important for present and future business opportunities. What made privacy advocates particularly unhappy was the report's agreement with marketers that they could carry out most data collection on an opt-out basis. That is, an advertiser didn't have to get permission to collect information from individuals except in highly sensitive areas. In fact, in some areas the staff agreed that companies didn't even need to offer an opt-out provision at all. For example, the staff report distinguished between first-party and third-party tracking, concluding that the two types involve different consumer expectations. The former involves a company tracking people only on its site and on other sites with the same brand—for example, Disney.com and Disney.net—while the latter involves a company that follows people across sites and uses the data to send ads to them.

> After considering the comments, staff agrees that "first party" behavioral advertising practices are more likely to be consistent with consumer expectations, and less likely to lead to consumer harm, than practices involving the sharing of data with third parties or across multiple websites. . . . In such case, the tracking of the consumer's online activities in order to deliver a recommendation or advertisement tailored to the consumer's inferred interests involves a single website where the consumer has previously purchased or looked at items. Staff believes that, given the direct relationship between the consumer and the website, the consumer is likely to understand why he has received the targeted recommendation or advertisement and indeed may expect it. The direct relationship also puts the consumer in a better position to raise any concerns he has about the collection and use of his data, exercise any choices offered by the website, or avoid the practice altogether by taking his business elsewhere. By contrast, when behavioral advertising involves the sharing of data with ad networks or other third parties, the consumer may not understand why he has received ads from unknown marketers based on his activities at an assortment of previously visited websites. Moreover, he may not know whom to contact to register his concerns or how to avoid the practice.[8]

This basic distinction became a key launching pad from which five industry groups—American Association of Advertising Agencies, Association of National Advertisers, Direct Marketing Association, Interactive Advertising Bureau, and Council of Better Business Bureaus—built their self-regulation policy.[9] The approach solidified around the use of an "advertising option icon" next to an ad to disclose that behavioral targeting has taken place. The icon would link the site visitor to the kinds of explanations and opt-out activities the FTC report suggested.[10] Industry representatives met with FTC staff intensively to make sure the emerging industry approach mapped onto the FTC report and intent.

Guidelines that the five industry groups released in 2009, however, used a narrower definition of the activity than that of the FTC's initial broad take. Online behavioral advertising, the report said, is "the collection of data online from a particular computer or device regarding Web viewing behaviors over time and across non-affiliate Web sites for the purpose of using such data to predict user preferences or interests to deliver advertising to that computer or device based on the preferences or interests inferred from such Web viewing behaviors."[11] Taking a cue from the FTC staff's sense of consumer expectations, the industry group excludes first parties from even the notion that behavioral advertising is taking place. That means a publisher doesn't have to display the icon if it buys off-line information about its site visitors or if it follows people around on its own site and on "affiliate sites." Affiliate sites are those the publisher owns or controls even if the names of the sites are so different as to make it unlikely a consumer could discern this; ESPN.com and Disney.com is an example of affiliate sites (Disney being the parent company of the cable sports channel ESPN). Therefore, if a publisher exerts management control over the advertising on one hundred sites that have totally different names, it can track people across those domains and not have to show them the icon.

The icon is supposed to be a company's portal to "clear, meaningful" notice about "data collection and use practices." In important ways, though, what it leads to is little different from a Web staple that should have helped with such disclosures but didn't: the privacy policy. As Wikipedia notes, a privacy policy "is a legal document that discloses some or all of the ways a party gathers, uses, discloses and manages a customer's data."[12] With the exception of certain information involving health, finances, and children, the United States does not have specific regulations requiring companies to explain themselves when they collect and use data about individuals. Nevertheless, in 1998 the FTC released "Privacy Online: A Report to Congress," which described what the Commission said were widely accepted "fair information practice principles" that companies ought to follow when collecting personal information from the public. They included: *notice* about the activities, *choice* about whether and how the personal information should be used beyond the initial purposes for which it was provided, *access* to the data to be able to judge its accuracy, and reasonable steps for *security*—that is, ensuring that the information collected is accurate and protected from unauthorized use. The FTC made clear that although no law mandated the principles and practices, they were norms to guide the drafting of privacy policies online. It also noted that *enforcement*—the use of a reliable mechanism to provide sanctions for noncompliance—was a critical component of any governmental or self-regulatory program.[13]

By the turn of the twenty-first century, many critics were already pointing out that overwhelmingly privacy policies did not fully follow the FTC's principles. Moreover, the legalistic formulations of the policies made them nearly impossible to understand. The FTC, implementing a privacy-policy requirement in the Children's Online Privacy Protection Act of 1998, tried to enforce clarity on those texts.[14] It didn't help; a systematic content analysis of ninety children's websites that I led in 2000 found major problems with their "completeness and complexity."[15] While no similar analysis of children's sites exists today, it is apparent nevertheless that complexity and incomplete adherence to the fair-information principles are hallmarks of websites in general. Just as important from the standpoint of advertiser power is a more subtle phenomenon: even if you can get through a site's privacy policy, you will find little that is direct and explicit about what advertisers do on the site. Put another way, part of the power advertisers hold over websites is manifested by the sites' behind-the-scenes responsiveness to advertisers.

Consider Google's privacy policy, which is obscure and scattered around its website. It's no easy task to find out what information Google makes available to its advertisers about people who visit Google Display Network sites. The main theme of the privacy policy appears to be that Google protects "personal information," the site explains while avoiding a central focus on advertising. For one thing, Google's privacy policy doesn't define this term directly. Instead, a link that brings you to a separate page describes it as "information that you provide to us which personally identifies you, such as your name, e-mail address or billing information, or other data which can be reasonably linked to such information by Google." The phrasing is ambiguous: does this mean that Google considers a detail to be personal information only if "you provide it to us"? If a marketer provides the same information, is it then not considered "personal"?

The privacy policy also simply states that cookies are used "to improve ad selection" but reveals nothing about their role in helping the firm create data for interest-based advertising. Much later in the policy a statement notes that "Google uses the DoubleClick advertising cookie on AdSense partner sites and certain Google services to help advertisers and publishers serve and manage ads across the web." But it does not offer any explanation of DoubleClick, AdSense, partner sites, and certain Google services. This section of the policy does go on to explain how site visitors can view, edit, and manage ad preference through an "Ad Preferences Manager" and select a "DoubleClick opt-out cookie." Here, too, the policy includes no direct explanation of the preference manager and opt-out cookie. Instead, hot links associated with those terms can start you on a journey across Google pages in hopes of learning about terms and the activities connected to them. After wading through the privacy policy an uninformed visitor (or even a viewer of Google's privacy videos) may well come away believing that Google doesn't help advertisers learn about them or tailor ads to them. As we saw in Chapter 5, Google executives are telling advertisers just the opposite.

But Google is by no means alone when it comes to obscuring disclosure of the tracking and data-sharing activities it shares with marketers. In fact, a mark of digital media outlets' sensitivity to advertisers' demands is a willingness to cloak the data marketers share, use, and trade across websites. At Pogo.com, the hugely popular casual gaming site owned by Electronic Arts, the welcome paragraph on the Pogo home page states that "Pogo is a great place to play free online games," and it encourages players to "earn tokens, enter for chances to win prizes, create your own personalized avatar and chat with other people while you play free online games." Those who click on the "Get Started!" button are taken to a "Create Your FREE Account" form. To allay any nervousness about filling in your e-mail address, a big sign on the right side of the form states, "We Protect Your Privacy," with the Electronic Arts logo positioned underneath. That promise may be enough on its own to keep you from feeling any need to read the privacy policy, but if you do choose to click on it, you'll see another comforting message in bold right at the top: "EA respects your privacy and understands the importance of protecting your personal information. We will only collect information we need to fulfill your requests and our legitimate business objectives. We will never send you marketing communications without your consent, and we will never share your personal information with third parties that are not bound by our privacy policy unless you tell us we can."[16]

A close reading of these assurances suggests the opposite of privacy protection. The paragraph is filled with deceptive ambiguities, as someone would learn provided the reader had the stamina to wade through the 5,136-word privacy policy as well as the knowledge to understand its technical terms. A large part of the reason for the evasiveness is EA's desire to satisfy advertisers without calling public attention to it. The privacy policy makes clear that the company collects both "personal information" and "non-personal" information. EA defines the former as "information that identifies you and that may be used to contact you on-line or off-line," a characterization it reserves for name, postal address, and e-mail address. It dubs as "non-personal information" most of the other information it collects about its visitors and members via cookies, Flash cookies, and Web beacons. These data range from information on your computer's IP address to "feature usage, game play statistics and scores, user rankings and click paths as well as other data that you may provide in surveys, via your account preferences and online profiles or through purchases, for instance." The company states that it will "never share your personal information with third parties without your consent." Nevertheless, EA also states that it may use your personal information to buy "either non-personal or public information" from third parties "in order to supplement personal information provided directly by you so that we can consistently improve our sites and related advertising to better meet our visitors' needs and preferences. To enrich our understanding of individual customers, we tie this information to the personal information you provide to us."[17]

In other words, EA is saying that it uses "personal information" to learn "non-personal" information, which it can then use to attract advertisers for targeting. This disclosure is difficult to discern, however. Nor would the uninitiated have a clue about the extent to which Pogo accommodates advertising networks not only in data it collects for them but in the data it allows them to collect via cookies and Web beacons. The privacy policy notes that "DoubleClick, the company that serves many of the ads that appear on www. pogo.com, also collects information regarding your activities online, including the site you visit." It adds that "other ad serving companies may also collect similar information." It doesn't discuss all the ways advertisers, ad networks, ad exchanges, and data providers can converge to use information obtained in the course of tagging you to decide which ads to send. Instead, it suggests going to DoubleClick for "opt out" information. And, to protect itself from the use of data by advertisers and ad networks that post cookie tags and beacons on Pogo but that are under no obligation to conform to its privacy policy, EA yet further down in the notice presents this alarming warning:

> If you click on a link to a third party site, including on an advertisement, you will leave the EA site you are visiting and go to the site you selected. Because we cannot control the activities of third parties, we cannot accept responsibility for any use of your personal information by such third parties, and we cannot guarantee that they will adhere to the same privacy and security practices as EA. We encourage you to review the privacy policies of any other service provider from whom you request services. If you visit a third party website that is linked to an EA site, you should consult that site's privacy policy before providing any personal information.[18]

This paragraph is rather common on ad-supported websites, and it sounds like a public service announcement. Reading the EA privacy policy without a decoder, one would hardly get the impression that Pogo itself is contributing information collected on the site and purchased elsewhere to help create segments that determine which ads will appear next to and in the games you play. Pogo also obscures the possibility that marketers will gather data about you on Pogo.com and that they will link this with other data and use this information elsewhere. The games you like and their relation to demographics, ad-click preferences, or various behaviors or lifestyle characteristics are additional elements that marketers and data providers might use to build up ideas about your preferences for particular products, services, or even ideologies. Here then, by drips and drabs, are the building blocks for a broadly shared reputation, virtually hidden in the interest of sponsors by the exhortation to follow links.

By 2010, the FTC concluded that the public lacked a clear understanding of privacy policies, and it encouraged the industry to help the public learn about behavioral targeting "outside the privacy policy." Ironically, though, the model adopted for the advertising option icon by the industry's self-regulatory group, Evidon, amounts to a well-established pattern of cloaking and ambiguity, as the icon has enabled many advertisers and ad networks to hide their activities behind jargon and rabbit-hole links. Moreover, despite the internet advertising industry's professed enthusiasm for the device, it is not omnipresent. It does appear with many Yahoo! sites' ads; for example, as of this writing the icon appears on the Yahoo! Sports' NHL site (http://sports.yahoo.com/nhl), where it is included in the top-right corner of an ad from the retail giant Target. For various reasons it may not be visible to some, one explanation being that Yahoo! is currently not targeting you by tracking your behavior across sites, though it may be targeting you through demographic or other categories. Even if the icon does appear you may not notice it; on Yahoo! it is a tiny gray drawing next to the wording "AdChoices," also in gray. But suppose you do notice it and click on it to learn more. Doing this in mid-2011 would have brought you to a Yahoo! page that, confusingly, has nothing to do with Target. It is a Yahoo! privacy page titled "AdChoices: Learn More About This Ad."[19] The page is divided into two parts, one "for consumers" and the other "for advertisers and publishers." The former presents a preamble about how "the Web sites you visit work with online advertising companies to provide you with advertising that is as relevant and useful as possible." It then lists three bulleted items: Who placed this ad? (answer: Yahoo!); Where can I learn more about how Yahoo! selects ads? (answer: a link to a page about Yahoo!'s "privacy and advertising practices"); and What choices do I have—about interest-based advertising from Yahoo!? (answer: a link to see the "interest-based categories" Yahoo! uses to serve you ads as well as to add to the category list or opt out). Click on the link to the choices and you may see that Yahoo! has tagged you in a few or many of the hundreds of interest categories.

Yahoo! is following the rules, and the rules say it doesn't have to give you detailed explanations about data mining or tracking right after you click on the icon. What Yahoo! actually says may sound completely innocuous, so you may not find it worth your bother to take additional action. Let's assume, though, that you decide you want to opt out of the company tracking you. You'll find a lot of language on the page and successive links that try to dissuade you. A prominent "Learn More!" notice on the AdChoices Web page exhorts the visitor to follow a link to "find out how online advertising supports the free content, products, and services you use online." Another link takes a person to the Network Advertising Initiative (NAI), which tells visitors at the top that allowing cookies is "a way to support the websites and products you care about." OK, but say you still want to stop Yahoo! from tracking you. Turns out, you can't do it. The only thing you can do is link to a part of the NAI site where you can tell that company and others that you don't want to receive their online behavioral ads. The company can still track you with a cookie so that it can use what it learns about you in statistical analyses of Web users. The rules don't allow you to tell it to stop doing that. In fact, when you go to the opt-out area, the site cautions you that your action to stop the firm's targeted ads will not enable you to stop receiving advertising. It will simply result in ads that are not necessarily relevant to your interests.[20] In view of the limitations—that you will continue to be tracked and have irrelevant ads sent to you—why would many people click to opt out?

That, of course, is exactly what the internet advertising industry hopes will happen. It may be a bit shocking that the self-regulatory apparatus is set up to guide people to accept tracking by behavioral marketers. An even deeper concern are four propositions that the digital advertising system's reports, websites, and leaders weave into their pronouncements, because each of them discourages people from taking seriously what is going on behind their screens. Randall Rothenberg's opinion piece discussed earlier in this chapter underscores the first proposition: marketers and regulators have dealt success-fully with the real privacy problems of the Web so that the only reason people worry about the use of their data in the new media environment is because it feels "creepy." This view sees the Web's real potential for harm as the leaking of information about a person that can damage a person's financial situation, reveal sensitive health information, or cause other forms of embarrassment that might corrode interpersonal or employment relationships. The 2007 FTC report quietly accepts this view. It does not present a summary of why we ought to be concerned about behavioral targeting, but its strongest state-ments of concern center on situations whereby people may be stung when their anonymity is unmasked without permission. This approach regarding first- and third-party tracking also shows up in the 2009 FTC report quoted above; the report accepts that some internet users' worries may relate to real estimations of misused or abused information, while some worries related to the creepiness of being followed. The internet industry generally accepts this view, though it argues that the FTC, like privacy advocates, overestimate the real dangers that exist.

The second proposition holds that regulators and the public should appre-ciate marketers for promoting anonymity and relevance as the two pillars of acceptable tracking by the advertising system. Marketers and websites state that while they reserve the right to learn and use people's names and e-mail addresses, they typically don't sell or reveal that personally identifiable infor-mation to other parties that are using their data. That said, the industry main-tains, the public and regulators should know that companies need to feed on individuals' data if they are to bring them relevant, enjoyable material. Giving up information, even personal information, will increasingly be the price of circulating "free" or inexpensive relevant content on the internet. But, according to the industry, the kind of information requested—and the protections of that information—are such that the worries are merely psychological.

This stream of logic leads to the third and fourth propositions. The third one declares that because privacy concerns about internet advertising are really emotional states not rooted in logical or valid concerns, people's reactions to marketers' data collection efforts are inherently unstable. After all, people may say they want to protect their information, but they will gladly relinquish it for token rewards. This contention has been analyzed in the trade press and at meetings for years. A 2001 *Advertising Age* article, for example, quoted industry analyst Rob Leathern as saying "flatly" that "consumers are very schizophrenic. They want their privacy, but they're willing to give out information for entry into an online sweepstakes."[21] In contrast, the fourth proposition sees audiences as more rational, arguing that while some Americans are simply unconcerned about their privacy online, most Americans make cost-benefit analyses about whether to release their information. Privacy consultant Alan Westin calls these people "privacy pragmatists." He noted in a 2003 survey analysis of Americans' attitudes on this topic that "they examined the benefits to them or society of the data collection and use, wanted to know the privacy risk and how organizations proposed to control those, and then decided whether to trust the organization or seek legal oversight."[22]

This description of most Americans as being aware of their online privacy options supports the industry's contention that self-regulation through opt-out mechanisms is a logical way to go and that the small opt-out numbers reflect rational choice. Those who champion the notion that consumers are illogical about privacy would probably agree that such mechanisms can't hurt but that in the end their decision not to opt out reflects fickleness more than anything else. Either assessment would click with Dave Morgan's view that quid pro quo arrangements with consumers is the best way to handle data collection. Morgan is a target-marketing entrepreneur who has founded companies (24/7 Real Media and Tacoda) that have exerted profound influence on the internet. "If you're giving medicine to a dog, you put it inside some peanut butter," he advised in 2001. "Tell consumers what you're going to do, but give them something for it."[23]

Morgan's recommendation that companies offer people a trade for their information resonates with the needs of marketers even more today. Publishers increasingly want visitors to register so that they can track them across different devices—for example, a desktop computer, a laptop, an iPad, a mobile device, or a home television set. In the heat of escalating competition, publishers will also want information from people—about their health, their travels, the value of their homes—that can attract advertisers to them but that individuals may think twice about providing. For some visitors a gift, a few kind words, and a nod to security will pry loose their data. These tactics likely will also escalate among marketers and third-party data providers, as these groups want to collect data of their own as well as to convince people not to opt out of their participation in behavioral advertising practices. When such schemes result in a willingness among people to offer up personal information, the industry can argue that people are inconsistent about their data or that they carefully consider their choices. Indeed, the industry is doing its best to convince the public and regulators that self-regulation guards against bad actions as well as educates people, thereby minimizing any risk to those offering personal information online. To hear Randall Rothenberg tell it, the risk may even be nonexistent, exaggerated, or trumped up by activists.

A series of national telephone surveys I've conducted with the help of well-known polling firms since 1999 demonstrates that neither *schizophrenic* nor *pragmatic* is an apt description of what is taking place when people willingly offer information about themselves. Rather, individuals seem to be facing an enormous deficit when they try to find a balance between their need to carry out activities online and their realization they are being tracked. Beyond knowing they are being tracked, they have little understanding of how companies are allowed to handle their data. In fact, they underestimate what marketers can legally do, and they overestimate the protection the government provides for them. These findings point to very different conclusions from the ones marketers and even regulators have been promulgating. This reality, linked to an alternative understanding of the importance of the data-collection system, also suggests very different courses of action than the ones we have seen to this point.

Consider first that, in 2005, 79 percent of 1,500 adults participating in a nationally representative survey I conducted agreed with the statement "I am nervous about websites having information about me."[24] We had cast our net broadly to include anyone eighteen years or older who answered yes to the question "Have you used the internet in the past month at home, work, or anywhere else?" The concern expressed was not a fluke; after more than a decade of tracking Americans' attitudes and ideas about online marketing, concerns about online data collection had become a persistent worry.

The picture accompanying this worry is complex and troubling. Eighty percent of the 2005 survey respondents believed that "companies today have the ability to follow my activity across many sites on the web." At the same time, large majorities of the internet-using U.S. public did not understand key practices and laws relating to profiling and behavioral targeting. They mistakenly believed that the government will protect them from online activities that put their data in danger or that create unfair differential pricing. We found that about half the adult population did not realize that most online merchants are allowed to share information with "affiliates" without the consumers' permission or that print magazines can sell information about them without their permission. About half were unaware of the scheme called "phishing," in which crooks posing as trusted banks or other institutions send e-mails to an unsuspecting public, requesting sensitive information such as credit card numbers and passwords. At the same time, half the respondents did not believe that banks "often send their customers emails that ask them to click on a link wanting them to verify their account."

If the fact that half the population was ill-informed doesn't seem shocking, many other topics in the survey demonstrated much higher percentages of unaware consumers. For example, 62 percent of our respondents thought that it was illegal "for an online store to charge different people different prices at the same time of day," and 71 percent thought the same of a brick-and-mortar store. Similarly, 68 percent did not know whether "by law, a site such as Expedia and Orbitz that compares prices on different airlines must include the lowest airline prices" (the answer is *false*). Sixty-four percent didn't know that it is legal for their supermarket "to sell other companies information about what I buy," and 72 percent didn't know that charities can legally sell names to other charities.

Nor has consumer awareness increased notably in the past few years. A 2009 survey I conducted with Chris Jay Hoofnagle and Jennifer King at Berkeley Law School asked similar questions about the legality of merchants sharing or selling people's information, and only half of the population or less answered correctly.[25] Moreover, the 2009 study confirmed the public's lack of understanding of Web privacy that was evident in three of my earlier surveys. Sixty-two percent falsely believed that "if a website has a privacy policy, it means that the site cannot share information about you with other companies, unless you give the website your permission" (16 percent answered that they didn't know). This ignorance is distressing: despite all the discussions in policy circles about online privacy, 78 percent of American adults still do not realize that the phrase "privacy policy" is merely an invitation to read how companies deal with their information. Some analysts—even some consumer advocates—have suggested to me in frustration that the widespread, continuing ignorance betrays an irritating lack of attention to what people ought to see as a key issue. My perspective is that, although people do see the use of their data by marketers as an important topic, they also have busy, complicated lives, which encourages shorthand assumptions that often turn out to be wrong.

Whatever their level of nervousness, and whatever misconceptions they have, a majority of Americans who go online say they don't want online content tailored to them. Our 2009 survey tackled this topic in a number of ways, with a telephone interviewer asking randomly selected participants:

- Please tell me whether or not you want the websites you visit to show you ads that are tailored to your interests.
- Please tell me whether or not you want the websites you visit to show you discounts that are tailored to your interests.
- Please tell me whether or not you want the websites you visit to show you news that is tailored to your interests.

If a respondent answered "yes" to any of these questions, a corresponding question would then be asked:

- Would it be OK or not OK if these ads [discounts/news] were tailored for you based on following what you do on the website you are visiting?
- Would it be OK or not OK if these ads [discounts/news] were tailored for you based on following what you do on OTHER websites you have visited?
- Would it be OK or not OK if these ads [discounts/news] were tailored for you based on following what you do OFFLINE—for example, in stores?

The interviewer also asked a general question about whether behavioral tracking for the purpose of tailored ads is acceptable if the tracking is anonymous. The lead-up to the question noted that marketers "often use technologies to follow the websites you visit and the content you look at in order to better customize ads." The interviewer then asked whether the respondent would "definitely allow, probably allow, probably not allow, or definitely not allow advertisers" to "follow you online in an anonymous way in exchange for free content."

It turns out that fully 66 percent of the respondents do not want advertisements tailored for them. The proportions saying no to tailoring are lower when it comes to tailored discounts and news, but they still represent around half the population—49 percent and 57 percent, respectively. When we add to them the respondents who reject tailoring when they learn they will be followed at the same website, on other websites, or off-line, the number saying no jumps strongly. If the tracking is "on the website you are visiting," 73 percent don't want it for ads, 62 percent don't want it for coupons, and 71 percent don't want it for news. If the tracking takes place on "other websites you have visited" or "offline—for example, in stores," more than 80 percent say they don't want tailoring for all three areas—advertisements, discounts, and news.

The assurance that the tracking is anonymous doesn't seem to lessen Americans' concerns about behavioral targeting. They are quite negative when it comes to the general scenario of free content supported by tailored advertising that results from anonymously "following the websites you visit and the content you look at." A total of 68 percent "definitely" would not allow it, and 19 percent would "probably" not allow it. While 10 percent would "probably" allow it, only 2 percent would "definitely" permit it; 1 percent say they don't know what they would do.

A final aspect of the findings that deserves highlighting relates to young adults (eighteen to twenty-four years old). Popular commentary suggests that America's youngest adults do not care about information privacy, particularly online. As evidence, many point to younger internet users' adoption and prolific use of blogs, social-networking sites, posting of photos, and general documenting and (over)sharing their life's details online, from the mundane to the intimate, for all the world to consume. "Young adults," exhorted one newspaper article to that segment of its readers, "you might regret that scandalous Facebook posting as you get older."[26] More broadly, Robert Iger, CEO of Disney, quipped in 2009 that "kids don't care" about privacy issues, contending that complaints generally came from much older consumers. Indeed, he said that when he talked to his adult children about their online privacy concerns, "they can't figure out what I'm talking about."[27] The contention is an important one, because at industry meetings one often hears internet practitioners claim that today's privacy concerns are confined to an older generation. The rising generation, they predict, will not have anywhere near the worries about privacy that their elders had—so tracking and targeting activities will have more freedom.

Iger is not alone in this view. Anecdotes abound detailing how college-age students post photos of themselves, unclothed and/or drunken, for the entire world—including potential employers—to see. It is not a leap to argue that these actions are hard-wired into young people. One psychological study found that adolescents (age thirteen to sixteen) and what they termed "youths" (those age eighteen to twenty-two) are "more inclined toward risky behavior and risky decision making than are 'adults' (those older than 24 years) and that peer influence plays an important role in explaining risky behavior during adolescence."[28] Their finding was more pronounced among adolescents than among youths, but differences between youths' and adults' willingness to take risks were striking—particularly when group behavior was involved. Although the authors do not mention social media, the findings are clearly relevant to these situations. There the benefits of looking cool to peers may outweigh concerns about negative consequences, especially if those potential consequences are not likely to be immediate. A related explanation for risky privacy behavior on social-networking sites is that they encourage users to disclose more and more information over time.

Young people's use of social media does not in itself mean that they find privacy irrelevant. Indeed, the Pew Internet & American Life Project found in 2007 that teenagers used a variety of techniques to obscure their real location or personal details on social-networking sites.[29] That study fits with the findings of other researchers, who have urged the importance of reframing the issue to ask, *what dimensions* of privacy concern younger adults? While differences between young and older adults may be important, other, more subtle commonalities may be ignored. In recent years older age groups have rushed to social networking in large numbers with discussions of personal issues and details. A common anecdotal observation is that young adults and adolescents are more likely than their elders to post racy photos or document episodes of unseemly or disreputable behavior. If research shows this distinction to be accurate, the question nevertheless remains: Do identical, higher, or lower percentages of Americans over twenty-four years old reveal perhaps more subtle but important private information about themselves that might lead to embarrassing or unfortunate incidents, such as identity theft?

In fact, we found that, unlike what many have suggested, attitudes toward privacy expressed by American young adults (age eighteen to twenty-four) are not nearly so different from those of older adults.[30] Indeed, large percentages of young adults are in agreement with older Americans when it comes to sensitivity about online privacy and policy suggestions. For example, both a large majority of young adults and those over twenty-four years old:

- have refused to give information to a business when they felt it was too personal or not necessary (82 percent for young adults, 88 percent for the entire sample);
- believe anyone who uploads a photo of someone to the internet should get that person's permission first, even if taken in public (84 percent and 86 percent);
- believe there should be a law entitling people to know all the information websites have about them (62 percent and 68 percent); and
- believe there should be a law that requires websites to delete all stored information about an individual (88 percent and 92 percent).[31]

In view of these findings, why do so many young adults behave in social networks and other online public spaces in such indiscreet and revealing ways? A number of answers present themselves, including suggestions that people twenty-four and younger approach cost-benefit analyses related to risk differently than do individuals older than twenty-four. Wrapped up in their desire to socialize online, they tend to overlook concerns that they may have in more quiet, rational moments. An important part of the picture, though, must surely be our finding that, among all age groups, higher proportions of the eighteen–twenty-four-year-olds had the poorest understanding of the meaning of the privacy policy label and the right of companies to sell or share their data with other firms. According to our findings, the online savvy many attribute to younger individuals (so-called digital natives) doesn't appear to translate to privacy knowledge. The entire population of adult Americans exhibits a high level of online-privacy illiteracy: 75 percent answered only two or fewer questions correctly, with 30 percent getting none right. But the youngest adults perform the worst on these measures: 88 percent answered only two or fewer correctly, and 42 percent could answer none correctly. One conclusion we can draw from these results is that younger people believe even more than their elders that the law protects their privacy online and off-line more than it actually does. This lack of online and legal literacy rather than a cavalier lack of concern for privacy seems to be an important factor in young people's much-hyped disregard for traditional privacy.[32]

In the conclusion to the full report, my colleagues and I suggest that "young-adult Americans have an aspiration for increased privacy even while they participate in an online reality that is optimized to increase their revelation of personal data." Actually, the findings of the surveys we conducted in 2005 and 2009 support this point not just for young adults but for more than 70 percent of adult Americans who go online. As we have seen, Americans worry that marketers are following them even as they participate in marketing activities online. But because the FTC does not dispute the industry's claim that truly anonymous targeting is not harmful, should we accept that our problem with tracking and tailoring is simply a visceral, mere psychological impression of creepiness?

The answer is no. There are crucial issues relating to privacy in the digital-marketing space that have not received the attention they deserve. This book tells the story of an advertising system that has embarked on a fundamental and systematic process of social discrimination. It's a new world, and we're only at the beginning. Nevertheless, the logic of social discrimination is already firmly entrenched in the advertising system and the media that serve it. The direction is basic: In their quest to separate "targets" from "waste," marketers buy access to data about users' backgrounds, activities, and friends that will allow them to locate the customers they deem most valuable. They surround those targets with commercial messages that match their views of them and that offer them incentives and rewards—discounts, personal messages, the possibility of relationships—that are designed to make them feel good about the product. And digital publishers help the marketers: by drawing on information about individuals acquired through registrations and purchase from data firms, they provide the targets with personalized content. This personalized content is designed for two purposes: to keep individuals on the site and thereby increase the chance that they will interact with the sponsor's ad; and to resonate with and reinforce the commercial message.

Industry claims of *anonymity* surrounding all these data may soften the impact of these sorting and labeling processes. But in doing so, it seriously undermines the traditional meaning of the word. If a company can follow and interact with you in the digital environment—and that potentially includes the mobile phone and your television set—its claim that you are anonymous is meaningless, particularly when firms intermittently add off-line information to the online data and then simply strip the name and address to make it "anonymous."

The logical end for marketers and publishers of all these practices is the creation of reputation silos: flows of advertising, information, entertainment, and news designed to fit profiles about individuals and people who statistically seem similar. The speed, variety, and texture of the targeting and person-alization work that defines the new media-buying system have progressed to such an extent over the past half-decade that the next half-decade and the decades beyond will see exponentially rising abilities to mine individuals' information, decide their value using probabilistic methods, and target and personalize mass-media content. Add to that the ever-widening sharing of information about customers among companies, and it is not at all difficult to see that media and advertisers are determined to present people who have been assigned specific reputations in the marketplace with preconceived views of the world and with opportunities based on those reputations.

Recall Larry and Rhonda, the fictional lower middle class family of fast-food aficionados I mentioned in the introductory chapter. By now it should be easy to see how this daisy chain of labels will be applied to them in the twenty-first-century marketing world. Although Larry had complained in conversation with his boss about the down-market Web he was seeing, not all labels reflect a downscale reputation. In fact, in view of the attributions and predictions publishers and marketers make about their targets (à la Eric Schmidt, as discussed in Chapter 6), the reputations people receive might even have an accidental, weird quality to them.

In that vein, consider Sasha, a fictional woman with many Facebook and Twitter friends who chat with her online about a particular upscale cosmetics line she uses. Marketers of trendy products begin to see her as a hub for trendy women's accessories. No matter that her salary as a receptionist in a law firm does not provide her with nearly enough money to buy all these products; some marketers have discovered that she had an Ivy League education and that she lives—with her well-off parents, it turns out—in upscale Roslyn, Long Island. Because of her educational background and current address, one data analysis tags her as selectively affluent. Another labels her as influential among women in the age eighteen to twenty-eight bracket. As a result, soon she is as surrounded by cosmetics products in the same way that Rhonda is surrounded by loan and weight loss ads. The barrage leads Sasha to start a blog about cosmetics, and it takes on a viral popularity after she posts a video in which her cat sports lots of different types of makeup. The numbers of visitors to her blog lead firms to send her a wide variety of cosmetics in the hope that she will offer favorable comments (recall the discussion on "earned media" in Chapter 6). Companies that make all sorts of upscale goods begin sending her products. She also finds that articles awaiting her when she goes online tend to be about fashion trends, and they are often sponsored by companies that make expensive dishware, travel cases, and writing implements. Unlike Larry and Rhonda, she has never received a discount coupon for a fast-food outlet, and the e-mails and ads she receives from fitness companies emphasize not weight but their high-quality equipment and elite air.

It remains to be seen how long the lives, or half-lives, of such reputations last as we move deep into the tailored-marketing century. Will reputations of some people endure, with news, entertainment, and commercial messages meshing consistently through many years? Will the reputations of others move among different reputation grades, with accordingly different opportunities and worldviews at different times? What will happen when people who are unhappy with what they perceive to be their profiles try to game the system, changing their digital habits in order to reconstruct and perhaps rehabilitate their reputations?

Whether one approves or disapproves, social discrimination via reputation silos may well mean having sectors of your life labeled by companies you don't know, for reasons you don't understand, and with data that you did not grant permission to use. As we have seen, marketing-driven synergies between advertising, information, human-interest stories ("soft news"), discount offers, and entertainment are becoming commonplace. We have also seen that technologies to tailor and target these activities are developing quickly. An increasing number of digital advertisers already expect that publishers will choose or craft editorial matter to reinforce the tailored ads that surround them. Not too many years from now your TV listings, the amount you pay for programs, and the commercials you see will significantly be determined by the reputation you develop with marketers and publishers that want to attract those advertisers.

Advertisers and publishers will reach out to form relationships with customers they value—targets—pushing away the "waste" whose purchase patterns suggest low margins and even losses. Better still, they will adopt data-analysis techniques that warn them against advertising to those people with those brands in the first place. They will have different brands for them, and a targeting and triaging process to get them there. This isn't a new idea. During the 1990s the Kroger supermarket company, which owns Smitty's and Ralph's in the same areas of California, sent certain Smitty's discount coupons and advertisements to Ralph's customers after deciding that this group fit the more downscale profile of that brand. In the years to come, these sorts of activities will become technologically easy, common, based on broadly shared data about people and households, and reinforced by associations with news, information, and entertainment that stream alongside, and even as part of, the commercial messages.

All this will take place under an umbrella of industry reassurance that individuals and households are receiving the most relevant, and therefore interesting, materials possible. Personalized customer relationship marketing by marketers and media firms will reach out to people to assure them of the benefits of tailored content. Lobbyists will similarly assure government officials, whom they will surround with the most desirable streams of marketing and media available in order to gain their favor. Individual clicks will still be key technologies in measuring results. They will indicate your activities online, measure your responses, determine what content environment promotes the buying of particular products, and help determine where you belong in the schemes of value that advertisers and publishers concoct. But as voice recognition technology takes off, the click will be less and less often defined by a finger on a mouse or a remote control, because your voice will register your interest, particularly in the mobile space and home television. Your role in the long click that links ads and content with purchases will also be traced by whatever technology replaces the credit-card swipe. Your mobile device will probably carry a near-field-communication chip that will automatically communicate with your bank or credit-advancing company. Eventually your voiceprint or some as-yet unknown technology will complete the deal in ways to ensure that your money is secure while they add to your profiles held by companies that have cultivated relationships with you.

So what are the social costs of such a world—a world in which discrimination through reputation silos has become the norm? One way to answer is to ask what a society needs from its media. I would suggest that a good society should have a balance between what might be called society-making media and segment-making media. Segment-making media are media that encourage small slices of society to talk to themselves, while society-making media are those that have the potential to get all those segments to talk to each other. A hallmark of the twentieth century was the growth of both types in the United States. A huge number of ad-supported vehicles—mostly magazines and newspapers—served as a way to reinforce, even create, identities for an impressive array of segments that advertisers cared about, from immigrant Czechs to luxury-car owners, to Knights of Columbus, and far more. At the same time, some ad-sponsored newspapers, radio networks, and—especially—television networks were able to reach across these groups. Through entertainment, news, and information, society-making media depicted concerns and connections that people ought to share in a larger national community.

For those who hope for a caring society, each level of media had, and continues to have, its problems. Segment-making media have sometimes offered their audiences narrow, prejudiced views of other social segments. Similarly, society-making media have marginalized certain groups, perpetuated stereotypes of many others, and generally presented an ideal vision of the world that reflects the corporate establishment sponsoring them at the expense of the competing visions that define actual publics. Nevertheless, the existence of both forms of media offers the potential for a healthy balance. In the ideal scenario segment-making media strengthen the identities of interest groups while society-making media allow those groups to move out of their parochial scenes to talk with, argue against, and entertain one another. The result is a rich and diverse sense of overarching connectedness: this is what a vibrant society is all about.

Yet the past three decades have marked a steady movement away from such a society, and this change is directly related to the profound shift in the long-term strategies of major advertisers and their agencies away from society-making media and toward segment-making media—media, that is, which have allowed them to search out and exploit differences between consumers. This is a slow process that will continue to evolve through the twenty-first century, but we can already see stages nevertheless. During the 1980s and early 1990s, with cable TV splintering channels to the home, advertisers' focus was on identifying segment-making vehicles. They encouraged the growth of electronic and print channels that reached segments of society that marketers found valuable. As this book has shown, though, the past decade has seen the rise of a new mini-industry within advertising that is upending not only traditional marketing practices but traditional media practices as well. The emerging media-planning and media-buying system is predicated on neither society-making nor segment-making advertising media channels. Rather, it is organized by a belief in the primacy of the chosen person: a belief which has motivated them to sort audiences, find individuals within them whom they deem "valuable," track those people, and serve them personalized ads and other content anywhere they show up.

This is not quite the world that technology writers such as Yochai Benkler, Henry Jenkins, and Clay Shirky celebrate when they note the immense value of the internet in people's collaborations. It is no less important, however, to note less-celebratory aspects of this same activity. Away from public view advertisers and their agents try to audit and exploit collaborations, sometimes to the point of attempting to influence them by stimulating buzz to hype a particular brand. People's contributions to Facebook, Twitter, Foursquare, Huffington Post, and even their own blogs become fodder for the advertising system's databases. Similarly, marketers' analyses of the "social graph" of an individual's friends may lead advertisers to shape the earned, paid, and owned media that those friends see to the extent that it affects the way they collaborate with each other.

This is also not quite the world political theorists such as Cass Sunstein predict when they talk about how Americans will increasingly self-select their news on the basis of their political values. In fact, behind the screen marketers and publishers are increasingly interested in selecting the news material that individuals are to be offered. To some extent, at least, a distinction needs to be drawn between so-called hard news and other information. Sunstein's focus is principally on hard news and associated editorial matters. By contrast, marketers and publishers so far have tended to stay away from personalizing straightforward political news and views. Rather, they are interested in positioning human-interest stories as well as advertisements, discounts, and television-viewing agendas in ways that fit the new marketing logic. This focus doesn't make the advertising and media system's activities any less political, though. The views people receive from advertising, soft news and information, and entertainment very much relate to the ongoing struggle over who will guide society. Media content presents dynamic portraits of which groups and people are "in" and which are "out"; who has claim to public attention and who doesn't; who in society has problems and why we should care; which corporate and government institutions work well and which work badly—and why; and how we fit into all of it.

These pictures are starting points for our interpretations; recall Sasha as well as Rhonda and Larry and their kids. People in consistently different reputation silos—fed different streams of material—will have very different starting points and different opportunities. From these understandings of power in everyday life and our relation to it come interpretations of the functions and success of capitalism, democracy, and the American ethos of equal opportunity. The advertising system clearly isn't creating these distinctions and nodes of power out of new cloth. Broadly shared stereotypes, prejudices, and resource struggles lie behind much of what is taking place. The advertising system is, however, placing the elements of social discrimination in striking new contexts. They now appear as individualized rather than group realities—a kind of report card of a person's social position. The ones who come out on top may find the grades exhilarating.

Even for them, though, the realization that marketers are doing the grading in secret and without permission may not be a sanguine thought. New ways to tweak formulas, a few bad marketing and media choices on an individual's part, social-media "friends" marketers decide are wrong for certain topics, the inevitable lack of marketer interest that comes with aging—these and other uncontrollable changes might throw a person down the reputation slope.

Of course, reputation silos will never be hermetically sealed. People will see other choices, and the serendipity of meeting untargeted, unlikely content will remain. So will the vagaries of individual interpretation. But the different starting points that personalization encourages and that feel comfortably related to people's life circumstances may well discourage some from exploring entertainment, information, and news that seem too far from the comfort zones. They will allow, perhaps even encourage, individuals to live in their own personally constructed worlds, separate from people and issues they don't care about and don't want to be bothered with. Such a preference may accelerate when antagonisms based on employment, age, income, ethnicity, and more rise up as a result of competition over jobs and political muscle. In these circumstances, reputation silos may accelerate the distance people feel between one another. They may further erode the tolerance and mutual dependence between diverse groups that enable a society to work.

People's awareness of differences in the content they receive may also create or reinforce a sense of distrust about the power of organizations over which they have no control to define and position them in the social world. The sense that advertisers are manipulating labels about people's value behind the scenes, but without the targets knowing how or with what information, is an invitation to social tension. It's hard not to be suspicious when articles appear in the popular press about certain people being charged different prices for the same merchandise by the same company at around the same time. As I discussed earlier in this chapter, Annenberg national surveys show quite clearly that Americans believe this sort of price discrimination to be illegal. Anecdotal evidence suggests that when citizens realize that price discrimination is legal they become angry at the businesses that carry it out and the government that allows it. Going forward, then, it seems likely that the new advertising system using data people wouldn't want marketers to have in order to choose winners and losers behind people's backs will produce a corrosive social atmosphere characterized by resentment and distrust of both government and marketers.

The way in which the new advertising system approaches individuals and society is difficult to understand. It is hidden behind multiple screens of industry jargon, claims of competitive secrecy, and links that pretend to lead toward explanations but actually enhance confusion. The confusion is accepted by a federal government that centers on narrow privacy issues instead of realizing that at the core this story is the health of consumer-business relations in the twenty-first century, and the extent to which marketers should be able to take consumers' own information, movements, friendships, and far more and turn these points into statistically driven profiles of them. These labels are often based on the analysis of far-flung data gathering and probability statistics. They may have little to do with the ways the individuals see themselves. Nor is it clear that the generalizations these labels imply have anything to do with truth or reality. Simply because an ad campaign yields positive results doesn't prove that the audience labels built into the campaign are correct. What remains after all the mathematical smoke clears, though, is that marketers' images of people, people's images of themselves, and media firms' approaches to traditional norms and society are irrevocably altered. Moreover, the new technologies that marketers and media firms have developed to track individuals and tailor materials to them are a template for the manipulation of citizens. Governments throughout the world can easily adapt them in their attempts to control populations for explicit political aims.

What can be done? To a large extent the train has already left the station in the United States. The media-planning and media-buying industry's new logics are quickly becoming part of our landscape. Despite bipartisan concerns about privacy, the Federal Trade Commission's mantra of self-regulation is unlikely to change in the foreseeable future. Advertising and media representatives will undoubtedly continue to be adept at defining a narrow problem and a narrow solution. Nevertheless, here are four major steps that need to be carried out if we take seriously the claim that the new rules of advertising are reshaping our world—and not for the better—and are doing so behind our backs:

• *Teach our children well—early and often.* Today, the overwhelming number of people who use the internet have had no formal training in it. In the rush and excitement of new technologies, they have adapted by figuring out what they need to do and getting help if something goes wrong. That method works on a day-to-day basis, but it's the wrong approach if we are to have a citizenry that can claim control over the rules of the game behind the screen. You don't have to be a computer engineer to be able to grasp the policy issues involved in the emerging media system. It is crucial, however, to have knowledge of the ABCs of digital technologies in order to understand what marketers, media firms, and technology companies are doing as well as to talk to experts who can evaluate their claims. This is a new language of the twenty-first century, and students from at least middle school onward should learn it. The claim that the curriculum is already too crowded is a poor excuse for a fascinating topic that can be easily accommodated across the curriculum—in science, math, history, and even literature and art. The more difficult challenge is to get teachers up to speed so that they can teach it effectively. But it has to be done. A serendipitous by-product might be an increase in the number of students who want to pursue engineering careers.

- *Let people know what is really going on with their data.* In 2008 I suggested to *New York Times* technology reporter Saul Hansell that the industry ought to post an icon on every tailored advertisement that when clicked would lead to a "privacy dashboard."[33] The dashboard would show you the various levels of information the advertising company used about you to create the specific ad. The information disclosed would not only show behavioral targeting but would include knowledge collected from any sources, including third-party data providers, the U.S. Census, and online discussions.[34] The dashboard would reveal precisely which companies provided that information, how certain data were mixed with other data, and what conclusions were drawn from this mixing. It would also allow you to suggest specific deletions or changes in various companies' understandings of you. Unfortunately, instead of the icon with the privacy dashboard the industry gave us the "advertising option icon," which, as noted earlier, does not seriously address the problem of people's complete lack of understanding of specific information that companies know about them. I appreciate the difficulty of carrying out a project such as this; after Hansell's blog post appeared I had lots of good discussions with people in the industry about it. But one great advantage of the dashboard approach is that it would facilitate individuals' involvement with their data and would encourage them to see in an uncomplicated yet compelling way just what does happen behind the screen. It may be quixotic to believe that major industry actors such as Google, Microsoft, Ford, Procter and Gamble, Publicis, and WPP would come together to implement it. Nevertheless, I'm still convinced that something far more informative than what we have now can be implemented.

- *Create a "Do Not Track" regime with rotating "relevance" categories.* This activity, too, will require industry will and creativity, but it must be done. As part of their bid to demonstrate to Congress and the FTC that they can self-regulate, some important internet actors, among them the browser divisions of Microsoft, Mozilla (maker of Firefox), and Google, have moved in different ways toward enabling Web users to choose not to be tracked by third parties. Of course, at the same time, marketers, websites, and advertising associations discourage the public from signing up with the reminder—by now a mantra—that by prohibiting advertisers from following them users will lose the ability to consistently be served relevant ads and offers.

  To counter this reminder, the public needs to be better informed that receiving relevant ads may come at the cost of control over their personal information as well as their self-definition. At the same time, a positive spin should be placed on the lack of specific ad relevance. Instead of sending people ads that are totally random, firms should be pressured to deliver ads that have been tailored to other categories of people—or to other specific people—and to inform them which types the ads are intended to serve. So, for example, a forty-year-old African American man might get an ad that, he will be told, is normally sent to a sixteen-year-old African American teenager—or to a forty-year-old Hispanic man. This sharing of tailored ads might well intrigue people and bring far more signups to such a list than the NAI list has now. In addition, it will allow people to witness the divisions advertisers are creating between people, encourage critical social conversation about this practice, and possibly help advertisers understand what limits various stakeholders would like to place on such categories of division.

- *Pass ground-level government regulations to force a playing field of good actors.* Industry actors naturally want to control their own activities, and they often make a claim that the digital environment is still too new to form rules that might stifle creativity. Not wanting to kill an American goose that is laying golden eggs both domestically and worldwide, regulators have come to accept their argument. In discussing data tracking and use with people throughout the industry, however, I have come to believe that some companies are pursuing paths of data intrusion they wouldn't otherwise if not for the competition. It may well be that a small but critical group of ground-level regulations is necessary to allow the good actors to prosper and at the same time to stop actions by firms that an intersecting community of privacy advocates, industry practitioners, citizens, and regulators believes may be going too far with collecting, analyzing, and implementing certain data. Consensus already exists generally about the delicacy of so-called sensitive data—information on people's sexual preferences, pharmaceutical drug use, and financial status. At this point, these areas tend to be treated as having opt-in status; maybe they should be fully off-limits. Perhaps, too, less-explosive categories should likewise be assigned opt-in or maybe even off-limits status when it comes to targeted advertising and publishing. For example, we might consider prohibiting data firms from using without permission what individuals say in the heat of social-media discussions or in chat rooms for the purposes of marketing to them. Such a step would assure people that some parts of the social world can be enjoyed without worrying that what they say might be used to follow them in ways they could hardly have considered.

These steps are not rigid; others may well have different, better ideas. The point of this process—in fact, the purpose of all four steps—is not only to make good rules; it is to encourage people from many backgrounds to examine, interrogate, understand, and critique the twenty-first-century advertising and media system and its rules. In the final analysis, this process of understanding will ensure that all of us can knowledgeably exert influence over the forces that define us as well as our value to ourselves and to the world at large.

Notes

CHAPTER 1. THE POWER UNDER THE HOOD

1. Nicholas Negroponte, *Being Digital* (New York: Knopf, 1995), p. 5.
2. Christopher Harper, introductory blurb, "The Daily Me," *American Journalism Review,* April 1997, http://www.ajr.org/Article.asp?id=268 (accessed November 20, 2009).
3. Yochai Benkler, *The Wealth of Networks* (New Haven: Yale University Press, 2006), p. 2.
4. Cass R. Sunstein, *Republic.com2.0* (Princeton, NJ: Princeton University Press, 2007), p. 5.
5. Henry Jenkins, *Convergence Culture* (New York: NYU Press, 2008).
6. Cheong Suk-Wai, "You're Powerful . . . Very Powerful," *Straits Times,* January 7, 2007, via Nexis.
7. See, for example, Mark Andrejevic, *iSpy* (Lawrence, KS: University Press of Kansas, 2007); also Mark Andrejevic, *Reality TV: The Work of Being Watched* (New York: Roman and Littlefield, 2003).
8. José van Dijck, "Users Like You? Theorizing Agency in User-generated Content," *Media, Culture & Society* 1 (2009): 41–58.
9. See, for example, the essays on advertising in Joseph Turow and Matt McAllister, eds., *The Advertising and Consumer Culture Reader* (New York: Routledge, 2010).
10. Eleftheria Parpis, "Ad Icons, Slogans Honored," Adweek.com, September 22, 2009, via Nexis; and Andrew Hampp, "Did AOL's Icon Run Off with the Advertising Week Election," *Advertising Age,* September 28, 2009, p. 29.

11. Advertising Age DataCenter, "100 Leading Advertisers, 2009," http://adage.com/article/datacenter-advertising-spending/100-leading-national-advertisers/144208/ (accessed February 28, 2011). The figure includes both measured and unmeasured media estimates. Measured media includes those (such as magazines, TV, radio, newspapers) in which reputable auditing firms report audience numbers. In the words of *Advertising Age,* unmeasured media include "direct marketing, promotion, internet paid search and other forms of spending not tracked in measured media."

12. Christina Merrill, "Media Agencies: What's in a Name? Lots!" *Adweek,* August 24, 1998, via Nexis.

13. Alasdair Reid, "Thirty Years of Independent Media," *Campaign,* July 21, 2006, p. 24, via Nexis.

14. Ibid.

15. Fred Danzig, "Interpublic's Marion Harper Dead at 73,"*Advertising Age,* October 30, 1989, p. 1.

16. Sandra Salmans, "Saatchi & Saatchi's Buying Binge," *New York Times,* July 14, 1985, via Nexis.

17. "Saatchis Closing In on Foreign Goals," *Advertising Age,* July 7, 1987, via Nexis.

18. "Advertising's Big Bang," *Economist,* January 28, 1989, p. 63 (U.S. ed.), via Nexis.

19. Ibid.

20. Eamon Quinn, "Zenith Sparks Off Media Rebellion," *Campaign,* September 8, 1988, via Nexis.

21. Ibid.

22. Ibid.

23. Reid, "Thirty Years of Independent Media."

24. "Media Agency Report: Media Gambit—The Scramble for Supremacy," *Adweek,* December 20, 1999, via Nexis.

25. "Media Buying," *Advertising Age,* August 2, 1999, p. S-2.

26. Chuck Ross and Laura Petrecca, "WPP's Ogilvy, JWT Shops Merge Their Media Clout," *Advertising Age,* April 7, 1997, p. 2.

27. Laura Petrecca, "Clients Should Pay for Exclusivity: Reinhard," *Advertising Age,* May 10, 1999, http://adage.com/article/news/clients-pay-exclusivity-reinhard-ddb-chairman-cites-conflict-policies-unfair/62480/ (accessed May 23, 2011).

28. Merrill, "Media Agencies: What's in a Name? Lots!"

29. Ibid.

30. Jack Neff, "P&G and Unilever's Giant Headaches," *Advertising Age,* May 24, 1999, p. 23.

31. Merrill, "Media Agencies: What's in a Name? Lots!"

32. Chuck Ross, "P&G Media Move Will Alter U.S. TV Landscape," *Advertising Age,* November 24, 1997, p.1.

33. "Media Buying & Planning," *Advertising Age,* August 2, 1999, p. S1.

34. Ibid.

35. Merrill, "Media Agencies: What's in a Name? Lots!"

36. Ibid.

37. Chuck and Laura Petrecca, "WPP's Ogilvy, JWT Shops Merge Their Media Clout," *Advertising Age,* April 7, 1997, p. 2.

38. Merrill, "Media Agencies: What's in a Name? Lots!"
39. Laura Petrecca, "Big Shop Media Units Emerge from Shadows," *Advertising Age,* July 22, 1996, p. S6.
40. Merrill, "Media Agencies: What's in a Name? Lots!"
41. Media Agency Report: "Media Gambit—The Scramble for Supremacy,"1.
42. Bill Harvey, "A Brief Personal History of Media Optimization," http://www.billharvey-consulting.com/articles/pdf/history-of-media-opt.pdf (accessed December 24, 2009).
43. Ibid., p. 5.
44. Ibid., pp. 5–6.
45. Erwin Ephron, "Advertising Moves to Made-up Metrics," *Advertising Age,* July 31, 2000, p. 32.
46. Ibid.
47. Merrill, "Media Agencies: What's in a Name? Lots!"
48. Tobi Elkin and Richard Linnett, "Media Moves Up; On Top," *Advertising Age,* July 9, 2001, p. 3.
49. Ibid.
50. Ibid.

CHAPTER 2. CLICKS AND COOKIES

1. Michael Schrage, "Out There: The Ultimate Network," *Adweek,* May 17, 1993, https://secure.mediaweek.com/aw/esearch/article_display.jsp?vnu_content_id=523498.
2. Ibid.
3. Valerie Mackie, "Electronic Newsstand to Add Ads," *Advertising Age,* November 1, 1993, p. 22. For a reference to the libertarian nature of early internet culture, see Frances Bula, "Two Sides to Sex Link," *Vancouver Sun,* January 30, 1993, p. C2. See also Esther Dyson, *Release 2.0: A Design for Living in the Digital Age* (New York: Broadway, 1997).
4. Mackie, "Electronic Newsstand to Add Ads."
5. Gary Levin, "Plugging into Interactive Early On: Ogilvy & Mather Martin Nisenholtz," *Advertising Age,* September 12, 1994, p. S-10.
6. Jonathan Anastas, "Media Laggards" (letter to the editor), *Adweek,* June 20, 1994, via Nexis.
7. Editorial, "Flamers on the Internet," *Advertising Age,* May 2, 1994, p. 24.
8. "Content Providers Learn Online Reality," *Billboard,* May 6, 1994, via Nexis.
9. Ibid.
10. Editorial, "Flamers on the Internet."
11. Edwin Artzt, "The Future of Advertising," *Vital Speeches,* September 1, 1994 (speech given May 12, 1994).
12. Ibid.
13. Debra Aho Williamson, "Web Ads Mark 2nd Anniversary with Decisive Issues Ahead," *Advertising Age,* October 26, 1996, p. 1.
14. Interview with Alec Gerster, February 4, 2010.
15. This point was made by Ariel Poler in an interview, February 9, 2010.
16. "Content Providers Learn Online Reality," *Billboard,* May 6, 1994, via Nexis.

17. Jack Kapica, "Cyberia: Why Fees Are Failing to Be Feasible," *Globe and Mail,* February 7, 1997, A8, via Nexis.

18. Michael Kinsley, "A Momentous Announcement: Slate Chickens Out," *Slate,* January 12, 1997, via Nexis.

19. Kapica, "Cyberia: Why Fees Are Failing to Be Feasible."

20. "Content Providers Learn Online Reality."

21. Without evidence, a Wikipedia entry notes that the website Global Network Navigator (GNN) sold the first clickable Web ad—later called a banner—on its home page in 1993 to a law firm with a Silicon Valley office. It claims that the Hotwired site was the first to sell clickable ads in large quantities. See "Web Banner," Wikipedia (English edition), accessed January 31, 2010.

22. "Banner Ads Get Smarter," *Advertising Age,* October 21, 1996, p. 50.

23. There arose a fieldwide discussion as to whether an impression should be considered the serving of an ad or the actual appearance of the ad in the person's browser. For various reasons, the two activities didn't always coincide.

24. Debra Aho Williamson, "P&G Fights to Recast Web CPMs," *Advertising Age,* April 22, 1996, p. 1.

25. Michael Krantz, "The Medium Is the Measure," *Adweek,* September 25, 1995, via Nexis.

26. The I/Pro-Nielsen outfit quickly became the leader at providing both reports of a site's traffic to help it with marketing and formal audits to certify the validity of its reports. Critics sneered that this represented a conflict of interest. There was talk I/Pro would outsource the audits to the gold-standard arbiter in the print business, Audit Bureau of Circulation, which was trying to break into internet work. Debra Aho Williamson, "I/Pro May Link with ABC to Audit Web Site Traffic," *Advertising Age,* November 11, 1996, p. 6.

27. "I/Pro (Internet Profiles Corporation) Announces First System to Deliver True Measurability of Internet Usage," Business Wire, April 10, 1995, via Lexis.

28. Krantz, "The Medium Is the Measure."

29. Ibid.

30. Ibid.

31. Ibid.

32. Williamson, "Web Ads Mark 2nd Birthday with Decisive Issues Ahead." According to eMarketer, a digital marketing and media analysis company, the number actually ended up being $175 million. See eMarketer, *The eAdvertising Report* (New York: Emarketer, 1999), p. 15.

33. Williamson, "Web Ads Mark 2nd Birthday with Decisive Issues Ahead."

34. Ibid.

35. Krantz, "The Medium Is the Measure."

36. Interview with Ariel Poler, February 9, 2010.

37. Jay P. Kessan and Rajiv C. Shah, "Deconstructing Code," *Yale Journal of Law and Technology* (2003–2004): pp. 279–389.

38. John Schwartz, "Giving Web a Memory Cost Its Users Privacy," *New York Times,* September 4, 2001, p. A1.

39. Williamson, "Web Ads Mark 2nd Anniversary with Decisive Issues Ahead."

40. Maddox and Patricia Riedman, "IMM: Research Firms Respond to Need for More Data," *Advertising Age,* September 8, 1997, p. 34.

41. Laurie Freeman, "Internet Visitors' Traffic Jam Makes Buyers Web Wary: Measuring Hits' Worth as Ad Medium Remains a Key Problem," *Advertising Age,* July 22, 1996, p. S14.

42. Scott Donaton, "Standards Required to Make Next Leap," *Advertising Age,* November 4, 1996, p. S-30.

43. Williamson, "Web Ads Mark 2nd Birthday with Decisive Issues Ahead."

44. Interview with Alec Gerster.

45. Ibid.; interview with Tom Hespos, April 27, 2011.

46. Laura Rich, "Measure for Measure; What Is the Web Worth?" *Advertising Age,* November 11, 1996, via Nexis.

47. Glen Fest, "AOL Opens North Texas Ad Trail via Digital City Dallas/Fort Worth," *Adweek,* November 18, 1996, via Nexis.

48. Editorial, "Echoes from the Big Bang; P&G Steps In," *Advertising Age,* April 29, 1996, p. 28.

49. Williamson, "Web Ads Mark 2nd Birthday with Decisive Issues Ahead."

50. Scott Hume, "Olds Sets HotWired Sponsorship," *Adweek,* October 7, 1996, via Nexis.

51. Williamson, "Web Ads Mark 2nd Birthday with Decisive Issues Ahead."

52. "Anatomy of An Interactive Ad," *Adweek,* May 26, 1997, via Nexis.

53. Ibid.

54. Freeman, "Internet Visitors' Traffic Jam Makes Buyers Web Wary."

55. Debra Aho Williamson and Laura Petrecca, "Interactive: Agencies Rev Up Separate Online Buying Units," *Advertising Age,* March 17, 1997, p. 30.

56. Ibid.

57. Ibid.

58. Freeman, "Internet Visitors' Traffic Jam Makes Buyers Web Wary."

59. Schwartz, "Giving Web a Memory Cost Its Users Privacy."

60. "Same Origin Policy," Wikipedia, http://en.wikipedia.org/wiki/Same_origin_policy (accessed November 7, 2010).

61. Schwartz, "Giving Web a Memory Cost Its Users Privacy."

62. "Interactive Quarterly: Network Formulas," *Adweek,* May 26, 1997, via Nexis.

63. Ibid.

64. Ibid.

65. Ibid.

66. IETF committee member David Kristol, quoted in Rick E. Bruner, "Interactive: Cookie Proposal Could Hinder Online Advertising," *Advertising Age,* March 31, 1997, p.16.

67. Rick E. Bruner, "Interactive: Cookie Proposal Could Hinder Online Advertising," *Advertising Age,* March 31, 1997, p. 16.

68. Ibid.

69. Ibid.

70. Schwartz, "Giving Web a Memory Cost Its Users Privacy."

71. Rick E. Bruner, "Interactive: Advertisers Win One in Debate over Cookies," *Advertising Age*, May 12, 1997, p. 62.

72. Ibid.

73. James Staten, "Navigator Tricks Raise Concerns," *MacWeek*, March 18, 1996, p. 18.

74. Ira Teinowitz, "The Pressure Is Building in Washington to Limit the Kind of Personal Information Marketers Can Ask of Kids Online," *Advertising Age*, June 23, 1997, p. 16.

75. Bruner, "Interactive: Advertisers Win One in Debate Over Cookies."

76. Richard M. Smith, "The Web Bug FAQ," Electronic Frontier Foundation, November 11, 1999, http://w2.eff.org/Privacy/Marketing/web_bug.html (accessed February 10, 2010).

77. Ibid.

78. Kim Cleland, "Media Buying & Planning: Marketers Want Solid Data on Value of Internet Ad Buys," *Advertising Age*, August 3, 1998, p. S18.

79. Ibid.

80. Ibid.

81. Ibid.

82. Ibid.

83. Kate Maddox, "Agency Pitch Heats Up," *Advertising Age*, August 10, 1998, p 18.

84. Kate Maddox, "P&G's Plan: Jump-Start Web as Viable Ad Medium," *Advertising Age*, August 17, 1998, p. 1. See also Patricia Riedman, "P&G Plans Pivotal Ad Forum About Net," *Advertising Age*, May 11, 1998, p. 4.

85. Maddox, "P&G's Plan: Jump-Start Web As Viable Ad Medium." Also, interview with Denis Beausejour.

86. I attended the 1998 P&G meeting with the kind permission of the organizers and remember AOL chief Steve Case giving an address arguing that Americans had no interest in broadband in the foreseeable future. Dial-up service was sufficient for the masses of Americans, he said, and dial-up was what AOL intended to keep giving them. The executives around me were chagrined.

87. Kate Maddox and Chuck Ross, "P&G Pushes Web Ad Sellers to Swallow Low-ball Rates," *Advertising Age*, January 18, 1999, p. 1.

88. Terry Lifton, "The Great Flameout," *Industry Standard*, March 19, 2001, p. 77.

89. Ted Sann, quoted in Lifton, "The Great Flameout." p. 76.

CHAPTER 3. A NEW ADVERTISING FOOD CHAIN

1. Verne Kopytoff, "Yahoo, Google Look to New Outlets," *San Francisco Chronicle*, April 26, 2005, p. C1.

2. David Court, Dave Elzinga, Susan Mulder, and Ole Jørgen Vetvik, "The Consumer Decision Journey," *McKinsey Quarterly*, June 2009, http://www.mckinseyquarterly.com/Media_Entertainment/Publishing/The_consumer_decision_journey_2373#.

3. Adrienne Mand, "IQ News: Unlaunched Site Making Digerati Google-Eyed," *Adweek*, July 12, 1999, via Nexis.

4. Imran Khan, "Nothing but Net," JP Morgan North American Equity Research, January 2, 2008, p. 17.

5. Stacy Straczynski, "AOL Search Boasts Highest Click-Through Rates," *Adweek*, December 10, 2009, via Nexis.

6. Brian Morrissey, "Marketers Find Search Ads Pay Off Beyond Online Sales," *Adweek*, March 14, 2005, via Nexis.

7. When Google officials noticed advertisers' attempts to place paid-search ads for "free" display, they did try to discourage the practice by refusing high bidders whose ads they found hadn't in the past yielded an acceptable number of clicks. Interviews for this book suggested that some advertisers continued to bid with the display angle in mind.

8. Lisa Phillips, "The Digital Home," eMarketer, November 18, 2009. As this report notes, eMarketer used the FCC's benchmark of the time as its definition for broadband: an internet connection of 200 kbps (kilobits per second) in at least one direction. While certainly higher than dial-up speeds, that standard fell well below global averages according to the second annual report on global broadband connections by the Said Business School, University of Oxford. The global average download speed in 2009 was 4.75 Mbps (megabits per second), the average upload speed 1.3 Mbps.

9. http://comscore.com/Products_Services (accessed November 8, 2010).

10. http://en-us.nielsen.com/content/nielsen/en_us/measurement/online.html   (accessed November 8, 2010).

11. Chris Anderson, *The Long Tail* (New York: Hyperion, 2006).

12. http://www.quantcast.com/info/marketer-overview (accessed April 23, 2010).

13. See "Advertising Terminology on the Internet," http://whatis.techtarget.com/definition/ 0,,sid9_gci211535,00.html#fast (accessed April 25, 2011). Also see Wikipedia's entry for impressions: http://en.wikipedia.org/wiki/Impression_(online_media).

14. "Audience   Targeting,"   http://www.nytimes.whsites.net/mediakit/online/audience/ audience_targeting.php.

15. http://www.nytimes.com/ref/membercenter/help/privacy.html#b (accessed April 9, 2010).

16. Searchable via http://www.claritas.com/MyBestSegments (accessed April 24, 2011).

17. http://www.audiencescience.com/media (accessed November 8, 2010).

18. See http://www.nytimes.whsites.net/mediakit/online/advertising/ad_programs.php and http://www.nytimes.whsites.net/mediakit/online/rates/online_ad_format_details.php (accessed November 9, 2010).

19. Emily Riley, "The New Ad Network," *Jupiter Research*, Volume 1, 2008.

20. http://advertising.aol.com/audiences/women (accessed April 15, 2010).

21. http://revenuescience.com/advertisers/advertiser_solutions.asp (accessed April 15, 2010).

22. "Transactional Advertising Driving Lower CPMs Says 24/7 Real Media Chairman Moore," Adexchanger.com.

23. Kahn, "Nothing But Net."

24. Interview with executive knowledgeable in this area but who requested anonymity.

25. Quoted in Jeff Chester, Ed Mierzwinski, and Pam Dixon, "Complain, Request for Investigation, Injunction, and Other Relief," presentation to the Federal Trade Commission, April 8, 2010, http://www.uspirg.org/uploads/eb/6c/eb6c038a1fb-114be75ecabab05b4b90b/FTCfiling_Apr7_10.pdf, p. 8 (accessed April 26, 2011).

26. "The Data-Driven Web," Winterberry Group, October 2009, p. 12.

27. "Data Marketplace," http://exelate.com/new/data-marketplace/marketers/ (accessed April 25, 2011).

28. Chester, Mierzwinski, and Dixon, "Complain, Request for Investigation, Injunction, and Other Relief." Also, "Data Marketplace," http://exelate.com/new/data-market-place/ (accessed April 24, 2011).

29. "BlueKai Exchange," http://bluekai.com/exchange.php (accessed April 25, 2011).

30. Julia Angwin, "The Web's New Gold Mine: Your Secrets," *Wall Street Journal*, July 30, 2010, http://online.wsj.com/article/SB10001424052748703940904575395073512989404.html?mod=WSJ_newsreel_technology.

31. http://www.pg.com/privacy/english/privacy_notice.html (accessed April 22, 2010).

32. Chester, Mierzwinski, and Dixon, p. 10.

33. http://www.pg.com/privacy/english/privacy_notice.html (accessed April 22, 2010).

34. Chris Jay Hoofnagle, "Beyond Google and Evil," *First Monday* 14, no. 4 (April 6, 2009), http://firstmonday.org/htbin/cgiwrap/bin/ojs/index.php/fm/article/view/2326/2156 (accessed May 23, 2011).

35. Chester, Mierzwinski, and Dixon, p. 17.

36. "Advertising Used to Be Straightforward," *New Media Age*, November 2010, http://live.nma.co.uk/downloads/tmc-the-future-of-online-display-advertising/MIRROR.pdf.

37. Pubmatic, "Understanding Real-Time Bidding (RTB) from the Publisher Perspective," February 2010, http://www.slideshare.net/PubMatic/understanding-realtime-bidding-from-the-publisher-perspective, pp. 9–10.

38. Ibid.

39. Discussion with David Cohen, April 21, 2010.

40. Pubmatic, "Understanding Real-Time-Bidding (RTB) from the Publisher Perspective."

41. eXelate, "DPAC4," PowerPoint presentation, October 23, 2009.

42. Tom Hespos, "Perplexing Ethical Dilemmas of Online Marketing," iMedia connection, January 21, 2010, https://www.imediaconnection.com/content/25704.asp.

43. Discussion with David Cohen.

44. See Joseph Turow, *Breaking Up America: Advertisers and the New Media World* (Chicago: University of Chicago Press, 1996).

45. See Erik Barnouw, *The Sponsor* (New York: Oxford University Press, 1971).

46. Mark Zagorski, quoted in Jack Marshall, "Data Costs Surpass Media Costs, Agencies Say," *ClickZ News*, http://www.clickz.com/clickz/news/1696083/data-costs-surpass-media-costs-agencies-say (accessed November 9, 2010).

47. For coverage of this address, see Zachary Rogers, "Millard Issues Plea for More Art, Less Science in Online Ads, *ClickZ News*, February 23, 2009, http://www.clickz.com/clickz/news/1696514/millard-issues-plea-more-art-less-science-online-ads (accessed November 9, 2010); Saul Hansell, "If Ads Were Traded Like Pork Bellies," in "Bits" online column, *New York Times*, March 3, 2008, http://query.nytimes.com/gst/fullpage.html?res=9900EEDC163BF930A35750C0A96E9C8B63&pagewanted=all (accessed November 9, 2010).

48. David Kaplan, "On Ad Networks: Pork Bellies, Diamonds, or the New Direct Marketing," paidContent.org, April 8, 2010, http://paidcontent.org/article/419-on-ad-networks-pork-bellies-diamonds-or-the-new-direct/.

49. Randall Rothenberg, "Like It or Not, We're All in This Together," *Ad Age Digital,* March 17, 2008, http://adage.com/article/digital//125730/.

CHAPTER 4. TARGETS OR WASTE

1. Don Pepper and Martha Rogers, *The One to One Future* (New York: Doubleday Business, 1993).
2. http://www.acxiom.com/Pages/Home.aspx (accessed November 12, 2010).
3. http://www.acxiom.com/products_and_services/cdi/Pages/CustomerDataIntegration. aspx.
4. Bradley Johnson, "Agency Report 2010," *Advertising Age,* April 26, 2010, p. 22.
5. Georgina Prodhan, "Global Ad Industry Grapples with New Spending Trends," Reuters, May 11, 2010, via Nexis.
6. Mike Shields, "NBC Digital, P&G Partner on Boomer Portal," *MediaWeek,* May 11, 2010, via Nexis.
7. http://www.pg.com/privacy/english/privacy_statement.html#tab2 (accessed May 16, 2010).
8. Michael Bus and Rupal Parekh, "More Marketers Want to Get to Know You," *Advertising Age,* August 25, 2008, p. 11.
9. Interview with Andy Pratkin, May 9, 2010.
10. Ibid.
11. Interview with Scott Lang, May 9, 2010.
12. Noreen O'Leary, "Ford, Google Put Banners in Context," *Adweek,* May 4, 2010, http://www.adweek.com/aw/content_display/news/digital/e3i7b2c50df9c8f86f-fa8e409aa4497fb50 (accessed November 12, 2010).
13. Interview with Andy Pratkin.
14. The quote is from the Acxiom website, Acxiom.com (accessed May 16, 2010). Also see "Acxiom Investor Day—Final [a transcript]," FD (Fair Disclosure) Wire, June 17, 2008, via Nexis.
15. Among the facts listed on Acxiom.com on May 16, 2010.
16. Tom Mangan, quoted in "Acxiom Investor Day—Final [a transcript]."
17. "Consumer Data Products Catalog: The Power of Insight," Acxiom Corporation, p. 28, http://www.acxiom.com/SiteCollectionDocuments/website-resources/pdf/pdf_brochures/AC-2507-09_Online_Data_Catalog.pdf (accessed May 16, 2010).
18. "Consumer Data Products Catalog," Acxiom Corporation, http://www.acxiom.com/SiteCollectionDocuments/website-resources/pdf/pdf_brochures/AC-2507-09_Online_Data_Catalog.pdf (accessed March 10, 2010).
19. Ibid.
20. Mangan, quoted in "Acxiom Investor Day—Final [a transcript]."
21. John Meyer, quoted in "Acxiom Investor Day—Final [a transcript]," FD (Fair Disclosure) Wire, June 17, 2008, via Nexis.
22. "Who's Buying, Who's Not and Why," Business Wire, January 27, 2009, via Nexis.
23. "eXelate Data Segments," eXelate, PDF available on home page, http://www.exelate.com/new/buyers-targetingsegments.html (accessed on May 24, 2010).

24. "Magnetic Delivers Search Re-targeting Data Solution for All Online Advertising," Magnetic, press release, March 22, 2010, http://magnetic.is/press/?id=1 (accessed May 24, 2010).

25. Josh Shatkin-Margolis, "Can Search Advertisers Play in Display's Backyard," Mediapost.com, May 17, 2010. Also, Laurie Sullivan, "Efficient Frontier Launches Platform Supporting Display, Search Ad Buys," Mediapost, April 27, 2010, http://www.mediapost.com/publications/?fa=Articles.showArticle&art_aid=126901 (accessed May 24, 2011).

26. http://medicxmedia.com/home/digital_advertising/agencies_advertisers.asp; http://medicxmedia.com/home/digital_advertising/aa_geomedical_targeting.asp.

27. "Mindset Marketing Solutions Debuts Zip+4 Geomedical Targeting with Launch of geoMEDICX," PRWeb, November 7, 2008, http://www.prweb.com/releases/2008/11/prweb1576174.htm.

28. Ibid.

29. *Omniture Test and Target Power User Training: Student Workbook* (Orem, Utah: Omniture, 2009), p. 41.

30. Chris Jay Hoofnagle, "Spoofing First Party Cookies Through DNS Aliasing," draft manuscript, Berkeley Law School, October 2010.

31. "Prospect Triggers," Experian, http://www.experian.com/consumer-information/prospect-triggers.html?cat1=customer-management&cat2—anage-customer-information-databases (accessed May 2, 2011); see "Manage Customer Information and Databases," Experian, http://www.experian.com/consumer-information/prospect-triggers.html?cat1=customer-management&cat2—anage-customer-information-databases (accessed May 2, 2011).

32. See Reed Elsevier's Lexis Nexis Risk Solutions, https://www.lexisnexis.com/risk/financial-services.aspx (accessed May 2, 2011).

33. Claire Cain Miller, "In Lean Times, Online Coupons Are Catching On," *New York Times,* November 25, 2008, via Nexis.

34. Todd Hale, "Nielsen Research: Consumer Insights: Innovate to Differentiate," *Progressive Grocer,* November 2009, via Nexis.

35. Miller, "In Lean Times, Online Coupons Are Catching On."

36. Ibid.

37. Stephanie Clifford, "Web Coupons Know Lots About You, and They Tell," *New York Times,* April 16, 2010, via Nexis.

38. Ibid.

39. Ibid.

40. Ibid.

41. http://www.couponsinc.com/corporate/MotivatingConsumers/CouponDistribution11Marketing.aspx (accessed May 28, 2010).

42. Coupons.com, privacy policy, http://www.couponsinc.com/Corporate/Privacy.aspx (accessed May 28, 2010).

43. Ibid.

44. Interview with Jonathan Treiber, May 25, 2010.

45. Interview with Don Batsford, May 10, 2010.

46. Ibid.

47. Andrew Martin, "Sam's Club Personalizes Discounts for Buyers," *New York Times,* May 30, 2010, B1.f.

48. Interview with Jonathan Treiber.

49. *Omniture Test and Target Power User Training: Student Workbook,* p. 1–6.

50. "Our Mission," Next Jump, http://www.nextjump.com/about/ourcompany (accessed November 12, 2010).

51. "The Most Secretive Startup in the World (Next Jump)," Takeaplunge.com, January 15, 2010, http://www.takeaplunge.com/the-most-secretive-startup-in-the-world-next-jump/ (accessed November 12, 2010).

52. Ibid.

CHAPTER 5. THEIR MASTERS' VOICES

1. Interviews with Rishad Tobaccowala, May 6 and August 26, 2010.

2. On advertising in magazines and newspapers, see John Tebbel, *The Media in America* (New York: Crowell, 1974). Regarding the early television industry's relationship with advertisers, see Erik Barnouw, *The Sponsor: Notes on a Modern Potentate* (New York: Oxford University Press, 1978).

3. See Joseph Turow, *Niche Envy* (Cambridge: MIT Press, 2006), pp. 50–52.

4. Interviews with Rishad Tobaccowala.

5. Brian Wieser, "Global Summary Simplified Model August 2010" (Excel spreadsheet), Magnum Global, August 2010.

6. Katy Bachman, "Kantar: Total Advertising Up 5.7% in First Half," *MediaWeek,* September 13, 2010.

7. Veronis Suhler Stevenson, *Communication Industry Forecast,* 2009–2013 (New York: VSS, 2009), p. 15-2.

8. Ibid., p. 12-2.

9. Wieser, "Global Summary Simplified Model August 2010."

10. Earl J. Wilkinson, "Newspaper Outlook 2008: Creating Value in a Multimedia Landscape," International Newspaper Marketing Association, 2008, http://www.inma.org/bookstore/2008-outlook.cfm.

11. Shira Ovide and Suzanne Vranica, "Magazines Use the iPad as Their New Barker," *Wall Street Journal,* March 24, 2010, http://online.wsj.com/article/SB10001424052748 704266504575141822475202814.html (accessed September 1, 2010). See also Nat Ives, "Wired's iPad Edition Has Finally Arrived," *Advertising Age,* May 26, 2010.

12. Interviews with Rishad Tobaccowala.

13. David Kaplan, "Google Finally Links Adwords to DoubleClick," PaidContent.org, September 17, 2009, http://paidcontent.org/article/419-google-finally-links-adwords-to-doubleclick/ (accessed July 15, 2010).

14. The exclusion of even demographic variables from paid search is hard to understand. People in the paid-search business are proud that they work in a pristine world of probabilities centered on anonymous individual intentions expressed only in words typed into the search box. Some suggest that the decision to keep search out of the data-mining business—a decision followed by Microsoft and Yahoo!, the other major search

powers—is political. Display advertising brings them enough flak from advocacy organizations and government regulators; they have no desire to add search to their headaches. In any event, Google's paid search has been a money gusher, accounting for an estimated $27 billion of its approximately $29-billion annual revenues. See Mike Shields, "Google Touts Display, Mobile Gains," Adweek.com, October 14, 2010, http://www.adweek.com/news/technology/google-touts-display-mobile-gains-116321 (accessed May 24, 2011).

15. Alison Diana, "Facebook Dominates Online Advertising," InformationWeek, November 9, 2010, http://www.informationweek.com/story/showArticle.jhtml?articleID=228200510 (accessed November 9, 2010).

16. "Advertising Policies," Google, http://adwords.google.com/support/aw/bin/static.py?hl=en&page=guide_toc.cs&path=policy (accessed July 14, 2010). Compare with Yahoo! ad specifications, which actually seem rigorous; see "Yahoo! Display Advertising," http://adspecs.yahoo.com/policies.php (accessed July 16, 2010).

17. Kaplan, "Google Finally Links Adwords to DoubleClick."

18. Gavin Dunaway, "Google Spills Display Beans at Barbecue," Adotas, July 1, 2010, http://www.adotas.com/2010/07/google-spills-display-beans-at-barbecue/ (accessed May 5, 2011).

19. Susan Wojcicki, "The Future of Display Advertising" (The Official Google Blog), March 15, 2010, http://googleblog.blogspot.com/2010/03/future-of-display-advertising.html (accessed November 12, 2010).

20. "Advertising and Privacy," Google, http://www.google.com/intl/en/privacy_ads.html (accessed July 14, 2010).

21. "BridgeTrack Customer Data Integration," http://www.bridgetrack.com/CustomerDataIntegration.aspx (accessed July 14, 2010).

22. Julia Angwin, "The Web's New Gold Mine: Your Secrets," July 30, 2010, http://online.wsj.com/article/SB10001424052748703940904575395073512989404.html (accessed November 12, 2010).

23. Interview with Edwin Wong, May 10, 2010.

24. Ibid.

25. Steve McClellan, "Starcom Names Branded Entertainment Chief," Adweek, February 10, 2010, via Nexis.

26. Interview with Kirk McDonald, May 9, 2010.

27. Interview with Imran Aziz, May 9, 2010.

28. Interview with Kirk McDonald.

29. Interview with Imran Aziz.

30. Interview with Gerald Hauser, May 11, 2010.

31. Randall Rothenberg, "Product Placement Carnival Rolls Back into Town," Advertising Age, September 10, 2001, http://adage.com/columns/article?article_id=32628 (accessed September 2, 2010).

32. For a history of product placement on television, see Turow, Niche Envy, pp. 50–62.

33. American Society of Magazine Editors, "American Society of Magazine Editors Guidelines for Editors and Publishers Thirteenth Edition, October 2005," Advertising Age.com, October 17, 2005, http://adage.com/images/random/asme101705.pdf (accessed September 2, 2010).

34. Nat Ives, "The Ad/Edit Wall Worn Down to a Warning Track," *Advertising Age,* August 23, 1010, http://adage.com/mediaworks/article?article_id=145501 (accessed September 2, 2010).

35. Ibid.

36. "ASME Guidelines for Editors and Publishers" (revised October 2010), http://www.magazine.org/asme/asme_guidelines/guidelines.aspx (accessed October 21, 2010).

37. Nat Ives, "ASME Calls ESPN, EW on the Carpet Over Covers," April 10, 2009, http://adage.com/mediaworks/article?article_id=135911 (accessed, September 2, 2009).

38. Ibid.

39. Nat Ives, "Ads Venturing Further into Magazines' Editorial Pages," *Advertising Age,* April 2, 2010, http://adage.com/mediaworks/article?article_id=143111 (accessed November 12, 2010).

40. Nat Ives, "The Ad/Edit Wall Worn Down to a Warning Track," *Advertising Age,* August 23, 1010, http://adage.com/mediaworks/article?article_id=145501 (accessed September 2, 2010).

41. From Brooke Erin Duffy, notes taken at the American Magazine Conference, Chicago, Illinois, October 3–5, 2010.

42. Meredith, "Our 360° Approach," http://www.meredith.com/marketing_solutions/360.html (accessed October 26, 2010).

43. See, for example, "Meredith and WE TV Team Up on Cross Media Promotion," Meredith press release published in Amanda Ernst, "Media WE Launch Cross Promotion," MediaBistro.com, May 18, 2009, http://www.mediabistro.com/fishbowlny/meredith-we-launch-cross-promotion_b11776.

44. Duffy, notes taken at the American Magazine Conference.

45. Matthew Creamer and Pupal Parekh, "Ideas of the Decade," *Advertising Age,* December 14, 2010, p. 8.

46. Michael Bush, "Unlike Last Major Downturn, Industry Experiencing Much Quicker Rebound," *Advertising Age,* August 23, 2010.

47. For these reasons Oscar Gandy describes marketing publicity as information subsidies. See Oscar Gandy, *Beyond Agenda Setting* (Norwood, NJ: Ablex, 1980).

48. "Content Farms," Wikipedia, http://en.wikipedia.org/wiki/Content_farms (accessed August 1, 2010); Peter Kafka, "Demand Media's Richard Rosenblatt and ProPublica's Paul Steiger Live at D8," June 3, 2010, http://d8.allthingsd.com/20100603/richard-rosenblatt-paul-steiger-session/?mod=ATD_search (accessed August 1, 2010).

49. Richard MacManus, "How Demand Media Produces 4,000 Pieces of Content a Day," ReadWriteWeb, November 12, 2009, http://www.readwriteweb.com/archives/how_demand_media_produces_4000_new_pieces_of_content_a_day.php (accessed September 16, 2010).

50. "Solutions for Publishers," Demand Media, http://www.demandmedia.com/solutions/publishers/ (accessed September 16, 2010).

51. Richard MacManus, "Ad-Driven Content—Is It Crossing the Line," ReadWriteWeb, November 13, 2009, http://www.readwriteweb.com/archives/ad-driven_content_is_it_crossing_the_line.php (accessed September 16, 2010).

52. Ibid.

53. Leslie Horn, "Demand Media Traffic Down 40 Percent After Google Search Change," *PCMag,* April 26, 2011, http://www.pcmag.com/article2/0,2817,2384348,00.asp (accessed May 5, 2011).

54. Leslie Horn, "Demand Media: Effects of Google Search Change 'Exaggerated,'" *PCMag,* April 18, 2011, http://www.pcmag.com/article2/0,2817,2383712,00.asp (accessed May 5, 2011).

55. Demand Media Q1 2011 Earnings Conference Call, May 5, 2011, streaming from the Demand Media website, http://ir.demandmedia.com/phoenix.zhtml?c=215358&p= irol-eventDetails&EventId=3960764 (accessed May 5, 2011).

CHAPTER 6. THE LONG CLICK

1. "Facebook F8," Wikipedia, http://en.wikipedia.org/wiki/Facebook_f8 (accessed February 24, 2010).

2. Andreas M. Kaplan and Michael Haenlein, "Users of the World, Unite! The Challenges and Opportunities of Social Media," *Business Horizons* 53, no. 1 (January 2010): p. 59–68.

3. Industry analysts were projecting that annual sales from virtual goods would reach $6 billion in 2013. See Jennifer Van Grove, "Target to Sell Facebook Credits as Gift Cards in Stores," Mashable, September 2, 2010, http://mashable.com/2010/09/01/ target-facebook-credits/ (accessed September 7, 2010).

4. http://about.bzzagent.com/ (accessed November 13, 2010).

5. "Code of Conduct," http://about.bzzagent.com/word-of-mouth/index/code-of-conduct (accessed October 16, 2010).

6. "A World Leader in Social Media Sponsorships," Izea, http://izea.com/about-izea/ (accessed May 16, 2011).

7. The claims show up as Flash Post-it style notes on the home page: http://about. bzzagent.com/ (accessed November 13, 2010).

8. "What We Do," http://izea.com/advertisers/social-media-sponsorship (accessed November 13, 2010).

9. Zach Hofer-Shall, "The Forrester Wave: Listening Platforms, Q3, 2010," Forrester Research, July 12, 2010.

10. Ibid.

11. Jeff Zabin, "The ROI on Social Media Monitoring," Aberdeen Group, October 2009.

12. Ibid.

13. Interview with Rohit Thawani, September 7, 2010.

14. "Social, SEO and the Open Graph: What to Do Now," Gigya, July 2010, pp. 7–9, posted on www.gigya.com.

15. Ibid.

16. Interview with John Nitti, September 20, 2010.

17. Emily Steel, "Marketers Watch as Friends Interact Online," *Wall Street Journal,* April 15, 2010, http://online.wsj.com/article/SB10001424052702304159304575184270077115444. html (accessed September 7, 2010). See also Jeff Jarvis, "The Hunt for the Elusive Influencer," BuzzMachine, April 1, 2010, http://www.buzzmachine.com/2010/04/01/the- hunt-for-the-elusive-influencer/ (accessed September 7, 2010).

18. Media6Degrees, "Social Data Targeting: New Internet Advertising Model," PowerPoint presentation, n.d.

19. Steel, "Marketers Watch as Friends Interact Online."

20. Ibid.

21. Jack Neff, "Point-of-Sale Focus: P&G Boosts Design's Role in Marketing," *Advertising Age,* February 9, 2004, p. 1.

22. Karl Greenberg, "Pepsi's Kaufman Talks About the Pepsico10," *Marketing Daily News,* September 20, 2010.

23. "Mobile Internet Users in the United States, 2009–2015 (in millions)," eMarketer, via University of Pennsylvania Libraries website (accessed May 24, 2011).

24. "Mobile Access 20210," Pew Internet & American Life Project, July 7, 2010, http://www.pewinternet.org/Reports/2010/Mobile-Access-2010/Summary-of-Findings.aspx (accessed May 24, 2011).

25. "Mobile Content Soars Thanks to Device and Network Advances," eMarketer, August 31, 2010, http://bx.businessweek.com/mobile-commerce/view?url=http%3A%2F%2Fwww.emarketer.com%2FArticle.aspx%3FR%3D1007899 (accessed May 24, 2011).

26. Ibid.

27. http://www.admob.com/advertise (accessed November 12, 2010).

28. "Privacy 101," Foursquare, http://Foursquare.com/privacy/ (accessed September 23, 2010).

29. "Foursquare Labs, Inc. Privacy Policy," https://foursquare.com/legal/privacy.

30. "Privacy 101."

31. Jack Marshall, "Device Fingerprinting Could Be a Cookie Killer," ClickZ, March 2, 2011, http://www.clickz.com/clickz/news/2030243/device-fingerprinting-cookie-killer.

32. Ibid.

33. Stephanie Clifford, "Web Coupons Know a Lot About You, and They Tell," *New York Times,* April 16, 2010, http://www.nytimes.com/2010/04/17/business/media/17coupon.html?ref=stephanie_clifford (accessed September 23, 2010).

34. See Joseph Turow, *Niche Envy* (Cambridge, MA: MIT Press, 2006), pp. 138–47.

35. http://catalinamarketing.com/brands/ (accessed September 27, 2010).

36. "The Consumer Truth," Catalina Marketing, http://catalinamarketing.com/company/why_shopper-driven_marketing.html (accessed September 27, 2010).

37. "Checkout Coupon," http://catalinamarketing.com/products/checkout_coupon.html (accessed September 27, 2010).

38. "Checkout Direct," http://catalinamarketing.com/products/checkout_direct.html (accessed September 27, 2010).

39. "Catalina Hires Head of Google's Affiliate Network to Lead Emerging Digital Business," Catalina Marketing Corporation press release, March 3, 2010, http://www.catalinamarketing.com/news/pressreleases/newsArticle_03-03-10.html (accessed May 16, 2010).

40. "Google Affiliate Network," http://www.google.com/ads/affiliatenetwork/publisher/index.html (accessed October 21, 2010).

41. Holman W. Jenkins Jr., "Google and the Search for the Future," *Wall Street Journal,* August 14, 2010.

42. Ibid.

43. Jon Gertner, "Our Ratings Ourselves," *New York Times Magazine,* April 10, 2005.

44. James L. McQuivey, "Why Google TV Is Bigger Than You Think," June 7, 2010, p. 3, Forrester Research, www.forrester.com.

45. Ibid.

46. David Graves, "Personal TV: The Reinvention of Television," August 25, 2008, Forrester Research, www.forrester.com.

47. Brian Weiser (global director of forecasting, Magna), in discussion with the author, September 2010.

48. Clay Shirky, "How Television Ratings Portend the Death of Mass Media," October 14, 1999, http://www.shirky.com/writings/television_ratings.html (accessed October 4, 2010).

49. Tim Arango, "Cable Firms Join Forces to Attract Focused Ads," *New York Times,* March 10, 2008, http://www.nytimes.com/2008/03/10/business/media/10cable.html?_r=1 (accessed October 4, 2010).

50. Andrew Hampp, "Addressable TV: an FAQ," *Advertising Age,* November 30, 2009, http://adage.com/mediaworks/article?article_id=140740 (accessed November 12, 2010).

51. Tim Arango, "Cable Firms Join Forces to Attract Focused Ads," *New York Times,* March 10, 2008, http://www.nytimes.com/2008/03/10/business/media/10cable.html?_r=1 (accessed October 4, 2010).

52. Steve McClellan and Brian Morrissey, "The Future of TV," Adweek.com, November 17, 2008, http://www.adweek.com/aw/content_display/special-reports/30-anniversary/articles/e3i33bb91d0a29fdfb15196b76bfaacd955 (accessed November 12, 1010).

53. Ibid.

54. Steve McClellan, "4A's: What's Delaying Ad Addressability?" March 3, 2010, http://www.adweek.com/aw/content_display/news/media/e3ib786618f922dfc1d-c4e59ece9082598f (accessed November 12, 2010).

55. Tom Cuniff, "Old vs. New Media," MediaBizBloggers.com, March 3, 2010, http://www.jackmyers.com/commentary/media-business-bloggers/86009407.html (accessed October 4, 2010).

56. "Television on the Web Is Redefining Must-See Viewing," Fast Company, September 1, 2010, http://www.fastcompany.com/magazine/148/the-new-fall-season.html.

57. Patrick J. Sauer, "Next New Networks Takes Grassroots YouTube Talent to the Next Level," FastCompany, September 1, 2010, http://www.fastcompany.com/magazine/148/next-new-networks.html (accessed May 17, 2011).

58. "About Next New Networks," http://www.nextnewnetworks.com/page/about-company (accessed October 4, 2010).

59. Aymar Jean Christian, "Research Update: Thinking About Web Series, Independent Production and Emerging New Media," Televisual, http://blog.ajchristian.org/2010/08/14/research-update-thinking-about-web-series-independent-production-and-emerging-new-media/ (accessed October 4, 2010).

60. Laurie Sullivan, "Google and Intel to Launch Social TV Platform," *Online Media Daily,* May 17, 2010, http://www.mediapost.com/publications/?fa=Articles.show Article&art_aid=128349.

61. Ibid.

62. Steve McClellan, "Google Invests in Invidi," Adweek.com, May 5, 2010, via Nexis.

63. McQuivey, "Why Google TV Is Bigger Than You Think," p. 3.

CHAPTER 7. BEYOND THE "CREEP" FACTOR

1. Miguel Helft and Tanzina Vega, "Seeing That Ad on Every Site? You're Right. It's Tracking You," *New York Times,* August 30, 2010, p. A-1.

2. Joanna O'Connell, interview by Laura Sydell, "Smart Cookies Put Targeted Online Ads on the Rise," *All Things Considered,* National Public Radio, October 5, 2010, via Nexis.

3. Randall Rothenberg, "Don't Fear Internet Tracking," *USA Today,* August 9, 2010, p. 10A.

4. Ibid.

5. Laurie Sullivan, "Report: Click Fraud Reaches New Heights," Online Media Daily, October 21, 2010, http://www.mediapost.com/publications/?fa=Articles.showArticle &art_aid=138061 (accessed October 21, 2010).

6. Tanzina Vega, "Code That Tracks Users Browsing Prompts Lawsuits," *New York Times,* September 21, 2010, p B-3.

7. "Online Behavioral Advertising: Moving the Discussion Forward to Possible Self-Regulatory Principles," Federal Trade Commission, 2007, http://www.ftc.gov/os/2007/12/P859900stmt.pdf (accessed May 24, 2011).

8. "Self-Regulatory Principles For Online Behavioral Advertising," Federal Trade Commission, February 2009, p. 27, http://www.ftc.gov/os/2009/02/P085400 behavadreport.pdf (accessed May 23, 2011).

9. See, for example, Thomas Clayburn, "Ad Industry Sets Seven Privacy Protection Principles," Information Week, July 2, 2009, http://www.informationweek.com/news/internet/search/showArticle.jhtml?articleID=218400278&subSection–ews (accessed November 4, 2010).

10. "Major Marketing/Media Trade Groups Launch Program to Give Consumers Enhanced Control over Collection and Use of Web Viewing Data for Online Behavioral Advertising," Interactive Advertising Bureau, press release, October 4, 2010, http://www.iab.net/about_the_iab/recent_press_releases/press_release_archive/press_release/pr-100410?gko=7b157 (accessed October 4, 2010).

11. "Self-regulatory Principles for Online Behavioral Advertising," American Association of Advertising Agencies, Association of National Advertisers, Direct Marketing Association, Interactive Advertising Bureau, and Council of Better Business Bureaus, July 2009, http://www.iab.net/insights_research/public_policy/behavioral-advertising-principles (accessed October 26, 2010).

12. "Privacy Policy," Wikipedia, http://en.wikipedia.org/wiki/Privacy_policy (accessed November 12, 2010).

13. "Privacy Online: A Report to Congress," Federal Trade Commission, June 1998, http://www.ftc.gov/reports/privacy3/toc.shtm (accessed May 19, 2011).

14. See Joseph Turow, *Privacy Policies on Children's Websites: Do They Play by the Rules?* (Philadelphia: Annenberg Public Policy Center, 2001), http://www.asc.upenn.edu/usr/jturow/Privacy%20Report.pdf (accessed November 10, 2010).

15. Ibid.

16. "Electronic Arts Privacy Policy," June 11, 2010, http://www.ea.com/1/privacy-policy (accessed July 8, 2010).

17. Ibid.

18. Ibid.

19. See http://info.yahoo.com/privacy/us/yahoo/relevantads.html (accessed November 4, 2010).

20. NAI, "Opt Out of Behavioral Advertising," http://www.networkadvertising.org/managing/opt_out.asp.

21. Larry Dobrow, "Tread Carefully on Privacy: Be Wary of E-consumer Backlash," *Advertising Age,* October 29, 2001, p. S6.

22. Alan Westin, "Social and Political Dimensions of Privacy," *Journal of Social Issues* 59 (July 2003): p. 445.

23. Dobrow, "Tread Carefully on Privacy," p. S6.

24. The 2005 study referenced here is: Joseph Turow, Lauren Feldman, and Kimberly Meltzer, *Open to Exploitation: American Shoppers Online and Offline,"* Report from the Annenberg Public Policy Center, University of Pennsylvania, 2005, http://www.annenbergpublicpolicycenter.org/Downloads/Information_And_Society/Turow_APPC_Report_WEB_FINAL.pdf (accessed November 4, 2010).

25. Joseph Turow, Chris Jay Hoofnagle, Jennifer King, Amy Bleakley, and Michael Hennessy, *Americans Reject Tailored Advertising and Three Activities That Enable It, Report from Annenberg School for Communication of the University of Pennsylvania and Berkeley Law School, 2009,* http://papers.ssrn.com/sol3/papers.cfm?abstract_id=1478214 (accessed November 4, 2010).

26. "There Is No Privacy," *Virginia Pilot,* April 4, 2009, p. B9.

27. Gina Keating, "Disney CEO Bullish on Direct Marketing to Consumers," Reuters, July 23, 2009, http://www.reuters.com/article/idUSTRE56M0ZY20090723?pageNumber=2&virtualBrandChannel=0.

28. Margo Gardner and Laurence Steinberg, "Peer Influence on Risk Taking, Risk Preference, and Risky Decision Making in Adolescence and Adulthood: An Experimental Study," *Developmental Psychology* 41, no. 4 (2005): 625–635. No person twenty-three or twenty-four years old was in the sample.

29. Amanda Lenhart and Mary Madden. "Teens, Privacy, and Online Social Networks," Pew Internet & American Life Project, April 18, 2007, http://www.pewinternet.org/Reports/2007/Teens-Privacy-and-Online-Social-Networks.aspx (accessed November 4, 2010); and more generally Danah Boyd's excellent bibliography of Social Networking Studies at http://www.danah.org/researchBibs/sns.html (accessed November 4, 2010).

30. Christopher Hoofnagle, Jennifer King, Su Li, and Joseph Turow, *How Different Are Young Adults from Older Adults When It Comes to Information Privacy Attitudes and Policies? Report from Annenberg School for Communication of the University of*

Pennsylvania and Berkeley Law School, April 14 2010, http://papers.ssrn.com/sol3/
papers.cfm?abstract_id=1589864 (accessed November 4, 2010).

31. Ibid.
32. Ibid.
33. Saul Hansell, "An Icon That Says They're Watching You," *New York Times,* March 19,
    2009,   http://bits.blogs.nytimes.com/2009/03/19/an-icon-that-says-theyre-watching-
    you/?apage=2#comments (accessed November 4, 2010).
34. Jeffrey Chester of the Center for Digital Democracy has added the intriguing and
    important point that "consumers and citizens . . . should be informed, for example,
    about any role neuroscience played in crafting the online message" (comment section,
    in ibid.).

Index